Ultimate Apache Superset for Data Visualization and Analytics

Leverage Apache Superset to Create Interactive Dashboards and Master Modern Business Intelligence

Bragadeesh Sundararajan

AF517162

AVA

www.orangeava.com

Copyright © 2025, Orange Education Pvt Ltd, AVA®

All rights reserved. No part of this book may be reproduced, stored in a retrieval system, or transmitted in any form or by any means, without the prior written permission of the publisher, except in the case of brief quotations embedded in critical articles or reviews.

Every effort has been made in the preparation of this book to ensure the accuracy of the information presented. However, the information contained in this book is sold without warranty, either express or implied. Neither the author nor **Orange Education Pvt Ltd** or its dealers and distributors, will be held liable for any damages caused or alleged to have been caused directly or indirectly by this book.

Orange Education Pvt Ltd has endeavored to provide trademark information about all of the companies and products mentioned in this book by the appropriate use of capital. However, **Orange Education Pvt Ltd** cannot guarantee the accuracy of this information. The use of general descriptive names, registered names, trademarks, service marks, etc. in this publication does not imply, even in the absence of a specific statement, that such names are exempt from the relevant protective laws and regulations and therefore free for general use.

First Published: April 2025

Published By: Orange Education Pvt Ltd, AVA®

Address: 9, Daryaganj, Delhi, 110002, India

275 New North Road Islington Suite 1314 London,
N1 7AA, United Kingdom

ISBN (PBK): 978-93-48107-33-6
ISBN (E-BOOK): 978-93-48107-58-9

Scan the QR code to explore our entire catalogue

www.orangeava.com

Dedicated To

My beloved Parents, Whose Unwavering Love, Sacrifices, and Wisdom Have Shaped My Journey – My Father, Sundararajan, and My Mother, Tamilmani – Whose Guidance and Values Are The Foundation of All That I Am.

To My Pillar of Strength and My Greatest Source of Inspiration – My Wife, Shalini, Whose Belief in Me Fuels My Dreams, and My Son, Ishan, Whose Laughter and Curiosity Make Every Moment Meaningful.

And to My Brother, Jagadeesh, My First Friend, My Confidant, and My Lifelong Support – Thank You for Always Standing by Me.

With Deepest Gratitude and Boundless Love,
This Book is for You

About the Author

Bragadeesh Sundararajan is a visionary leader in artificial intelligence, data science, and analytics, with over 15 years of experience transforming data into measurable business impact. A passionate advocate for technology-driven decision-making, he has been at the forefront of AI innovation, crafting scalable, intelligent solutions that empower organizations and individuals alike.

Bragadeesh has been recognized as one of India's Top 100 AI Influential Leaders (2023) by Analytics India Magazine and honored as a Standout Thought Leader (2024) by 3AI. He has made significant contributions to AI and data science, pushing the boundaries of generative AI, predictive modeling, and real-time analytics. His pioneering work includes designing a self-booking vaccination slot system during the COVID-19 pandemic, demonstrating the power of AI to serve humanity at scale.

With a postgraduate degree in Artificial Intelligence and Machine Learning from The University of Texas at Austin, an MBA from IIT Madras, and a Computer Science degree from BITS Goa, Bragadeesh blends technical expertise with strategic acumen. He also holds multiple certifications in AWS, PyImageSearch, and Big Data Analytics, showcasing his deep proficiency in cloud computing, advanced analytics, and full-stack development.

Bragadeesh's mission is simple yet powerful: to bridge the gap between technology and real-world impact. He believes AI should not be a privilege but a tool for empowerment, and he continuously strives to make data-driven decision-making more accessible, ethical, and transformative. His vision is to build AI-driven ecosystems that revolutionize industries, optimize human potential, and create a future where technology enhances lives rather than replacing them.

As an author, thought leader, and mentor, Bragadeesh is dedicated to demystifying AI and data science, enabling professionals to leverage technology for strategic decision-making. His work is a testament to the belief that curiosity, learning, and innovation are the driving forces of progress.

This book is a reflection of his passion for analytics and his unwavering commitment to empowering the next generation of data leaders.

About the Technical Reviewers

Ananth Packkildurai is a recognized thought leader in data engineering and the author of the popular *Data Engineering Weekly* newsletter. With over 15 years of experience, he has built large-scale data infrastructure at companies including Slack and Zendesk, focusing on data pipelines, search infrastructure, customer analytics, and observability.

Ananth is a frequent speaker at global conferences, a panelist, and a podcast guest, where he shares insights on modern data platforms, AI-driven automation, and the evolving data landscape. His expertise in designing scalable and efficient data systems has influenced industry best practices.

As an advocate for knowledge-sharing within the data community, Ananth regularly reviews technical books and contributes to discussions on emerging trends in data engineering. His work continues to shape how organizations build and manage their data ecosystems.

Jatinder Singh is an experienced technology professional with over two decades of expertise in driving digital transformation and utilizing advanced technologies, including AI and machine learning. As a Senior Technical Account Manager at Amazon Web Services (AWS), he spearheads initiatives to modernize legacy systems, enhance performance, and develop innovative cloud-native solutions. His broad skillset encompasses solution and enterprise architecture, data security, governance, and cloud financial management, with a strong emphasis on delivering valuable insights through data-driven analysis.

His career trajectory, starting as a mainframe systems developer and advancing through leadership roles in ETL and business intelligence, has equipped him with a deep understanding of the software development lifecycle and modern data strategies. Over the past decade, Jatinder has been instrumental in assisting organizations with AWS cloud migrations, providing tailored solutions to meet each client's unique needs. He also specializes in FinOps, helping companies optimize cloud spending. A recognized public speaker and contributor to technology publications, Jatinder shares his expertise with the wider technical community. Based in Virginia, USA, he is known for his ability to lead cross-functional teams and ensure successful project implementations within budgetary constraints.

Acknowledgements

Writing a book is never a solitary journey, and I am incredibly grateful to all those who have supported, guided, and encouraged me along the way.

First and foremost, my deepest gratitude goes to **my parents, Sundararajan and Tamilmani**, whose unwavering faith in me has been my greatest strength. Their love, encouragement, and wisdom have shaped my path, and without them, this book would not have been possible.

I thank **my wife, Shalini**, and **my son, Ishan** for their endless patience, love, and understanding as I spent countless hours immersed in writing. Their unwavering support kept me going through every challenge.

A special note of appreciation to **my brother, Jagadeesh**, for always being there, pushing me forward, and believing in me, even when I doubted myself. Their encouragement has been invaluable.

I am also deeply grateful to the organizations, mentors, and experiences that have played a pivotal role in shaping my knowledge and expertise. The journey of learning never stops, and I owe a great deal to the courses, companies, and individuals who have enriched my understanding.

A heartfelt thanks to Ananth Packkildurai and Jatinder Singh, my technical reviewers, whose keen insights and meticulous scrutiny have helped refine this book. His expertise and guidance have been instrumental in making this work more precise and impactful.

Lastly, to my colleagues, friends, and readers – thank you for your encouragement and belief in my work. Writing this book has been an incredible journey, and I hope it adds value to your learning, just as the process of writing it has enriched mine.

Preface

In an era where data drives decisions, the ability to transform raw numbers into meaningful insights is more crucial than ever. Business leaders, data analysts, and technology enthusiasts all seek powerful tools to navigate the complexities of data visualization and business intelligence (BI). Apache Superset has emerged as a game-changer—an open-source, modern BI tool designed to empower organizations with self-service analytics, interactive dashboards, and scalable data exploration.

This book is a comprehensive guide to mastering Apache Superset, from its foundational concepts to advanced customization and real-world deployment. Whether you are a data analyst looking to build interactive dashboards, a data engineer integrating Superset into enterprise data pipelines, or a business leader seeking better insights, this book provides a structured, hands-on approach to leveraging Superset effectively.

Through 13 chapters, we explore everything from installation and configuration to advanced data visualization techniques, security best practices, and scaling Superset in production environments. We dive into exploratory data analysis (EDA), hypothesis testing, and business reporting, ensuring that readers not only learn how to use Superset but also understand how to extract real business value from their data.

What sets this book apart is its practical approach—each chapter builds upon the last, introducing key concepts alongside hands-on examples and industry use cases. By the end of this book, you will not only be proficient in Apache Superset but also be equipped to deploy it at scale, integrate it with your data pipelines, and enable self-service BI within your organization.

Whether you are a beginner looking to get started or an experienced professional wanting to deepen your expertise, this book serves as your definitive guide to Apache Superset. Let's embark on this journey together and unlock the full potential of modern data visualization.

Welcome to the future of Business Intelligence!

Get a Free eBook

We hope you are enjoying your recently purchased book! Your feedback is incredibly valuable to us, and to all other readers looking for great books.

If you found this book helpful or enjoyable, we would truly appreciate it, if you could take a moment to leave a short review with a 5 star rating on Amazon. It helps us grow, and lets other readers discover our books.

As a thank you, we would love to send you a free digital copy of this book, and a **30%** discount code on your next cart value on our official websites:

www.orangeava.com

www.orangeava.in (For Indian Subcontinent)

☑ **Here's how:**

Leave a review for the book on Amazon.

Take a screenshot of your review, and send an email to **info@orangeava.com** (it can be just the confirmation screen).

Once, we receive your screenshot, we will send you the digital file, within 24 hours.

Thank you so much for your support – it means a lot to us!

Downloading the code bundles and colored images

Please follow the links or scan the QR codes to download the ***Code Bundles and Images*** of the book:

https://github.com/ava-orange-education/Ultimate-Apache-Superset-for-Data-Visualization-and-Analytics

The code bundles and images of the book are also hosted on ***https://rebrand.ly/de18ec***

In case there's an update to the code, it will be updated on the existing GitHub repository.

Errata

We take immense pride in our work at **Orange Education Pvt Ltd,** and follow best practices to ensure the accuracy of our content to provide an indulging reading experience to our subscribers. Our readers are our mirrors, and we use their inputs to reflect and improve upon human errors, if any, that may have occurred during the publishing processes involved. To let us maintain the quality and help us reach out to any readers who might be having difficulties due to any unforeseen errors, please write to us at :

errata@orangeava.com

Your support, suggestions, and feedback are highly appreciated.

DID YOU KNOW

Did you know that Orange Education Pvt Ltd offers eBook versions of every book published, with PDF and ePub files available? You can upgrade to the eBook version at **www.orangeava.com** and as a print book customer, you are entitled to a discount on the eBook copy. Get in touch with us at: **info@orangeava.com** for more details.

At **www.orangeava.com**, you can also read a collection of free technical articles, sign up for a range of free newsletters, and receive exclusive discounts and offers on Print Books and eBooks.

PIRACY

If you come across any illegal copies of our works in any form on the internet, we would be grateful if you would provide us with the location address or website name. Please contact us at **info@orangeava.com** with a link to the material.

ARE YOU INTERESTED IN AUTHORING WITH US?

If there is a topic that you have expertise in, and you are interested in either writing or contributing to a book, please write to us at **business@orangeava.com**. We are on a journey to help developers and tech professionals to gain insights on the present technological advancements and innovations happening across the globe and build a community that believes Knowledge is best acquired by sharing and learning with others. Please reach out to us to learn what our audience demands and how you can be part of this educational reform. We also welcome ideas from tech experts and help them build learning and development content for their domains.

REVIEWS

Please leave a review. Once you have read and used this book, why not leave a review on the site that you purchased it from? Potential readers can then see and use your unbiased opinion to make purchase decisions. We at Orange Education would love to know what you think about our products, and our authors can learn from your feedback. Thank you!

For more information about Orange Education, please visit **www.orangeava.com**.

Table of Contents

CHAPTER 1

Introduction to Apache Superset

Introduction

Apache Superset is an open-source data exploration and visualization platform, that enables organizations to transform unanalyzed data into actionable insights. It falls in the modern data analytics ecosystem where users can create interactive dashboards and rich visualizations and perform exploratory data analysis in a very intuitive and user-friendly manner. Its goal is to empower both technical and non-technical users in analyzing and understanding their data, being thus an all-round solution for data analysts, scientists, and other business professional types.

Superset does offer visualization, from simple charts such as bar and line graphs to more advanced explorative tools such as heatmaps, geographical maps, and time-series analysis. Real-time data can be accessed with one click, then start exploring it using the drag-and-drop interface features of the platform. A user can create dashboards without any necessity for knowledge in coding at all; however, more complex queries can be developed using SQL-based querying.

Apache Superset is an open-source tool that any organization, big or small, can freely use. Not only do licensing costs disappear, but also customization and adaptability are actively encouraged. There is an active community of developers continuously contributing to its growth and ensuring that the tool stays at the cutting edge of modern data visualizations.

Structure

In this chapter, we will cover the following topics:

- History and Evolution
- Apache Superset: A New Dimension in Modern Business Intelligence/BI
- The Benefits of Choosing Superset

- Key Features of Superset
- SQL Lab: A Powerful SQL IDE in Apache Superset
- Basic Overview of BI Concepts
- Data-Driven Decision Making in Contemporary Business

History and Evolution

Airbnb developed Apache Superset, later handled by the Apache Foundation. The origination of Apache Superset initially began as an internal project back in 2015 at Airbnb, aimed towards data exploration and visualization. This was started because, at the time, the then BI tools available at Airbnb were either too complex to use for nontechnical users or incapable of handling huge amounts of data produced daily.

Maxime Beauchemin, who was an engineer at Airbnb at the time, began developing what would eventually become Superset, recognizing a much more intuitive, scalable, and flexible tool.

It was initially named "*Caravel*" but quickly gained popularity across the company because it is so easy to use, very interactive, and can easily attach itself to sources of information. It thus became the most used data visualization tool in the company. This way, various teams could have meaningful dashboards and reports with little effort.

In 2017, Airbnb opened its project and therefore all the functionalities of Airbnb became open to the rest of the tech community. Its user base went up rapidly as Superset started becoming a sought-after tool among data enthusiasts and organizations looking for a free, open-source alternative BI solution. Reaching such a potential, Apache Software Foundation took Superset back into its Incubator program in 2017.

In 2021, Apache Superset graduated to become one of the Top Level Projects (TLPs) under the Apache Foundation, which points out the maturity and stability of its acceptance globally. Presently, Apache Superset is indeed one of the leading open-source business intelligence tools as it has more than thousands of contributions from developers around the globe and also worked in many sectors such as finance, healthcare, technology, and e-commerce.

Apache Superset: A New Dimension in Modern Business Intelligence

High-speed data exploration and analysis is one of the necessities for business competitiveness, along with an enlightening provision of modern technologies toward decision-making. Traditional Business Intelligence tools involve a high cost of learning, and expensive licensing fees, and are not easily adaptable, making them inaccessible to most organizations. Apache Superset bridges this gap by providing an open-source, user-friendly, and highly customizable BI solution that meets modern analytics requirements.

Perhaps the most crucial role Apache Superset plays in the BI ecosystem is democratizing access to data. The tool allows users with and without technical knowledge to browse data, create visualizations, and build dashboards with as little coding knowledge as possible. That self-service approach to BI allows organizations to push a data-driven culture, letting users answer questions as quickly as possible, cutting out reliance on data engineers or IT for knowledge.

Superset can be easily used for companies with a very heterogeneous landscape of data. This means that it can connect to a good range of data sources from SQL-type traditional databases all the way to modern big-data engines such as Druid and Presto in such a way that any business could unify its data analysis efforts within one platform. This will ensure that decision-makers are always updated on the latest information available by processing large datasets and providing real-time data visualization. Another critical role in which modern BI plays is extensibility. Organizations can tailor Superset to match their needs whether proprietary data source integration, custom visualizations, or the embedding of Superset into another application. That flexibility makes it a powerful solution for those organizations looking for a BI platform for growth and support.

Example Use Cases: Data Discovery, Interactive Dashboards, and Self-Service Analytics

Applications of Apache Superset

The Apache Superset can be applied in most use cases across most industries being pretty versatile. Some of the most common applications are as follows:

- **Data Exploration:** Data exploration means winnowing through raw data to identify trends, patterns, or insights. Users can use Superset to quickly connect to the source of the data, write SQL queries, and then apply a variety of chart types to see the results. It reveals correlations, outliers, and trends that might go unnoticed in a tabular report. For example, a retail organization can leverage Superset to delve deep into the sales data of a company to determine the top products along with ascertaining changes in customer preferences over time.
- **Interactive Dashboards:** Dashboards stand as one of the best ways in which data insights can be communicated clearly and presentably. This allows for very interactive dashboards with filters, drill-downs, and cross-filtering by Superset. In this way, people get data in a very dynamic fashion useful in those situations where stakeholders need to grasp complex information quickly. For example, an example of using Superset is the dashboard that the marketing team came up with to follow the performance of several campaigns. Filter values can bc changed in real-time to see by region, by time, or by advertising channel.

- **Self-Service Analytics:** This is probably the most significant takeaway from using Apache Superset: self-service analytics. In other words, this means that business users can simply explore data, make reports, and create visualizations on their own and not depend on IT or data specialists. Because organizations empower end-users to analyze on their own, they remove bottlenecks in data processing and accelerate the whole process of making decisions. For example, a financial analyst can use Superset to explore transaction data, segment customers, and build insights into spending without waiting for technical assistance.

The Benefits of Choosing Superset

The increased organizations within the new world of data, with data originating from various sources including but not limited to, customers through sales transactions, social media, and internal business processes create so many types of data. This explosion represents one side of the coin and creates a challenge: only organizations that can make meaning out of raw data by using tools such as Apache Superset can harness the potential for better decision-making.

Perhaps one reason that Apache Superset has quickly become the modern standard in business intelligence is the fact that it is free, flexible, and empowering. Here are a few of the key reasons why Superset stands out in the BI landscape:

- **Demand for Data Visualization Tools in a Data-Driven Organization:** Today, modern organizations make strategic decisions, optimize operations, and look for opportunities to grow based on a humongous amount of data. However, raw data is complex, voluminous, and to some extent, cumbersome to interpret. Hence, data visualizations are highly sought after because they take the raw dataset and convert them into charts, graphs, and dashboards that are easier and even more comfortable to understand and analyze.
- **The Role of Visualization Tools:** Visualization of complicated rich data is made visual by visualization tools. Decision-making persons can thus grab trends, patterns, or anomalies. For example, a simple line graph would certainly show sales trends over time and is much more likely than a spreadsheet of numbers to do so.
- **Fast Decisions:** The dashboards allow direct viewing of real-time data, so the decision-makers can draw information in order to make judgments without heavy reports of data.

  Improving Data Communications Visualizations are better for communicating insights across various teams, so each one of them can understand the story the data tells, irrespective of the technical background.

  This is where Apache Superset really shines. It can offer a wide set of visualizations, from the simplest line and pie charts up to the most complex time series or geographical maps, and more. Its interface is interactive and intuitive, and it is very much prompting users to explore data, create visualizations, and build dashboards that immediately deliver value.

- **The Growth of Self-Service BI and Data Democratization:** It was an IT and data specialist-owned field of BI and Data Analysis. Reports and visualization requests had to be made by business users. This meant delays and bottlenecks. This model is not tenable in a fast business world where timely insights are necessary to be competitive.

  Self-service BI addresses this challenge by allowing non-technical users to access, explore, and analyze data without bothering the IT or data specialists. On that account, one of the trends created came to be tagged as data democratization, that is the availability of data access and insight to virtually connect everyone within an organization, regardless of technical proficiency.

- **Importance of Self-Service Business Intelligence:**

  Empower End User: With self-service BI, business users including marketing managers, sales teams, and HR professionals are allowed access to the data and enabled to produce reports on their own, thereby curtailing reliance on technical teams and accelerating the decision-making process.

  Improves Agility: The dynamic business environment requires high-velocity adaptation toward trends and challenges. Through self-service BI tools, the end-user can scrutinize data and draw insights in real time that improve the agility of an organization.

This creates a data-driven culture because, with data available to all levels of employees, such a culture develops toward data-driven decision making. This process will eventually lead to more informed strategies and better performance with a common business understanding.

Apache Superset is targeting self-service BI. It puts itself in a good place as a service that empowers business users to explore and analyze data with minimum technical know-how owing to its drag-and-drop UI, SQL Lab-an integrated SQL IDE, and ease of integration with multiple sources. Users own their visualization-a brief and effective way of customizing dashboards and sharing insights without needing to be technical experts.

Meeting the Demands of Today's BI Users with Apache Superset

Modern BI users require flexibility and scalability, as they prefer to handle different demands of their data. Such demands are addressed by Apache Superset through its key features:

- **Open-Source and Low-Cost:** Apache Superset is open-source and free of licensing fees. And this, in particular, similar to most proprietary BI tools, has become a reason to use it for all possible business entities, starting with startups and ending with large enterprises. Another aspect that makes it open to organizations is its open-source nature, where this can be tailored by the organization to fit their needs better including adding new visualizations, integrating it with proprietary data sources, or even building custom features.
- **High Visualization Power:** Superset has very diverse chart types from simple to more complex ones, so data may be visualized in the best possible way according to analysis requirements. It supports creating informative and also beautifully pleasing visualizations. The tool supports interactive features such as filters, drill-downs, and cross-filtering, and provides users with the opportunity to inspect data from multiple angles without leaving the dashboard.
- **More Integrated Heterogeneous Data Sources:** Modern organizations work with different sources of data from traditional databases, such as MySQL and PostgreSQL, to big data engines such as Druid and Presto. What makes Superset such a powerful unifier of data analysis efforts is compatibility with dozens of data connectors. Since Superset supports SQLAlchemy, it is pretty flexible with the integration of data and supports any connection to that data source with a supported SQLAlchemy dialect.
- **Scalability and Performance:** Apache Superset is developed to efficiently handle enormous datasets and can easily accommodate more organizations within big data. The caching mechanism is integrated along with Celery for working, so any task initiated asynchronously is managed with perfect ease. This way, it ensures an appropriate performance even at complex queries and large datasets. Its architecture supports horizontal scaling; therefore, an organization's ability to explore can scale along with the quantity of accrual of data.
- **Strong Security and Access Controls:** All BI tools handle data that is most critically sensitive and must therefore remain private. Superset, therefore, provides strong authentication and authorization. The tool supports Role-Based Access Control, or RBAC, by which the right access is controlled by administrators and data security is assured. It also supports enterprise authentication systems, such as LDAP and OAuth, for hassle-free security management in large enterprise environments.
- **Customization and Extensibility:** Modern BI users need to be able to customize the tools offered to them depending on the requirements of their business. Superset extensible architecture allows developers to create custom

visualization, add plugins, or integrate Superset with existing workflows using its API. The aforementioned flexibility allows organizations to adapt Superset to the changing needs of a business, hence making it a future-proof solution for BI.

Apache Superset is a new, open-source Business Intelligence that supports data-driven organizations. Businesses also generate and rely on data continuously at all times to make decisions that affect various aspects of it; hence, there will always be a growing need for better data visualization tools. Superset fulfills the need with a platform that is powerful and extremely rich in features, yet accessible to users from diverse backgrounds of technical expertise. It provides self-service analytics, detailed options for visualization, and connects sources of diverse origin in itself. It can, therefore, be considered a good choice for organizations looking to democratize access to data and propagate a culture of data. Due to such a finish for modern BI user needs including flexibility, scalability, cost-effectiveness, and security; Apache Superset positions itself in the list of leaders among the tools in the BI landscape, transforming raw data into actionable insights driving business success.

Open Source and Community

It is also one of the characteristic strengths of Apache Superset that it is open-source, making it an attractive and powerful choice for any organization looking to adopt business intelligence tools in place of costly licenses or vendor lock-in. Superset offers openness, flexibility, and a collaborative development model driving continuous innovation-something that proprietary solutions cannot. Let us dig deeper into the pros of open-source BI tools, and the dynamism of the Apache Superset community, and make a comparison with leading proprietary BI solutions such as Tableau and Power BI.

Advantages of Open-Source BI Tools

In the past few years, open-source BI tools have gained much popularity, and the following are some of the key advantages for picking them over proprietary solutions:

- **Cost-Effectiveness**

  Zero Licensing Fees: Apache Superset is an open-source tool that does not attract notorious licensing fees, which is usual in proprietary BI solutions such as Tableau or Power BI. That alone brings huge advantages to startups, small businesses, and large enterprise entities who are looking to save on cost departments in software.

  Lower TCO: Since open-source BI tools are free, the TCO is also low in cost because customers do not pay their support and upgrade fees to the respective vendors. Organizations can use the money towards building and extending the tool rather than in license payments.

- **Heterogeneity and Customization**

  Open-source BI tools are open to the source code fully, and thus, allow organizations to change the tool according to the need it has. This kind of customization is valuable to organizations that have unique needs for themselves or integrate the BI tool with other existing systems.

  It is highly modular and extensible so developers can easily include new visualizations, plugins, or integration of diverse requirements in Superset. It makes Superset flexible enough to adapt to changing business needs and evolving data landscapes.

- **Transparency and Control**

  With open-source software, one has a complete view of how the tool works - openness and control over its functioning and security. This is very important for any organization that may handle sensitive data. It helps to ensure their BI tool meets such organizations' security standards and complies with their compliance.

This community regularly issues updates, security patches, and improvements to make Apache Superset a secure and up-to-date framework for development.

Comparison with Proprietary BI Tools (Tableau and Power BI)

While Apache Superset offers numerous advantages as an open-source BI tool, it is essential to understand how it compares to popular proprietary BI tools such as Tableau and Power BI.

Here is a breakdown of the key differences:

Feature	Apache Superset	Tableau	Power BI
Cost	Free and open-source	Expensive licensing (per user)	Affordable but with licensing fees
Customization	Highly customizable, full access to code	Limited customization	Limited customization
Data Connectivity	Supports a wide range of data sources, especially SQL-based	Extensive support, but some connectors require additional licenses	A broad range of connectors, tightly integrated with the Microsoft ecosystem

Community and Support	Community-driven, active forums, and GitHub support	Strong vendor support, but at a cost	Vendor support available; active user community
Ease of Use	Moderate; requires some technical knowledge	Highly intuitive, user-friendly	User-friendly with integration into Microsoft tools
Scalability	Scalable for large data sets; performance depends on deployment	Scalable but requires expensive enterprise solutions	Scales well with Microsoft's Azure infrastructure
Data Visualization	Wide variety of charts, with support for custom visualizations	Extensive visualization options, polished and refined	Solid visualization capabilities, with built-in Microsoft Office integration
Security and Governance	Role-Based Access Control (RBAC), integrates with enterprise authentication systems	Robust enterprise-level security features	Enterprise-grade security, and integration with Microsoft Active Directory

Table 1.1: *Comparison of BI Tools*

Key Comparisons

- **Cost**: Superset is open-source and, therefore, incurs no licensing fee. An attribute that most organizations budgeted in preferring to pay. Tableau and Power BI charge required licenses; huge prices are incurred on big teams.
- **Customization and Extensibility:** Superset offers much more flexibility than elsewhere, meaning that one can continue to customize the tool fully to their needs. Though customization is available in Tableau and Power BI, it is relatively much more limited as compared to full open-source-based access.
- **Ease of Use:** Tableau and Power BI are both extremely well-known for having friendly interfaces and polished looks to their visualizations. Superset has more of a steep curve and really should be left for those who have at least some technical knowledge, or SQL skills.
- **Scalability**: In terms of scalability, all these tools can handle large files. Scalability for Superset would heavily depend on deployment and configuration, and scalability solutions from Tableau and Power BI offer enterprise solutions optimized to scale but cost a pretty penny.

Hence, Superset is comparatively more flexible and low-cost in comparison with proprietary BI tools such as Tableau and Power BI. However, the cost may be higher, in terms of the time spent understanding the software, which is another con side for open-source software. Yet, as Superset is open-source, it becomes a great solution for organizations looking to drive their teams with data-driven insights without the lock-in of vendor solutions.

Key Features of Superset

One of the most prominent reasons Apache Superset has gained recognition globally is the variety of visualizations available and as much freedom it gives its users to build insightful and interactive dashboards. This section is going to include chart types, customization options for charts and dashboards, and the drag-and-drop interface that makes the process quite smooth, even for non-technical users.

Superset comes with a variety of chart types to cater to the numerous kinds of visualization that are required. The charts easily represent complex insights from data making it understandable and aesthetically pleasing to the visual senses.

Chart and Dashboard Customization

One of the strengths of Apache Superset lies in its customization of charts and dashboards according to the needs of your data visualization. The customization aspect is critical to ensure that visualizations communicate insights effectively to your audiences and are fashioned according to them.

Customize Charts

- **Data Configuration:** Select appropriate columns, metrics, and filters that you want to apply in your chart. You may aggregate data, apply transformations, or add calculated fields.
- **Colors**: Different built-in color schemes or import your own custom color scheme to add beauty and readability.

  This includes tooltip and labeling in order to personalize your tooltips and labels to show out data as one hovers over the chart for more interaction and information.
- **Sorting and Filtering**: Switch sorts to and apply filters in order to see select subsets of a dataset such that charts show the most relevant information.
- **Annotations and Trend Lines** Create annotations, trend lines, or reference lines to focus attention on interesting values, trends, or threshold data.

Customize Dashboard

- **Flexible Layout:** Graphics, tables, and all contents on the dashboard can be laid out by using a grid layout. Components can be resized, moved, and organized for producing a great and useful dashboard.

- **Interactive Filters:** Can introduce interactive filters such as dropdown menus, sliders, or date range pickers to allow users to dynamically investigate data; this makes dashboards more engaging and user-friendly.

  Superset supports cross-filtering in which a user can click one chart for an update about related charts by tying in the same data point. This way, users allow for greater depth by discovering relationships between different data sets.

  Text, Headings, and Custom HTML Add any context, explanations, or branding elements you require; you can add text boxes, headings, or even custom HTML components to make the dashboard even more informative and harmonious with your organization's identity.

- **Embed and Share:** Dashboards can be embedded into other web applications, or shareable URLs allow access to insights without a login to Superset.

Using these personalization features, the user gradually constructs interactive and personalized visualizations for any group of interested readers, from a summarized executive report to an extremely detail-rich analytical report, all the way to real-time operation dashboards.

A drag-and-drop interface allows for friendly interaction.

The drag-and-drop interface of Apache Superset, one of the most noted features with regard to ease of use, allows almost anyone to create beautiful charts and dashboards with minimal technical background in order to produce the same.

Primary Features of the Drag-and-Drop Interface

- **Intuitive chart builder:** The interface of the chart builder will allow users to drag and drop columns from data, metrics, and filters into fields. The learning curve decreases so that even non-technical users can quite easily make complex visualizations without writing SQL queries themselves.
- **Dashboard Design:** Users may add and arrange dashboards by dragging and dropping charts, tables, text boxes, and so on onto the canvas. The layout is grid-based, thus easy to resize and reposition components to enable the ability to design the dashboards according to your specific needs.
- **Instant Preview:** It constructs or changes charts and dashboards and, during the process, provides an instant preview so you can see exactly how your visualizations will look and make changes right away.
- **Responsive Design:** Drag-and-drop interface can support charts and dashboards such that it can be responsive with the automatic adaptation of various screen sizes as well as resolutions. It is more useful while sharing dashboards with users accessing on different devices.

- **Advantages of Drag-and-Drop Interface:** Since no SQL queries or code has to be written while creating charts and dashboards, it is also available for non-technical people to be used, such as business analysts, marketers, and executives.
- **Rapid Prototyping:** Drag-and-drop functionality enables rapid prototyping and testing of a wide range of possible visualizations so that fast data exploration and ensuing insight are possible.
- **Collaboration:** Ease of use makes collaboration possible between data experts and business users in order to work together on creating meaningful visualizations.

Interactive and Personalizable Dashboards

One of the most powerful features of Apache Superset is its ability to build interaction with customizable and user-friendly dashboards, viewing data dynamically and in an engaging manner. It allows you to create a deeper understanding, real-time interaction with data, and sharing findings with others. Let us talk about how you can build and edit an interactive dashboard, and apply filters, drill-downs, and cross-filtering in order to embed visualizations and share insights.

Building and Editing Interactive Dashboards

1. **Building a Dashboard from Scratch**

Almost mesmerizing in the creation of an Apache Superset dashboard is that it is almost intuitive due to its drag-and-drop facility.

Plot Personal Graphs: Previous to the days of the dashboard, it used to be done chart-wise.

Charts: Comes from the superset menu + Chart.

Select your dataset and chart type (for example, bar chart, line chart, pie chart) and configure your chart by selecting the proper dimensions, metrics, and filters.

Save each chart with a descriptive name, as you will add them to the dashboard later.

Create a New Dashboard

1. Go to Dashboards and click the `+ Dashboard` button to create a new dashboard.
2. Name it Dashboard and add a brief description; then click `Save`.
3. Set charts on the dashboard.

Once your dashboard is created, open it, then click `Edit Dashboard`.

You can now just drag and drop your saved charts directly onto the dashboard canvas. Arrange as you like, and resize to fit your design.

2. **Dashboard Version**

Superset offers numerous choices to make or update your dashboards:

- **Resizing and Rearranging Charts:** You can resize, drag, or rearrange a chart on the dashboard by dragging its edges or repositioning.
- **Adding Text, Headings, and Images:** Add text boxes, headings, and images. That should be the understanding in using the Add Component button from where all will help explain, describe, or brand your dashboard.
- **Add Tabs**. Using tabs, you can categorize your rows in a dashboard into relevant charts for better structuring, especially on complex dashboards with many sections or data categories.
- **Styling and Theming**: Superset's built-in theming is fully utilizable to provide your dashboard with an identically branded look and feel for your organization or any design preferences.

These features make it easy to create dashboards that are not only functional but also good-looking and understandable at first glance.

Applying Filters, Drill-Downs, and Cross-Filtering

Interactive dashboards in Superset also advance by applying filters, drill-down capabilities, and cross-filtering, allowing users to go deeper into data from a variety of perspectives.

- **Filter Use**

  Filters enable the user to choose specific data they would want to have on the dashboard. It is more effortless to just zero in on the most appropriate subsets of data such as a specific time period or region.

  - **Filters Global:** All the graphs would be affected by global filters. Adding a "*Date Range*" filter, for example, would thus enable an entire user to change the time frame for all visualizations on the dashboard with one click.
  - **Global Filter:** It appears by right-clicking Edit Dashboard> Add Filter, the following selects type of filter: dropdown, multi-select, date range; it then applies this to appropriate data fields.
  - **Chart-Specific Filters:** Each chart can also have its very own filters, which are separated from any other charts within the dashboard. Filters open up by clicking the filter icon from a given chart and then choosing your preferred criteria.

- **Drill-Down Capability**

  The more granular every level of opportunity is to drill down into the specific data points. For example, you might probably find sales by year and then drill from there into monthly or even daily sales.

How to Activate Drill-Downs:

1. Allow drill-down capabilities into the data through its hierarchical structure, for instance: **`Year`** → **`Month`** → **`Day`**.
2. While appearing under the "**`Group By`**" or "**`Columns`**" section of the interface, drill-downs can be configured to let the users click points of data to open up more detailed views in setting up your chart.

- **Cross-Filtering**

Cross-filtering is a very important feature in general, and will make charts interactive depending upon what the user does, for instance when a user clicks a point in one chart then related charts update automatically showing the filtered data.

How to Enable Cross-Filtering: Activate cross-filtering on when in edit dashboard for your charts. Charts that support cross filtering will react to what the user does, for example clicking a bar within a bar chart or on a point within a map.

For instance, clicking a "**`Region`**" in one graph might result in another graph displaying only data relevant to that region.

Filter options, drill-downs, and cross-filtering capabilities make interactive analyses more accessible and useful to users while offering more interesting, meaningful, and participative content as users can explore data in real-time.

Embed Visualizations and Share Insights

Once you build an interactive dashboard within Superset, there are many ways to share and embed visualizations, so it is easy to disseminate insights across your organization or with external stakeholders.

- **Inline Visualizations**

You can include individual charts or full dashboards in other web applications, intranet pages, or even external websites. This helps integrate Superset visualizations into your company's existing analytics tools or portals.

How to Insert a Visualization:

1. Now, select which chart or dashboard you want to embed. Click the **`Settings`**, or the gear icon, and select **`Embed Code`**.

2. Copy this code for the generated `HTML <iframe>`. Then, paste it into the target web page or application.

That is, by integrating with Superset visualizations, the insights regarding data reach one's hands, even without users' login to the Superset platform.

- **Sharing Dashboards**

  Superset allows for multiple ways of sharing dashboards with other people:

  - `Share Links`: You can share the link to the dashboard directly from a web browser, and copy it across. This way, other users accessing permissions can view your dashboard in their own instance of Superset.
  - `Exporting Dashboards`: Dashboards are exported as JSON files. It is easy to share them between different Superset instances. Such export enables one to migrate dashboards between environments or, for instance, from the development environment to production.
  - `Report Scheduling`: Reporting and Alerting can also be utilized to schedule periodic emails containing snapshots of your dashboard or specific charts. This allows stakeholders to receive the current information instead of accessing the dashboard.

- **Permission Settings for Sharing Role-Based Access Control**

  Superset allows controlling who can view or modify a dashboard through roles and associated permissions. One would, for example, use "`Viewer`" access only to let business users view the dashboard, but apply "`Admin`" access to data analysts who need to edit or manage a dashboard.

  Public Access: If you would like to share a dashboard with users outside your organization, you can make public access. This creates a public link, through which anyone might access the dashboard without needing to log into Superset. It also adds visualizations and makes use of such sharing possibilities so that the insights from Superset reach the right audience, be it internal teams, clients, or even external partners. Summing up, Apache Superset can develop interactive dashboards and can be customized at all levels, so it is versatile when it comes to data visualization and analysis.

SQL Lab: A Powerful SQL IDE in Apache Superset

One of the most powerful and flexible features of Apache Superset is SQL Lab. It provides a very rich SQL Integrated Development Environment for data exploration and writing SQL queries with previewing of results and management of your query history. It is supposed to be, on the one hand, a self-service tool, convenient both to a data analyst and business user, capable of conducting ad-hoc data analysis entirely independent from reliance on any data engineer.

Exploratory Data Analysis Using the Integrated SQL Lab

The SQL Lab is intuitive, and interactive, and makes it very easy for a user to experiment and explore their data; it can connect directly to your data sources and lets you query and interact directly with the data in real-time.

The SQL Lab Key Features

Many information sources are accessible.

SQL Lab supports most data sources configured via Superset, as well as PostgreSQL, MySQL, Oracle, Amazon Redshift, and Google BigQuery.

Databases and schemas allow the users to enable them to choose and analyze tables, columns, and data.

- **Interactive Table Browser:** In the left panel, SQL Lab will provide you with a way of browsing the available databases, schemas, and tables of connected data sources.

  The extended version of the table presents its columns, along with the data types including sample data. Then one can easily know the structure of data prior to writing any query.

- **Schema and Metadata Discovery:** Column details can also be accessed for users to provide support in more insight into their data model.

  It is very handy when one is working with unknown sets of data or is teaming up with others to analyze data.

- **Exploring Data with SQL Lab Getting Started**

  1. Open SQL Lab.
  2. Navigate to SQL Lab and then click SQL Editor from the Superset navigation menu.
  3. Select a database and schema:
     a. Select the database and schema of your choice using the dropdown menus at the top.
     b. You can use the left-hand side table browser to browse all tables available in the schema selected.

- **Analyze Table Structures**

  Expand tables to see columns and their data types; you will learn what is in your data and prepare you to write SQL queries. SQL Lab is useful in exploratory data analysis in real-time and can be a tremendous tool to get a first-hand overview of your datasets prior to getting into deeper analysis. Writing, Saving, and Sharing SQL Queries. The SQL Lab offers a very powerful SQL editor, which is useful for writing, running, saving, and sharing SQL queries.

This makes it useful for ad hoc analysis, data explorations, and report generation.

1. **SQL Query Creation Intelligent SQL Editor:** The SQL Lab comes with an intelligent SQL editor that supports syntax highlighting, autocompletion, and query validation for SQL writing.

Query Execution: Subsequent to writing a query, clicking the `Run` button runs it. SQL Lab sends the query to your data source, retrieves the results, and displays them in the result pane.

Example SQL Query:

```
SELECT customer_name, SUM(order_amount) AS total_sales
FROM orders
WHERE order_date >= '2023-01-01'
GROUP BY customer_name
ORDER BY total_sales DESC
LIMIT 10;
```

This query retrieves the top 10 customers based on total sales since January 1, 2023.

2. **Saving SQL Queries**

Save Queries to Run Them Again: You can save frequently run queries for later or even share them with other members of your team. Once you have run your query click the Save button. You name it, include a description, and save it to your list of personal queries.

Saved Queries: Saved queries can be placed into folders. This way, many queries about various projects or origins of data can be managed easily.

3. **SQL Queries Sharing**

Query Sharing Options: SQL Lab allows you to share saved queries with other users by sharing a direct URL or exporting the query as a JSON file that then can be imported into their instance of Superset.

Shared Questions Support Common Sense-Making: As teams strive to answer each other's questions, each refines findings for the others, revises existing questions, or generates new visualizations based on common results.

This enables SQL Lab to be an effective instrument for building up a library of reusable SQL queries, facilitating collaboration, and accelerating the workflow of data analysis.

Preview of Data and Query History

SQL Lab provides a full preview of data and also features a query history to track queries, see how the data changed, or track older analyses.

1. **Preview Data**

Instant Preview of the Result: When you run a SQL query from SQL Lab, your result will pop right into view in the result pane following the editor. You can instantly test the result and then modify the SQL code if needed.

SQL Lab has pagination and sorting capabilities so that it can be easier to work with large-scale data. Columns can be sorted directly in the result pane for further data analysis.

Export Data: The result of every query can be exported in multiple formats such as CSV, Excel, JSON in order to analyze it outside Superset or share it with other stakeholders.

2. **Query History**

Access Previous Queries: SQL Lab saves copies of all the queries you run by the user in your history and lets you recall them so you can edit and re-execute them instead of retyping them.

All the files of history would comprise query status, execution time, and the source of data. It may maintain the performance of the queries and may help discover the cause for the non-working of particular queries.

Search and Filter History: SQL Lab has query history that one can easily search and filter based on date, database, schema, or keywords.

All these features provide the user with an effortless way of monitoring their progress in analyzing, validating transformations in data, and keeping an organized record of activities in their data exploration.

Advantages of Using SQL Lab in Superset

The advantages the SQL Lab in Apache Superset offers to its users make it one of the better tools for data analysis.

- **Self-Service Analytics:** Users will find data, build their own queries, and develop insights without wholly relying on the data engineers or IT.
- **Ad-hoc Analysis:** SQL Lab supports ad-hoc analysis and thus can answer business questions on the fly by validation of data trends.

- **Reusability and Team Collaboration:** Saving and sharing queries and reusing them contributes to team-based work and quickens the analysis done by teams.
- **Data Exploration and Visualization:** This makes easy transformation of results from your query into visualizations or dashboards-bridging data exploration to data storytelling.

Adding Custom Visualization Plugins

While Superset comes with a rich set of built-in visualization options, there may be scenarios where you need a chart type or visualization that is not natively supported. Superset's plugin architecture allows you to add custom visualization plugins, enabling you to create unique and specialized visualizations that meet your specific data analysis needs.

Although Superset comes pre-loaded with a large set of visualization options, you will always find moments when you need a kind of chart or visualization that is not natively available. Superset has a plugin architecture, so you can add your own visualizations at your side to create unique and specialized visualizations that tend to specifically meet your needs in data analysis.

The Importance of Including Custom Visualizations

Specialized Data Requirements: Some organizations require special types of charts; these may be waterfall charts, funnel charts, or even very complex geospatial visualizations, which may not be included natively.

  - **Interactive Multimedia:** You can add interactive elements, animations, or data-driven effects to your customized visualization in dashboards, which makes it more attractive.
  - **Brand Consistency:** Custom visualizations can always be restyled to support your organization's brand guidelines for greater visual consistency across reports and dashboards.

1. **How to Add a Custom Visualization Plugin:**

Here is a high-level overview of the process for adding custom visualization plugins to Superset:

   a. Set Up a Development Environment:

      i. Install Node.js and npm, as the frontend part of Superset is built using JavaScript and React.

      ii. Clone the Superset GitHub repository:

- git clone https://github.com/apache/superset.git
- `cd superset`

2. **Introduce a New Visualization Plugin:**
   a. Superset also comes with a plugin template with which you can make your personalized visualizations. You may make a new plugin using either npm or yarn command.
   b. Define logic for visualization, data processing, and configuration options in React and D3.js or any other JavaScript charting library.
   c. Register the Plugin:
      i. Once ready, you should register your plugin with Superset using the setupPlugins.js to import and use it in the code. When it loads all the plugins, it should recognize and include your visualization.
3. **Build and Deploy:**
   a. Let us rebuild the frontend assets using the command npm run build.
   b. Restart the Superset server, and your custom visualization is now available.
   c. The aforementioned will make your custom visualization plugin appear in the list the next time you create or edit a chart within Superset. In this regard, you can easily extend the visualization capabilities of Superset to fit your special data analysis needs.

Examples of Custom Visualization Plugins:

- Advanced scatter plot with regression lines
- Color scale and heat map, custom-designed
- An animated line chart with transition effects
- Networking graphs for representing relationships among entities

Using APIs to Integrate Superset with Other Systems

Superset includes a set of RESTful APIs, which you can use to interface with another system when automating tasks, such as when embedding visualizations into third-party applications or managing Superset programmatically; it could make it easier to add Superset to an existing data ecosystem.

- **Common Uses of APIs**
  - **Automation:** Automate repetitive tasks such as dashboard creation and update, user management, or refreshing of the data connections.

   - **In-Embedding Visualizations**: Embed Superset charts and dashboards within other web applications, internal portals, or custom analytics platforms.
   - **Custom Workflows**: Superset integrates seamlessly with your existing data pipelines, ETL tools, and CI/CD systems to trigger updates or refresh workflows of the dashboards or visualization.

- **Key Superset API Endpoints**

  Here are some commonly used API endpoints that you can leverage for integration:

   - **Dashboard API**: Create, update, delete, or fetch information about dashboards.
   - Example: `GET /api/v1/dashboard/` retrieves a list of dashboards.
   - **Chart API**: Manage individual charts, including creating new charts or updating existing ones.
   - Example: `POST /api/v1/chart/` creates a new chart using the specified configuration.
   - **Dataset API**: Work with datasets, including adding new data sources, editing dataset properties, or retrieving dataset metadata.
   - Example: `PUT /api/v1/dataset/<dataset_id>` updates a specific dataset.
   - **Authentication API**: Manage user authentication and obtain access tokens for secure API interactions.

     Example: `POST /api/v1/security/login` authenticates a user and returns a session token.

- **How to Use the APIs**
   - **Authentication**: Most Superset API endpoints require authentication. You can obtain an access token by sending your username and password to the `/api/v1/security/login` endpoint.
   - **Making API Requests**: Use tools such as curl, Postman, or custom scripts (for example, Python, JavaScript) to interact with the Superset APIs. Include the access token in the request headers for authentication.

Example: Using Python to Fetch Dashboards

The following figure illustrates the use of Python to fetch Dashboards:

```python
import requests


superset_url = "http://localhost:8088"
login_endpoint = f"{superset_url}/api/v1/security/login"
dashboard_endpoint = f"{superset_url}/api/v1/dashboard/"


credentials = {
    "username": "admin",
    "password": "your_password",
    "provider": "db",
}

response = requests.post(login_endpoint, json=credentials)
access_token = response.json()["access_token"]


headers = {"Authorization": f"Bearer {access_token}"}
dashboard_response = requests.get(dashboard_endpoint, headers=headers)

dashboards = dashboard_response.json()
print(dashboards)
```

Figure 1.1: *Python to Fetch Dashboards*

This example demonstrates how to authenticate with Superset and retrieve a list of dashboards using the API.

Custom Theming and Branding for Organizations

Custom theming and branding allow organizations to personalize the look and feel of Superset to align with their brand identity. This helps create a consistent visual experience for users and stakeholders.

The Value of Customizing Themes and Branding:

- **Brand Consistency**: Apply your organization's colors, fonts, and logos to ensure the platform matches your brand guidelines.
- **Enhanced User Experience**: Create a more engaging user experience by customizing the UI to suit your audience's preferences.
- **Professional Appearance**: Custom theming gives Superset a polished, professional appearance that matches your company's internal tools and portals.

2. **Applying Custom Themes and Branding**

There are two main ways to customize the theme and branding in Superset:

a. **Custom CSS and LESS Files**

Superset uses CSS and LESS for styling, and you can customize the look of the platform by modifying these files.

Step 1: Access the CSS Files

Locate the main CSS or LESS files in the Superset frontend source code (for example, superset/assets/stylesheets).

Step 2: Modify the Styles

Apply your custom styles by editing these files, such as changing colors, fonts, button styles, and layout properties.

Step 3: Rebuild and Deploy

Rebuild the frontend assets using npm run build and restart the Superset server to apply the changes.

b. **Custom Configuration File (superset_config.py)**

You can also customize branding through the `superset_config.py` configuration file, which allows you to define global settings for Superset.

Logo and Favicon: Define paths to your custom logo and favicon.

```
APP_ICON = "/static/assets/images/your_logo.png"
FAVICON = "/static/assets/images/your_favicon.ico"
```

Branding Colors: Override the default color scheme by specifying your brand colors.

```
CUSTOM_CSS = "/static/assets/stylesheets/custom_theme.css"
```

Custom Welcome Message: Display a custom welcome message or instructions on the login page or dashboard.

```
APP_NAME = "My Company BI Platform"
```

3. **Applying Custom Themes Using Plugins**

If you prefer a more structured approach to theming, you can develop custom themes as plugins using React and the Superset plugin infrastructure. This allows you to create reusable themes that can be shared across different Superset deployments.

Basic Overview of BI Concepts

BI and Its Importance: Business intelligence relates to the acquisition, analysis, and process of data into useful and action information that helps make adequate decisions for organizations. Business intelligence can be described as the assembling of tools, technologies, methodologies, and practices to enable an improved understanding of the business's operations, marketplace trends, customers' behavior, and performance.

At its core, BI involves:

- **Data Collection:** Collect data from various sources such as a database, spreadsheets, CRM, or third-party APIs.
- **Data Analysis**: Statistical and analytical techniques that may reveal patterns, trends, and correlations.
- **Data Visualization**: Complex data will be represented in a presentable manner by the use of charts, graphs, dashboards, and reports.

The Importance of Business Intelligence: From this, BI, as the source that gives real-time data-backed insights enables decision-makers to identify opportunities and risks. BI integrates data from various sources, automates the analysis of data, and thus enables the organization to improve its processes so that data no longer is handled manually.

Competitive Advantage: Business organizations that use Business Intelligence have a better position for understanding market trends, customer preferences, and the dynamics of competition and respond in due course to such changes. The platform would help in identifying improvement areas, optimizing product offerings, and new revenue streams by basing decisions on the analysis of data. Put simply, BI is one of the enabling factors for any organization to succeed in the data-driven world of today, where raw data turns into actionable insight that in turn drives better business results.

Data-Driven Decision Making in Contemporary Business

Practically, data-driven decision making is used in analytical insights and data-driven business strategies, actions, and decisions. Rather than relying on intuition, gut feeling, or assumptions, they use data to reinforce their decisions because it ensures that based on the information collected, they are factual and objective.

Key Benefits of Data-Driven Decision-Making

- **Accuracy Increases:** The business reduces errors and biases to lead toward the achievement of more accurate and reliable outcomes in proper data support for decisions.

- **Agile**: Data-driven organizations are responsive to market changes, customer needs, or internal challenges thus more agile than others in a dynamic business environment.
- **Better Understanding of Customers**: There could be a better understanding of customer behavior, preferences, and trends on account of data-driven decision-making with better products and services for various groups of customers.
- **Optimized Operations**: Data analysis identifies inefficiencies and therefore allows businesses to have optimized processes, cutting costs and increasing productivity. Today, data-driven decision-making is no longer a luxury but a necessity to keep a person agile and innovative in the modern business scenario.

BI Workflow and Components

The BI workflow, therefore refers to the process from raw data towards actionable insights. It is made up of three fundamental basic components that can therefore be broken down into data extraction, transformation, and loading, data modeling, and storage, and lastly, visualization and reporting.

ETL: Extraction, Transformation, and Loading

This is the very broad range of ETL data processes in BI, which means extraction of data from multiple locations, transforming it into some analyzable mode, and then loading it into a data warehouse or database for preparation.

- **Extraction**: The fetching can be done from many sources, which include databases, spreadsheets, CRM systems, APIs, and external data feeds. Data type is usually unstructured and erratic with lots of formats.
- **Transformation**: All the extracted data is cleaned and formatted in order to ensure good quality and consistency. In fact, it can include such operations as, removing duplicate records, filling up missing values, changing data types, and applying business rules.
- **Loading**: Transformed data is loaded into a warehouse, lake, or some database for use and further analysis by BI tools.

Importance of ETL:

- Validates the information is correct, consistent, and in place for analysis.
- Data consolidation from the sources aforementioned gives a holistic view for further insight.
- Some of the most popular ETL tools include: Apache Nifi, Talend, Microsoft SQL Server Integration Services (SSIS), AWS Glue, and so on.

Data Modeling and Storage

Once the data is loaded onto a central repository it must be structured in a way that allows easy access, for analytical and reporting purposes. This process is referred to as data modeling.

- **Data Modeling:** The process of mapping the logical structures, in terms of tables, relationships, and hierarchies, into which the data will fit is known as data modeling. These make easy querying and analysis possible. There are several types such as star schema, snowflake schema, or normalized schema.
- **Data Storage** This kind of data may be held in a data warehouse, data lakes, or database that allows for effective query and retrieval. Examples of data warehouses include Amazon Redshift, Google Big Query, and Snowflake. It is designed to have high-complex analytical queries, and store massive amounts of data.

Importance of Data Modeling and Storage: Enable fast query and analysis of big datasets. It ensures the given data is structured according to the needs of business and analysis requirements.

Data Visualization and Reporting

The BI workflow culminates into data transformation with the help of tools for data visualization and reporting as visual insights. Here, tools such as Apache Superset come into the picture.

- **Data Visualization:** These visualization tools translate information into graphs, charts, maps, and dashboards that become intelligible to users regarding complex information. The trends, patterns, or anomalies are indeed a correct display of data.
- **Reporting**: Reporting tools create structured reports summarizing data insights, which are fed to stakeholder decisions. Reports are scheduled and automated with distribution to the concerned teams or clients.

Why Data Visualization and Reporting Matter: This brings complex data insights to the boundaries of nonspecialist users. Enables organizations to monitor KPIs, track performance, and identify areas of improvement. Some of the other BI tools still gaining popularity succeeding Apache Superset include Tableau, Power BI, and Looker.

Apache Superset's Role in the BI Workflow

Apache Superset, therefore, fits right into the data visualization and reporting piece of the BI workflow but engages other parts of the workflow process so it becomes an all-around valuable tool within modern BI ecosystems.

Data Connection and Integration: Superset connects directly to a number of data sources; including SQL databases-PostgreSQL and MySQL, also, data warehouses such as Amazon Redshift and Google BigQuery, and further big data engines such as Apache Hive, and Presto.

It effectively functions as an interface by which users will engage with the data residing in such systems, and no extraction or transformation should take place outside of this system.

- **Exploratory Data Analysis:** It has a SQL Lab, allowing its users to be comfortable at writing and running direct SQL queries over connected data sources in a SQL IDE, which explores data by a data analyst while testing hypotheses and executing ad hoc analysis.

  Then, the capabilities of data exploration from Superset will rapidly transform raw data into meaningful insights.

- **Data Visualization and Dashboarding:** It does an excellent job of creating highly interactive and customizable dashboards. The users can transform their data into different visualization types, including bar charts, line charts, pie charts, time-series charts, or geospatial maps.

  These can be assimilated into holistic dashboards that can provide an overview of key business metrics for the stakeholders to monitor and track performance and extract actionable insights.

- **Self-Service BI and Data Democratization:** Superset enables a non-technical user to view data with its drag-and-drop interface, filters, and ability for cross-filtering. This results in a distinct version of self-service BI culture where insights are freely generated without dependency on the skills of experts in data or IT teams.

- **Real-Time Data Analysis:** Through direct connectivity with live data sources, Superset facilitates users to have access to real-time visualizations and analysis of data giving them the freshest information for actual decision-making processes.

Advantages of Open-Source BI Tools

One of the major open-source business intelligence tools that answer to this is Apache Superset. In fact, it provides several important benefits for an implementation organization intent on really leveraging the opportunity of data visualization and analytics, released from proprietary software costs.

Let us continue with three key advantages of open-source BI tools: freedom from licensing fees, the power to customize and change as needed, active community benefits, and faster innovation.

Reduction in License Fees

Possibly, the most attractive benefit of open-source BI solutions is that these are free, while proprietary BI solutions charge through their nose for the licensing fee.

Cost Savings Proprietary BI tools include the likes of Tableau and Power BI, which cost an arm and a leg, as well as pricey licensing models based on cost per user or month/ year basis. Open-source tools such as Apache Superset are free, allowing organizations to plow more money into the necessary infrastructure, training, or data experts.

- **Scalability that does not Increase Cost:** As your organization grows, so do the users who need BI tools. With open-source solutions, you can scale up as many users as you want to have in your organization without experiencing the movement of your cost upwards.
- **No Vendor Lock-in:** Open-source BI tools do not lock the organizations into a given vendor's platform and then raise the price or otherwise restrict terms or force dependence on specific vendor technologies used.
- **Real-Life Application**: A low-capital small startup could be able to design dashboards and analytics that rival the highest, richest, and complex dashboards companies can build with many employees while paying zero dollars in licensing costs by using open-source tools such as Superset.

Personalization and Flexibility

Open-source BI tools give an organization many customizations and flexibilities, such that the organization gets a platform that is designed according to its needs.

Key benefits:

- **Custom Visualization Plug-ins:** This offering is open source; users can write their own custom visualization plug-ins in order to support specific needs in data visualization. For example, if the business needs a certain kind of chart, it can develop that and add it right into the tool.
- **Flexibility to Business Needs:** The open-source tools will be quite flexible and adapt easily to your organization's workflows, branding, and integration of data requirements. You will have direct access to the source code, which means you can modify the user interface, data connectors, add new features, and everything according to your business process.
- **Integration with Other Systems:** It will supposedly integrate well with open-source or proprietary systems you have as part of your data stack. This gives flexibility to building a single data ecosystem that can encompass various tools and technologies; for instance, you might want to integrate Superset into the ETL pipeline, a data warehouse, or any other data visualizations.
- **Example In-Practice:** A data-driven marketing organization might want

to create specific dashboards that collate information from one or more sources, mostly CRM systems, but potentially also social media analytics and website traffic data. They might use an open-source BI tool and customize the platform for their organization to add all these data sources and come up with visualizations to meet the reporting requirements they have in mind.

Active Community of Fast Innovation

The open-source BI tools are characterized by a living, breathing active community of developers, contributors, and end-users who constantly improve the platform. This allows for faster innovation and periodic updates.

Key advantages:

- **Continuous Improvement:** The open-source BI tools are under constant change, introducing new features, fixes to bugs, and improvement of the platform very frequently. In fact, this has become possible by developers who cumulate in the aim of making the tool even better, ensuring that the software always stays relevant to current trends and technologies in data analytics.
- **Access to a Wealth of Knowledge:** Active communities behind open-source tools often provide far-reaching documentation, tutorials, forums, and support channels that make it easier for the user to troubleshoot problems, learn best practices, and even share insights.
- **No Waiting for Feature Releases:** In contrast, proprietary BI tools make you wait until the vendor releases new features, whereas in open-source BI tools, the community provides feedback that propels its evolution. This will enable you to implement and start benefiting from the application of cutting-edge data visualization techniques and integrations much faster.
- **Real-World Example:** The moment there is a critical bug in an open-source business intelligence tool such as Superset, the community immediately contributes its fix so that organizations do not lose their productivity and are less affected by the problem. Of course, the community-driven nature also means that feature requests and even user improvement suggestions can be implemented much faster than proprietary solutions.

Conclusion

The business intelligence world has gained itself a versatile and powerful tool through Apache Superset, features that cater to the modern BI landscape. From its birth as an internal tool for Airbnb, it has grown to be a robust open-source platform perfectly fine-tuning diverse BI needs through data visualization, dashboard creation, and ad-hoc exploration.

By considering these needs and how Superset addresses them, we can thereby see how the tool empowers organizations with the insights they need to drive data-informed decisions. SQL Lab presents a powerful environment in which users can query data and build reports. Furthermore, the sheer range of customization options available also allows for tailoring the user experience to suit an organization's specific branding and requirements.

Comparing Superset with other BI tools, it pretty quickly became apparent that the open nature and flexibility it offers make it stand out from other BI tools. Whether it is something being integrated into a large-scale BI workflow or used for multiple parts of individual components, users at every level enjoy a seamless and efficient experience.

Apache Superset, in essence, meets the current needs of the demands of BI by offering a holistic, scalable, and customizable solution that develops with the growth of a company's data.

The next chapter will build upon the foundation of the knowledge created in the installation and configuration guide. It will focus on how to use Apache Superset to create effective data visualizations practically. This chapter will walk you through creating your first charts in Superset and selecting appropriate chart types for a variety of data sets; it will also introduce basic customization options available to enhance your visualizations. You will be able to become proficient in using Superset's easy-to-use drag-and-drop interface through a number of step-by-step tutorials, which will help you craft a compelling visual narrative that makes your data both accessible and high-impact. This will lay the foundation for more advanced data analysis and visualization techniques presented in later chapters.

CHAPTER 2

Installing and Configuring Apache Superset

Introduction

Apache Superset offers several ways of installing the product, allowing flexibility based on your environment and technical preferences. If you want to test or develop quickly, you could set up Superset using Docker, which encapsulates all dependencies in a container and reduces setup to an item of a few lines of code. Alternatively, if you like things more old-school, you can install Superset directly to a server in Python and pip. This provides more control over the environment and configurations. The approach you choose, and proper configuration ensures smooth integration with the superset with your sources of data and meets the requirements of security, scalability, and performance required to solve your specific problem in the organization. Knowing your options and configuring them to suit your needs maximizes this platform's capabilities to create valuable insights into your data.

Structure

In this chapter, we will cover the following topics:

- Installation and Initial Setup
- Understanding Superset's Architecture
- Data Flow in Superset

Installation and Initial Setup

Preceding you can start using Apache Superset, it is essential to understand the prerequisites needed to ensure a smooth installation and setup process. This section will guide you through the hardware and software requirements, as well as the supported operating systems.

Prerequisites

- **Hardware Requirements**

  To run Apache Superset effectively, your machine or server should meet the following hardware specifications. These requirements may vary depending on the size of your datasets and the number of concurrent users.

- **Minimum Requirements:**
  - CPU: Dual-core processor (2 GHz or faster)
  - RAM: 4 GB
  - Storage: 10 GB of free disk space
  - Network: Internet connection for downloading dependencies and connecting to data sources
- **Recommended Requirements for Optimal Performance:**
  - CPU: Quad-core processor (2.5 GHz or faster)
  - RAM: 8 GB or more (especially if working with larger datasets or multiple users)
  - Storage: 50 GB or more of free disk space
  - Network: Stable high-speed internet connection

Note: *For production environments, it is advisable to use a dedicated server or cloud instance with higher specifications to ensure stability and scalability, especially if you expect many users or need to handle large volumes of data.*

- **Software Requirements**

  Apache Superset relies on various software dependencies. Here is a list of the essential software components needed to install and run Superset:

  - **Python:**
    - **Version:** Python 3.8 or later
    - **Why it is Needed:** Superset is a Python-based web application, and Python is required to run the backend server.
    - **Installation:** Download from python.org and follow the installation instructions. Make sure to check the box "`Add Python to PATH`" during installation.

- `pip` **(Python Package Installer):**
  - **Version:** Comes bundled with Python, but make sure it is up-to-date by running
  - pip install --upgrade pip
  - **Why it is Needed:** Used to install Apache Superset and its dependencies.
- **Node.js and npm:**
- **Node.js Version:** 16.x or later
- **npm Version:** 7.x or later (comes bundled with Node.js)
- **Why They are Needed:** Superset's frontend is built using JavaScript and React, which require Node.js and npm for building and managing JavaScript dependencies.
- **Installation:** Download from nodejs.org. The recommended method is to install the Long-Term Support (LTS) version, which comes with npm.
- **Web Browser:** A modern web browser is required to access and interact with Superset's user interface. Recommended browsers include:
  - Google Chrome
  - Mozilla Firefox
  - Microsoft Edge
- **Database Backend:** Superset requires a database to store its metadata, which includes information about users, dashboards, charts, and data source connections. Supported metadata databases include:
  - **SQLite:** Suitable for testing or small-scale deployments (default option during installation).
  - **PostgreSQL or MySQL:** Recommended for production environments.

Note: *It is advisable to set up a* PostgreSQL *or* MySQL *database if you plan to scale Superset for multiple users or larger datasets.*

- **Redis (Optional but Recommended):**
  - **Why it is Needed:** Superset can use Redis as a caching layer and message broker, particularly when configured with Celery for asynchronous query execution. This is useful for improving performance in production environments.
  - **Installation:** You can install Redis via package managers such as apt on Ubuntu (`sudo apt-get install redis-server`) or download it from redis.io.

- **Supported Operating Systems**

  Apache Superset is a cross-platform application, meaning it can be installed and run on various operating systems. The following is a list of the supported operating systems along with any special considerations for each:

- **Linux (Recommended)**
  - **Supported Distributions:** Ubuntu 18.04 or later, CentOS 7 or later, Red Hat Enterprise Linux (RHEL) 7 or later, Debian 9 or later
  - **Advantages:** Most commonly used for production deployments due to its stability and performance. It also provides better support for system-level packages and dependencies.
  - **Special Considerations:** Ensure that your Linux distribution has apt, yum, or similar package managers for installing prerequisites such as Python, Node.js, and Redis.
- **macOS**
  - **Supported Versions:** macOS 10.14 (Mojave) or later
  - **Advantages:** Great for local development and testing, with easy access to tools such as brew (Homebrew package manager) to install dependencies.
  - **Special Considerations:** Use Homebrew (brew install python node) to manage software installations.
- **Windows**
  - **Supported Versions:** Windows 10 or later
  - **Advantages:** Suitable for local development, but not typically recommended for production environments.
  - **Special Considerations:**
    - It is advisable to use the Windows Subsystem for Linux (WSL) to create a Linux environment on Windows, as it provides a more consistent and reliable setup process.
    - If using WSL, make sure you enable it and install a Linux distribution such as Ubuntu from the Microsoft Store.

Table 2.1 gives a quick summary of the prerequisites as follows:

Component	Minimum Requirement	Recommended for Production
CPU	Dual-core (2 GHz)	Quad-core (2.5 GHz or faster)
RAM	4 GB	8 GB or more
Storage	10 GB	50 GB or more
Python	Version 3.8 or later	Version 3.8 or later

Node.js	Version 16.x or later	Version 16.x or later
npm	Version 7.x or later	Version 7.x or later
Database Backend	SQLite for testing	PostgreSQL/MySQL for production
Supported OS	Linux/macOS/Windows	Linux (Ubuntu/CentOS/RHEL)
Optional: Redis	Not required for testing	Recommended for caching/queueing

Table 2.1: *Summary of Prerequisites*

Once you have ensured that your system meets the hardware and software requirements, you can proceed to install Apache Superset. In the next section, we will cover the step-by-step installation process, including setting up the Python environment, installing Superset via pip, and configuring the web server.

By meeting these prerequisites, you ensure that your Apache Superset installation runs smoothly and efficiently, providing a solid foundation for your data visualization and business intelligence needs.

Installing Apache Superset

In this section, we will explore the two main installation options for Apache Superset: a **`Local Setup using pip`** and a **`Docker Setup`** using Docker Compose. Both methods have their own advantages, and the choice depends on your requirements and familiarity with these tools.

Let us begin with a quick comparison of both options and then proceed to the detailed step-by-step guide for each.

Installation Options: Local Setup versus Docker Setup

Step 1: Creating a Virtual Environment

Creating a virtual environment isolates your Python dependencies, ensuring that the Superset installation does not interfere with other projects.

a. Open a terminal (or Command Prompt on Windows)

b. Navigate to your desired project directory:

   i. `mkdir superset-setup`

   ii. `cd superset-setup`

c. Create a virtual environment using **`venv`**

   i. `python3 -m venv venv`

d. Activate the virtual environment

   i. On **Linux/macOS:**

   ii. `source venv/bin/activate`

e. On **Windows:**

   i. `venv\Scripts\activate`

Step 2: Installing Superset via pip

With the virtual environment activated, you can now install Apache Superset:

a. Upgrade pip to the latest version:

   i. `pip install --upgrade pip`

b. Install Apache Superset using pip:

   ii. `pip install apache-superset`

This command will install Superset along with all the necessary dependencies.

Note: *Use the latest version of apache-superset*

Step 3: Initializing the Superset Database

Superset uses a metadata database to store information about users, charts, dashboards, and data sources.

a. Initialize the database, this command sets up the initial database tables and schema:

   i. `superset db upgrade`

b. Create an admin user:

   i. `export FLASK_APP=superset`

   ii. `superset fab create-admin`

You will be prompted to enter your username, password, email, and other details.

Step 4: Loading Examples (Optional)

a. If you want to explore Superset's capabilities using example data, you can load the sample datasets:

```
superset load_examples
```

Step 5: Starting the Superset Server

a. Initialize Superset assets:

```
superset init
```

b. Start the Superset web server:

```
superset run -p 8088 --with-threads --reload --debugger
```

The server will start on **http://localhost:8088**. Open this URL in your web browser to access Superset.

Docker Setup: Benefits and Detailed Instructions Using Docker Compose

The Docker setup is an ideal choice for quickly setting up Superset with all its dependencies in a self-contained environment. It is also a great option for deploying Superset in production.

Benefits of Docker Setup

- **Portability**: Easily deploy Superset on any machine with Docker installed.
- **Scalability**: Use Docker Compose to manage multiple services such as Redis, PostgreSQL, and Superset itself.
- **Consistency**: No need to worry about dependency conflicts or system-specific issues.

Step-by-Step Guide to Installing with Docker Compose

Step 1: Install Docker and Docker Compose

a. Install Docker and Docker Compose from the official Docker website

b. Verify the installation:

   i. `docker --version`
   ii. `docker-compose --version`

Step 2: Clone the Superset GitHub Repository

a. Open a terminal and clone the Superset repository:

   i. `git clone https://github.com/apache/superset.git`
   ii. `cd superset`

Step 3: Start the Official Release of Superset

```
docker compose -f docker-compose-image-tag.yml up
```

Step 4: Access Superset

a. Open your web browser and go to http://localhost:8088 to access Apache Superset.

b. Login with username and password, both as admin.

Initializing the Superset Database

For both the Local and Docker setups, initializing the database is an essential step.

This process creates the necessary tables and configurations needed for Superset to function correctly.

- **Local Setup:**
```
superset db upgrade
superset fab create-admin
```
- **Docker Setup:**

  Initialization is done automatically when you run **`docker-compose up`** and **`superset-init`**.

Starting the Superset Server

- **Local Setup:** Start the server using:
```
superset run -p 8088 --with-threads --reload --debugger
```
- **Docker Setup:** The Superset server will start automatically when you run docker-compose up.

You can now access Superset through http://localhost:8088 in your web browser, where you will be greeted with the login page.

You now have two options to install and set up Apache Superset: a **`Local Setup`** using Python's pip or a **`Docker Setup`** using Docker Compose. Both methods enable you to run Superset efficiently, with the Docker setup providing a more streamlined and portable solution suitable for production environments.

By following these instructions, you should have a running instance of Apache Superset ready for data exploration, visualization, and building interactive dashboards.

First-Time Configuration

Once you have installed Apache Superset successfully using a local or a Docker setup, the last part of this installation puzzle is to configure the platform for the first time. In this chapter, we walk you through important configurations: setting up an admin user, connecting to a database, and getting accustomed to the look and feel of the Superset product. We also go through some common issues in installation that you might face.

1. **Setting Up an Admin User**

   The admin user is the primary user account with full access rights to manage all aspects of Apache Superset. During the initial setup, you need to create this user to access and configure the platform.

Local Setup: Creating an Admin User

a. Activate your virtual environment (if not already activated):

   - On Linux/macOS:
```
source venv/bin/activate
```

- On Windows:

  ```
  venv\Scripts\activate
  ```

b. Create an admin user using the following command:

```
superset fab create-admin
```

You will be prompted to enter details including:

- **Username**: (for example, admin)
- **User First Name**: (for example, John)
- **User Last Name**: (for example, Doe)
- **Email**: (for example, admin@example.com)
- **Password**: (Choose a secure password)

c. Initialize Superset: `superset init`

Docker Setup: Creating an Admin User

a. Run the following command:

```
docker exec -it superset_app superset fab create-admin
```

You will be prompted to enter the same details as aforementioned.

b. Subsequent to creating the admin user, run the initialization command if not already executed:

```
docker exec -it superset_app superset-init
```

You can now log in to Superset at http://localhost:8088 using the admin credentials you just created.

2. **Configuring a Database Connection**

   Superset requires a connection to one or more databases from which it retrieves data for visualization. You can connect to a variety of databases, such as PostgreSQL, MySQL, SQLite, or cloud-based databases.

Steps to Add a Database Connection:

a. Log in to the Superset UI using your admin credentials.

b. Navigate to the Database Configuration Page:

   i. Click **`Settings`** icon (gear) in the top-right corner.

   ii. Select **`Data`** → **`Databases`**.

c. Click "**`+ Database`**" in the top-right corner to add a new database connection.

d. Configure the Database Connection:

i. `Database`: Choose your database from the dropdown menu (for example, PostgreSQL, MySQL, SQLite).

ii. `Display Name`: Give your connection a recognizable name (for example, `"My Postgres Database"`).

iii. `SQLAlchemy URI`: This is a connection string that specifies how to connect to your database. It follows the format:

iv. `PostgreSQL`: `postgresql+psycopg2://username:password@hostname:port/dbname`

v. `MySQL`: `mysql+pymysql://username:password@hostname:port/dbname`

vi. `SQLite` (local file): `sqlite:////absolute/path/to/your/database.db`

vii. `Secure Extra (Optional)`: If you want to provide additional SSL settings, input them here.

viii. `Expose in SQL Lab`: Check this box if you want this database to be available for querying in SQL Lab.

ix. `Test Connection`: Click this button to ensure the connection is successful.

e. **Save the Configuration:** Click `Save`, and your database should now appear in the list of databases.

You can now start building visualizations using the connected data.

3. **Basic UI Walkthrough: Understanding the Interface**

   The Apache Superset interface is designed to be user-friendly and intuitive. Here is a quick walkthrough of the main components:

The Superset Menu Bar

a. `Home`: Takes you to the dashboard page, where you can see an overview of your dashboards, charts, and recent activities.

b. `SQL Lab`: This is where you can explore your data using SQL queries. It provides a powerful SQL editor with autocomplete and a history of queries.

c. `Charts`: View, create, and manage your charts. You can build visualizations using different data sources and chart types.

d. `Dashboards`: The heart of Superset, where you create and manage interactive dashboards that combine multiple charts.

e. `Data`: Manage your databases, datasets, and columns. You can define new data connections, tables, and data models here.

f. **`Settings (Gear Icon)`**: Access configurations, user management, roles, and other administrative settings.

Creating Your First Chart and Dashboard

a. To create a chart, navigate to **`Charts`** → **`+ Chart`**.

b. Choose a dataset and **`chart type`** (for example, bar, line, pie).

c. Customize your visualization by selecting dimensions, metrics, filters, and aggregations.

d. Save the chart and add it to a new or existing dashboard via the **`Dashboards`** section.

4. **Quick Tips for Troubleshooting Common Installation Issues**

   While setting up Apache Superset, you may encounter some common issues. Here are some troubleshooting tips:

Issue 1: "*Command not found*" or "*superset: command not found*"

- **Cause**: This usually means that the superset command is not recognized by your terminal.
- **Solution**: Ensure your virtual environment is activated (for local setup). If using Docker, make sure the containers are running (docker-compose up -d).

Issue 2: Database Connection Errors

- **Cause**: Incorrect SQLAlchemy URI or the database server is not running.
- **Solution**: Double-check your database connection string (username, password, hostname, port, database name). Ensure the database server is running and accessible.

Issue 3: Unable to Start the Superset Server

- **Cause**: Missing dependencies or incorrect installation.
- **Solution**: Ensure all dependencies are installed. For local setup, ensure you have Python, pip, Node.js, and npm correctly installed. You can check installed versions using:

```
python --version
pip --version
node --version
npm --version
```

Issue 4: Slow Performance When Loading Dashboards or Charts

- **Cause:** Superset may be running in debug mode or not using caching mechanisms.

- Solution:
  - For production, set up Redis and configure caching. This significantly improves performance.
  - Disable debug mode by setting DEBUG = False in your Superset configuration file.

Issue 5: Docker Container Issues

- **Cause**: Docker containers not starting or exiting unexpectedly.
- **Solution**: Check container logs using:

```
docker logs superset_app
```

Recreate containers if needed:

```
docker-compose down && docker-compose up -d
```

By following this guide, you should have successfully set up an admin user, connected a database, and familiarized yourself with the Apache Superset interface. These initial configurations will help you get started with building visualizations and exploring your data. With the troubleshooting tips provided, you can resolve common installation issues and enjoy a seamless experience as you dive into data exploration and visualization with Apache Superset.

Understanding Superset's Architecture

Apache Superset is an ambitious piece of architecture, aimed at being scalable enough to handle big data and support multiple users having an interactive yet intuitive experience. A critical understanding of the architecture of Superset lies in how it deploys, scales, and, more importantly, optimizes within the platform. The following section introduces Superset's architecture and explains further its core components at a high-level overview.

High-Level Overview of Superset Architecture

At a high level, Apache Superset follows a three-tier architecture, which consists of the following layers:

- Frontend layer (User interface)
- Web Application Server or Backend Layer
- Database Layer: metadata and data sources

Another important benefit is that Superset often has integrations for caching and asynchronous task processing to improve performance and scalability. Overall, the architecture is pretty modular, so one can customize and integrate this into various data sources, databases, and authentication systems.

Core Architecture Components

Frontend: The frontend is created with React, JavaScript, and Bootstrap, and at this layer, the user interfaces and interactions occur where users create charts, dashboards, and visualizations.

A Python-based backend using a web framework such as Flask, would process all user requests and appropriately take care of authentication features, data sources, and querying.

- **Metadata Database**: Here, metadata about the configuration of Superset is there, including saved charts, dashboards, user information, data connection, and query history.
- **Data Sources**: These will be the databases that your real data resides in, which may be SQL databases, NoSQL databases, or big data engines.
- **Caching and Task Queue**: These are two optional components that, apart from task asynchronous processing, also optimize performance.

Explanations of the Various Parts

Let us break down the individual components into further detail to understand how each works within the Superset architecture.

- **Layer Frontend (User Interface)**

  Modern UI, Using React: Attach your frontend creations with modern JavaScript libraries that allow full-featured interaction for building responsive and interactive user interfaces, from drag-and-drop facilities up to dashboard configuration tools, and much more.

  - **Visualizations**: Superset uses the Apache ECharts and D3.js libraries to provide a visualization. This way, one can create any type of chart such as bar, line, pie, heatmaps, geographic maps, and more.
  - **A Single Page Application**: The frontend, of course, will be a SPA. That is to say, users can accomplish their functions such as SQL Lab, Dashboards, and Charts by switching between them, without reloading the complete page, and hence improves user experience.

- **Backend Layer**
  - **Web Application Server:** The backend is a core part of Superset, handling both data processing and authentication and security with interactions of data. It is built using:
  - **Flask Web Framework**: The Flask frontend layer is used as a very light Python web framework for servicing HTTP requests, managing the user

session, and servicing API endpoints. Interaction between the frontend layer and the database layer is serviced by it.

- **SQLAlchemy ORM:** Superset utilizes SQLAlchemy as the ORM for handling interactions with the database connection. It operates as an SQL query executer and fetches data from various sources into the visualization layer.
- **Data Query Engine**: This would be the backend that executes SQL queries on connected data sources. For queries created by a user via a chart or by exploring data in SQL Lab, the backend should forward to the database and further forward the results back to the frontend for visualization.

The backend of Superset offers its RESTful APIs that let the front and back ends interact with one another. Some of them include retrieval of data, saving dashboards, handling users, and operations such as Create, Read, Update, and Delete (CRUD).

- **Metadata Repository**
  - **Purpose:** It is full of configuration, setting, and every line of information needed to make Superset work, which in reality would hold end-user accounts, access permissions, charts, dashboards, SQL queries, and database connections.
  - **Databases**: Superset natively uses SQLite as the underlying metadata database, although replacing it with a more robust RDBMS such as PostgreSQL or MySQL is suggested in serious production environments, especially in cases of really huge datasets and huge concurrent users.
  - Key Tables in the Metadata Database
    - **Users and Roles**: Details about users, roles, and access.
    - **Dashboards and Charts:** Definition of configurations, layout, and filter for dashboard and chart.
    - **Database Connections:** Details of the connected databases, including their corresponding connection strings and the credentials.
    - **Query History:** This retains the record of SQL queries run for auditing and debugging purposes.
- **Data Sources**
  - **Purpose**: Data Sources are the databases or data engines in which your actual business data resides. Superset can connect to a wide variety of data sources including SQL databases such as PostgreSQL and MySQL or Oracle; NoSQL databases such as MongoDB; big data engines such as Apache Hive or Presto; as well as cloud-based data warehouses such as Amazon Redshift or Google BigQuery.
  - **SQLAlchemy Connectivity:** Superset uses SQLAlchemy dialects connecting to these data sources. That is how it accomplishes a single

interface connecting and querying all kinds of databases through the use of SQLAlchemy so that it can easily use different data engines.

- **Security:** Superset respects database-level security and access controls; therefore, data access is strictly based on the user account permissions.

- **Caching and Task Queue (Optional Features)**

  To achieve higher performance and scalability, Superset will make use of other modules, particularly Redis, to enforce the following:

Caching (Redis)

- **Purpose**: Cache frequently executed queries and visualizations of dashboards locally on the client to avoid overloading the data source and improve responsiveness.

- **How it Works:** When a user makes some data request, Superset very first checks if the result is either cached or not. If yes then it directly serves the result from the cache; otherwise, it retrieves it directly from the source and then caches it in advance.

Asynchronous Task Processing: Celery

- **Purpose**: Celery enables running such codes such as SQL queries, plotting graphs, or refreshing dashboards, asynchronously and without blocking in long-running or resource-intensive tasks.

- **How It Works:** Once the task is initiated, Superset would asynchronously dispatch the task to Celery workers so that the main application can continue processing other requests, and Redis would be a message broker between Superset and Celery.

- **Security and Authentication**

  This product uses RBAC for permission and access control, thus allowing the definition of roles, such as Admin, Analyst, Viewer, and permissions related to view, edit, or manage data sources, charts, and dashboards.

  - **Authentication Mechanisms**: Superset accepts multiple authentication mechanisms via database authentication, LDAP, OAuth, and OpenID Connect, which makes it easily consumable by any enterprise authentication system.

  - **Interaction of These Parts User Interaction:** The user interacts with the frontend - the React-based UI - to form visualizations, and dashboards, or execute SQL queries.

  - **Request Handling:** All the requests received from the frontend layer are answered through the backend using Flask by making a connection with the source of data via SQLAlchemy.

- **Query Execution:** The backend sends SQL queries to the connected data source, such as PostgreSQL, MySQL, or Presto, and retrieves a result set.
- **Data Visualization:** The frontend really gives one the feel of processed backend data by the help of interactive visualizations.
- **Caching and Asynchronous processing:** If the cache is enabled, query results are cached to Redis when accessed very often; hence, long-running tasks are managed by Celery workers to make the application responsive.

Architecture has been designed for Apache Superset to be highly modular, flexible, and scalable and manage an increasing number of workloads in order to manage the functions of data visualization and exploration efficiently. It has a rich, interactive user experience frontend based on React, while its Python/Flask backend handles data processing, authenticates users, and deals with multiple data sources. This level of integration-caching and task queues can become pretty effective in ensuring that Superset will run at considerable speed and responsiveness, thus turning out to be more powerful for modern business intelligence implementations from organizations.

Data Flow in Superset

This requires a good understanding of where data goes and flows through the eyes of Apache Superset in order to fine-tune performance and extract the best from these capabilities. The following chapter will describe how data gets from source to visualization; the interactions occurring between the UI, metadata database, and sources, and then take it further to discuss query execution and caching mechanisms that make Superset efficient.

Data Journey from Source to Visualization

The data flow inside Superset can be explained at the following stages:

- **User Interaction**: A user creates or interacts with a chart, a dashboard, or an SQL query by Superset's frontend.
- **Data Source Querying:** Superset would then translate such user activities into SQL queries and feed these to the appropriate connected data source, which is either PostgreSQL, MySQL, or a combination of other cloud data warehouses.
- **Data Retrieval:** It executes the query on the data source and returns the result to Superset's backend.
- **Data Processing and Caching:** The backend processes the data. The result will be cached in a layer if the 'caching' flag is set.
- **Data Visualization:** Processed data is now forwarded to the frontend to render it as interactive visualizations, using libraries such as Apache ECharts or D3.js.

- **Dashboard Interaction:** Each action of the user with the dashboard (applying filters, drilling down, and so on) is repeated, new data being plugged into the visualizations.

This flow ensures real-time (or near real-time) fetch of data, efficient processing, and interactive visualization; hence, insight into the datasets of users is provided.

Interaction of the User Interface, Metadata Database, and Data Sources

Superset's architecture implies ongoing interaction between three very large components: the User Interface (UI), Metadata Database, and Sources of Data. Here is how these elements interact with each other as the data flows:

1. **User Interface (UI) Interactions**

   Creating Visualizations and Dashboards: The Superset UI lets users build charts, browse datasets, and create dashboards. For the most part, the interface is pretty intuitive about selecting data columns, defining metrics, use of filters, and chart types. Interaction with SQL Lab SQL Lab allows one to compose SQL queries, execute such queries, and preview data from the linked data sources. The backend captures the input of the user and forwards that input for processing.

2. **Backend Processing and Metadata Database**

   The backend interacts with a metadata database and processes all the requests coming from the UI:

   The process of creating or updating charts and dashboards is queried and executed as the frontend sends configuration data to the backend, which is further parsed through SQLAlchemy to SQL queries.

- **Metadata Management:** It maintains a metadata database on the backend to store and retrieve the details of the configuration.
- **Chart and Dashboard:** All chart and dashboard structure, filters, visualization settings, and data source connections.
- **User Information:** User profiles, user roles and permissions, and query history.
- **Data Source Information:** All the connection strings, table definitions, and metadata related to columns of connected data sources.

3. **Interaction with Data Sources Executing**

- **SQL Queries:** As soon as the backend has created an SQL query, it transmits that over to the database that it is connected to using SQLAlchemy. Of course, the results of this get fetched from the data source, for example, a PostgreSQL database.

- **fetching Data:** The server fetches the query results from the source data with successive processing for display.

Example of an Interaction Workflow

Let us consider a typical example where a user wants to create a sales dashboard with a bar chart that shows monthly sales by region:

Step 1: User Creates a Chart

a. The user selects a data source (for example, a PostgreSQL database) and chooses the columns for "`Month`," "`Sales`," and "`Region`" in the UI.

b. The frontend sends this configuration to the backend.

Step 2: Backend Generates and Executes a Query

a. The backend generates the following SQL query:

```
SELECT Month, Region, SUM(Sales) AS Total_Sales FROM sales_data
GROUP BY Month, Region;
```

b. This query is executed on the connected data source.

Step 3: Data Source Returns Results

The PostgreSQL database processes the query and returns the results to Superset's backend.

Step 4: Data Processed and Cached

The backend processes the data and stores the result in the cache (if caching is enabled) to optimize future requests.

Step 5: Data Visualization

The processed data is sent to the frontend, where the bar chart is rendered and displayed to the user.

Query Execution and Caching Mechanisms

Queries are probably the most critical pieces in Superset's data flow, both in terms of execution and caching, with a significant impact on performance and scalability. This is how it works:

1. **Query Execution Process**

   SQL Generation: Every user action on the UI is rendered to SQL queries that will support its execution with the backends' help from SQLAlchemy.

Data Source Execution: The SQL code generated will be executed directly against a connected data source. The backend will actually manage interactions with any type of database, and the specifics of the actual data source are what would define the proper syntax of that query.

Succeeding which, once the data source has finished executing the query, the results are passed back to the backend of Superset. Then, Superset processes the data and passes it back to its frontend for visualization.

Note: *Superset allows both synchronous as well as asynchronous query execution.*

Synchronous Execution: The query is immediately executed, and its result is returned. Useful for very short queries or small ones.

Asynchronous Execution (Celery): Celery is implemented for the asynchronous execution of long-running or complex queries. As a result, the core application maintains responsiveness to the processing of long queries.

2. **Cache Mechanism**

   With regard to performance and minimizing the load on data sources, Superset employs caching mechanisms that store query results once they have been executed.

   Caching Layers: Superset uses Redis as the caching layer, however, lets the user define their preferred caching backend.

Working of Caching

- If the user requests a chart or dashboard, it checks if the result of the query is actually in the cache.
- It will retrieve and display if it is available; otherwise, it will not repeat the execution of the SQL query.
- If data is not cached or if the cache has expired then a query is executed on the data source, and those results are stored in cache for future requests.

Advantages of caching

- **Reduced Latency:** Cache provides faster results so that dashboards and every kind of visualization respond much faster.
- **Reduced Database Load:** Superset fetches the data from cache rather than querying the same source time and again, which reduces the load on databases and, therefore, enhances performance. This can be configured from the configuration settings for Superset, `superset_config.py`. Here, you could define a certain cache timeout period, for instance, caching backend, and whatever other parameter related to the cache according to your needs.

Conclusion

We covered the basics of installing and getting Apache Superset up-and-running, from understanding installation prerequisites to initializing the setup, the and most common issues you might face. You have also gained some insight into the architecture of Superset and the flow of data in the platform, allowing you to perceive how its components work in harmony with each other to support powerful data visualizations and BI capabilities.

With this knowledge, you are now equipped to deploy and configure Apache Superset confidently, ensuring a smooth and efficient setup that meets your organization's needs. Whether you are preparing to use Superset for development, testing, or production, this guide provides a solid foundation for getting started and maximizing the potential of your Superset instance.

As you proceed in your journey with Apache Superset, the next chapter will dive deeper into the practical aspects of data visualization. We will walk through creating your first chart, choosing the right chart types, and exploring basic customization options. This chapter will give you a solid knowledge base on using Superset's interactive drag-and-drop interface—setting the scene for more advanced visual analytics in later sections. Be prepared to transform your data into compelling visual stories that speak to your audience.

Chapter 3
Getting Started with Data Visualization

Introduction

Data visualization is a symbolic representation of data and information using visual elements, such as charts, graphs, maps, and infographics. It transforms raw data into more intuitive visual formats to help people understand complex data patterns, trends, and insights more intuitively. Presentation in a visual context of information helps individuals spot relationships more easily, identifies outliers, and supports data-driven decisions.

Structure

In this chapter, we will cover the following topics:

- Converting Raw Data into Forms of Visualization
- Emergence of Data Visualization
- Big Data, Artificial Intelligence, and Business Intelligence Era
- Role of Data Visualization in the Modern Digital World
- Types of Data Visualization
- Role of Apache Superset in Data Visualization
- Data Sources in Apache Superset
- Configuring the Database Connection Using MySQL
- Steps to Create a Chart in Apache Superset
- Creating a Dashboard
- Accessing Data Sources: Starting Point in Exploring Data
- Building Charts Using Superset: Visualizing Your Data
- Dashboard Building: Aggregation of Charts into Visualization

Converting Raw Data into Forms of Visualization

Data is typically raw since it is neither structured as text nor structured more specifically such that the data points map onto graphical elements. This type of data tends to be overwhelming and difficult to understand. Data visualization maps data points into graphical elements, to change this data into visual formats. For instance:

- The bar charts are useful for comparing quantities across various categories.
- Line graphs display trends over time.
- Heat maps show areas of concentration or richness within datasets.

These graphics take highly complex data and turn it into digestible and meaningful graphics, allowing viewers to understand it at a glance.

Emergence of Data Visualization

Data visualization is not an invention of this generation; it has been in existence for thousands of years. The history of data visualization is portrayed as follows:

- **Early Civilizations**: Ancient civilizations, such as the Egyptians and the Babylonians, created maps and even ancient charts for pictorial representations of agricultural information, astronomical observations, and territorial lines. The earliest known data visualization is a map drawn on a Babylon clay tablet around 2300 B.C.
- **18th to 19th Century – The Birth of Statistical Graphics**: The wide range of graphs, including line, bar, and pie charts were invented in the late 18th century by William Playfair. Florence Nightingale was one of the pioneers of data visualization. She used polar area charts or coxcomb charts in the 1850s to inform mortality rates in military hospitals that forced healthcare reforms.
- During the **20th century**, computers were developed to produce far more complex visualizations. In the 1960s and 1970s, researchers such as John Tukey, who developed exploratory data analysis, and Edward Tufte, with his work "*The Visual Display of Quantitative Information*," laid the groundwork for contemporary principles of data visualization.
- The **21st century** saw an explosion in data visualization as data became digital and bigger than ever before. The advent of the internet, artificial intelligence, and machine learning opened the doors to new possibilities, making visualization more interactive, dynamic, and accessible through platforms such as Tableau, Power BI, and D3.js.

Big Data, Artificial Intelligence, and Business Intelligence Era

Data visualization has finally come of age today. It can handle big data and can be acquired from several sources: social media, sensors, financial transactions, and customer interactions. The rise in AI and machine learning has augmented visualizations with the ability to generate more intelligent predictions and analytics by providing automatic insights. Business intelligence tools are now available with dashboards that provide a real-time view of performance, irregularities, and trends.

Role of Data Visualization in the Modern Digital World

Usage Overview of Visualization in Multiple Industries:

Data visualization is an important component in most industries as it aims to turn complex data into actionable insights.

- **Finance**: Visualizations such as candlestick charts and heat maps help analysts monitor stock performance, detect market trends, and assess risk. For instance, dashboards track real-time stock prices, aiding investors in making quick trading decisions.
- **Health**: Data visualization can be found in tracking patient outcomes, monitoring disease spread, and distributing resources in hospitals. For instance, during the COVID-19 pandemic, real-time dashboards displaying infection rates allowed governments to make policy decisions on when to implement control measures.
- **Marketing**: Marketers use visualization to understand campaign performance, monitor the behavior of customers, and understand their demographic audience. Google Analytics allows for visual dashboards to report traffic sources, conversion rates, and user engagement.
- **Sports**: Visualizations help assess a player's performance, track the strengths and weaknesses of an athlete, and assist in developing game strategies. For instance, in basketball, shot charts indicate where players are most likely to shoot at different moments.

Such scenarios of everyday life may include:

- **Retail Business**: A global retail chain uses data visualization to understand the trend of sales performance in different regions. It clearly identifies which regions are top performers by showing sales on an interactive map, thus helping to improve targeted marketing campaigns and inventory control.

- **Health Monitoring**: While using patient data visualizations, hospitals monitor real-time changes in the patient's vital signs. Spikes in heart rate or blood pressure are immediately highlighted, and timely intervention can save lives. In soccer, data analysts make heat maps, which tell where the players spend most of their time in the field. This allows the coach to make appropriate adjustments in formations and strategies for optimized output.

Types of Data Visualization

The process of transforming raw data into visual formats to enable easier comprehension, analysis, and communication is called data visualization. Visualization is very important in dealing with huge datasets since it discovers hidden patterns, trends, and correlations within them. In this chapter, we will cover the many types of charts and visualizations that Apache Superset provides, a project that makes data visualization open-source and interactive. From this point forward, you will be much better equipped to pick just the right, most effective visual representation of your data once you learn how to use different kinds of visualizations. We go further to outline the difference between static and interactive visualizations and how Apache Superset supports dynamic data exploration, thereby improving decision-making using data.

Basic Chart Types

Visualizations come in various forms, each designed to present data in a way that best fits a particular analytical need. Here, we will explore some of the most common chart types used in Apache Superset and their practical applications:

Bar Charts

- **Description:** Bar charts use rectangular bars to represent data values, with the length of each bar corresponding to the data's magnitude. Bars can be oriented horizontally or vertically.
- **Use Case**: Ideal for comparing different categories or groups, such as sales performance across product categories.
- **Example**: Displaying monthly sales for different regions using Apache Superset, where each bar represents the sales for a specific region.
- **When to Use**: When comparing discrete categories or groups, especially when you want to highlight differences or similarities.

Line Charts

- **Description**: Line charts connect data points using lines, making them ideal for showing trends and changes over time or across another continuous variable.
- **Use Case**: Best for tracking metrics such as stock prices, website traffic, or sales trends over time.

- **Example**: Visualizing daily temperatures or sales trends over a year using Superset, where each point represents a specific day.
- **When to Use**: When you need to analyze trends or changes over time or any continuous variable.

Pie Charts

- **Description**: Pie charts are circular charts divided into slices to represent the relative proportions of the whole.
- **Use Case**: Useful for showing the distribution of categories within a dataset, such as market share or budget allocations.
- **Example**: Visualizing the percentage distribution of different customer age groups using Superset, where each slice represents an age category.
- **When to Use**: When you want to show how different parts contribute to a whole, but they are less effective with more than five or six categories.

Scatter Plots

- **Description**: Scatter plots use dots to represent the values of two variables, showing relationships or correlations between the two.
- **Use Case**: Ideal for identifying patterns, correlations, or clusters in datasets.
- **Example**: Plotting customer age versus spending amount in Superset to understand spending behavior across different age groups.
- **When to Use**: When exploring relationships between two continuous variables, such as for identifying correlations.

Area Charts

- **Description**: Similar to line charts, but with the area below the line filled with color to emphasize the volume or magnitude.
- **Use Case**: Demonstrates trends over time, such as showing cumulative sales or revenue growth.
- **Example**: Visualizing the growth in total revenue month-over-month using Superset.
- **When to Use**: When you want to emphasize the overall volume or the trend over time.

Histograms

- **Description**: Histograms display the distribution of a dataset by grouping data into ranges (bins) and showing the frequency.
- **Use Case**: Useful for understanding the distribution of data, such as customer ages, product prices, or transaction amounts.

- **Example**: Displaying the distribution of transaction amounts using Superset, where each bar represents a range of values.
- **When to Use**: When analyzing the distribution or frequency of a single continuous variable.

Heatmaps

- **Description**: Heatmaps represent data using colors, where color intensity indicates the magnitude of the values.
- **Use Case**: Ideal for showing correlations or performance metrics over time.
- **Example**: Visualizing website traffic by hour and day using Superset, where darker colors indicate higher traffic.
- **When to Use**: When you want to convey relationships or intensity across two dimensions.

Box Plots

- **Description**: Box plots visualize data distribution using five summary statistics including minimum, first quartile, median, third quartile, and maximum.
- **Use Case**: Great for identifying outliers and skewness and understanding data spread.
- **Example**: Analyzing sales data distribution across different stores using Superset, where each box represents a store.
- **When to Use**: When you want to understand the spread, variability, or outliers in the data.

The usefulness of each chart type for different data representations:

- **Comparison**: Use Bar Charts or Grouped Bar Charts to compare different categories or groups.
- **Trend Analysis**: Use Line Charts or Area Charts to observe trends over time.
- **Distribution Analysis**: Use Histograms or Box Plots to understand data distribution and variability.
- **Proportion**: Use Pie Charts or Donut Charts to display parts of a whole.
- **Correlation**: Use Scatter Plots or Heatmaps to explore relationships between variables.

Interactive versus Static Visualization

Static Visualization

- Description: Visuals that are fixed and unchangeable once generated (for example, printed charts or static images).

- Pros:
  - Easy to create and share.
  - Suitable for reports or presentations where data do not change frequently.
- Cons:
  - Limited flexibility and less engagement for dynamic data analysis.
- Example: A printed pie chart showing last quarter's sales distribution.

Interactive Visualization

- Description: Visualizations that allow users to interact with the data, such as filtering, zooming, and hovering for details.
- Pros:
  - Dynamic and engaging, allowing users to explore data in real time.
  - Facilitates deeper analysis and decision-making.
- Cons:
  - Requires more processing power and may be more complex to create.
- Example: A line chart in Superset where users can hover over data points to see values or filter data by specific time ranges.

Role of Apache Superset in Data Visualization

A superset is ideal for creating interactive visualizations for the following reasons:

- **Open-Source and Highly Customizable**: It offers flexibility to suit different data visualization needs.
- **Easy Integration with Various Data Sources**: Connect to SQL databases, CSV files, cloud data warehouses, and more.
- **Intuitive Drag-and-Drop Interface**: Makes data visualization accessible, even for non-technical users.

Static Visualization Options in Superset

- Superset allows you to export static images (PDFs, PNGs, and more) of visualizations for use in reports and presentations.

Interactive Visualization Options in Superset

- Using Superset's dashboard functionality to create interactive data stories that enable real-time filtering, drill-downs, and dynamic data exploration.

Data Sources in Apache Superset

A data source in Superset refers to the datasets or tables that you can connect to and analyze through the platform. The source of data can come from any place, ranging from SQL databases to cloud data warehouses, or local CSV files.

Superset primarily supports SQL-speaking databases, including but not limited to:

- PostgreSQL
- MySQL
- Presto
- Google BigQuery
- Amazon Redshift
- Snowflake
- SQLite

A data source is, in essence, a bridge between your data storage (database) and the visualization layer in Superset. Subsequent to connecting a data source, you can build charts, graphs, and dashboards based on that data.

Sources of Data Types

There are two primary types of data sources available for use within Superset:

- **Tables**: These are single tables in a database that you can connect to Superset. Each table holds rows and columns that form your data.
- **SQL Queries (Virtual Datasets)**: Superset allows users to create virtual datasets by writing SQL queries on top of existing tables. These virtual datasets are roughly like views, where the result of the SQL query can be treated as a new dataset that can be viewed and analyzed.

Connecting to Data Sources in Apache Superset

This is a comprehensive data exploration and visualization platform that supports integration with most databases. Superset does not have native connectivity to existing databases. The appropriate database drivers must be installed in order to connect an external database to Superset.

Database Drivers Installation: To connect Superset to a database, one must have a Python DB-API database driver and an SQLAlchemy dialect for the engine of each database that you want to connect. Every database driver is unique and must be installed within your Superset environment. These drivers can be added using pip commands.

For example, to connect to MySQL, you would install the **`mysqlclient`** package:

```
pip install mysqlclient
```

Supported Databases: Superset supports various databases, each requiring specific Python packages. Here is a list of some commonly used databases, along with their corresponding packages and connection strings:

- AWS Athena
  - Install packages:
    ```
    pip install pyathena[pandas]
    pip install PyAthenaJDBC
    ```
  - Connection string:
    ```
    awsathena+rest://{access_key}:{secret_key}@athena.{region}.
    amazonaws.com/{schema}
    ```
- AWS Redshift
  - Install package:
    ```
    pip install sqlalchemy-redshift
    ```
  - Connection string:
    ```
    redshift+psycopg2://{user}:{password}@{endpoint}:5439/
    {database}
    ```
- PostgreSQL
  - Install package:
    ```
    pip install psycopg2
    ```
  - Connection string:
    ```
    postgresql://{user}:{password}@{host}:{port}/{database}
    ```
- MySQL
  - Install package:
    ```
    pip install mysqlclient
    ```
  - Connection string:
    ```
    mysql://{user}:{password}@{host}/{database}
    ```
- Google BigQuery
  - Install package:
    ```
    pip install sqlalchemy-bigquery
    ```
  - Connection string:
    ```
    bigquery://{project_id}
    ```

These are just a few examples, and many more databases are supported.

Installing Drivers in Docker Images

When running Superset in Docker, the drivers must be installed inside the Docker container. The steps to install a driver are as follows:

1. **Driver Package List:** For instance, if you want to connect to MySQL, you will need the **`mysqlclient`** package.
2. **Create a Requirements-local.txt file:** List your package in this file.

   ```
   echo "mysqlclient" >> ./docker/requirements-local.txt
   ```
3. **Restore the Docker Image:** If you have a personal Docker image, you should:

   ```
   docker compose build --force-rm
   ```

Subsequent to successfully installing the driver, return to the Superset web UI and navigate to **`Settings`** -> **`Data`**: **`Database Connections`** to configure and test your database connection.

Troubleshooting Connections

If your connection fails, check the Docker logs or manually test the connection using Python within the container to isolate the problem. For example:

```
docker exec -it <container_name> bash
```

This helps determine if the issue lies with Superset or the connection itself.

Connecting Through UI

Here is what connecting through the UI appears as:

1. Open Superset and open the Database Connection UI.
2. **Log into Superset:**

   Open a web browser and navigate to the URL where Superset is installed. For implementation on your local machine, this usually would be http://localhost:8088. Log in with your Superset credentials (admin or user with database connection permissions).
3. **Transition to Settings:**

   Once signed in, scroll to the top right-hand corner and locate the menu titled "Settings." Many of the admin-level configurations are available here. Continuing with this is the option, from the pull-down menu provided, for Database Connections under Data, which opens the interface to manage your database connections.

Click the "**+ DATABASE**" Button: From the Connections to Databases page, click the **+DATABASE** button. Use **+DATABASE** to add new databases and specify how Superset connects to them.

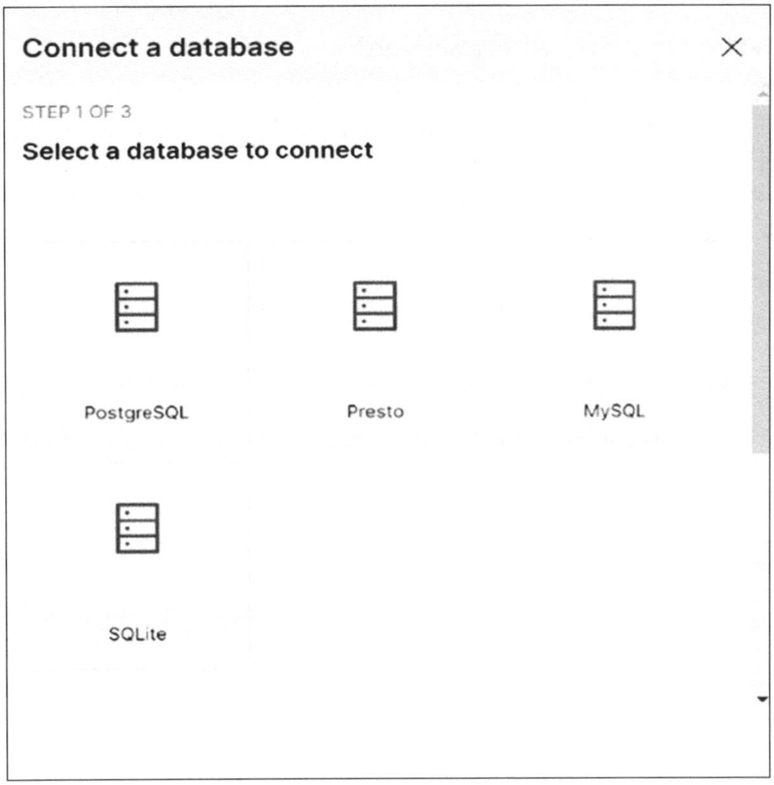

Figure 3.1: *Connecting a Database*

Configuring the Database Connection Using MySQL

Here is how you can configure the database connection using MySQL:

1. Choose MySQL as the type of database.
2. In the "**Add Database**" configuration page, there is a list of supported database engines. Scroll through the list or search for MySQL.
3. Click MySQL. This indicates to Superset that you are actually connecting to a MySQL database, which will then know the specific configuration requirements for MySQL.
4. Complete the following connection parameters:

Now, add the connection details to your database in MySQL.

- **DATABASE NAME:** Your chosen MySQL database name, for example, **my_database**.
- **USERNAME**: The MySQL user authorized for the database, such as the root.
- **PASSWORD**: The MySQL user password.
- **HOST**: The hostname or IP address of the host running the MySQL server. If MySQL is running on the same machine as Superset, use localhost or 127.0.0.1. If MySQL is running elsewhere on the network, use the IP address or domain name of the server running it.
- **PORT**: MySQL typically uses port 3306. If your MySQL server is using a different port, use that one here.

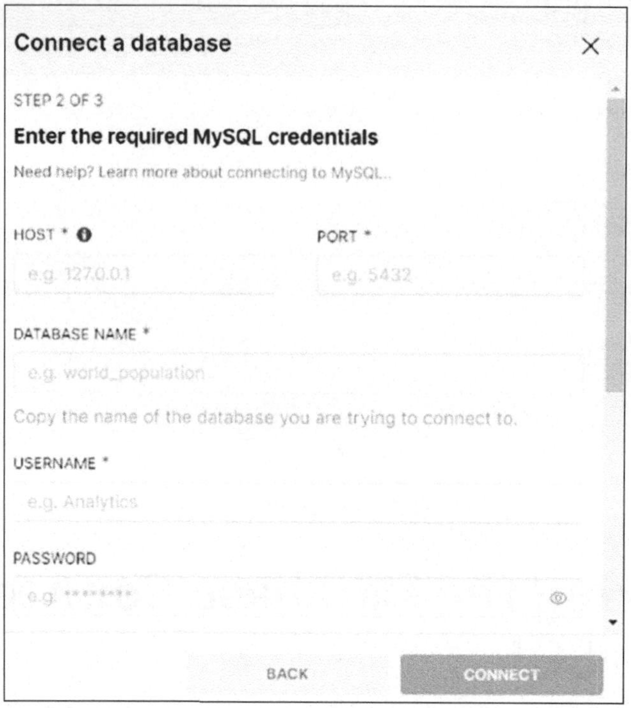

Figure 3.2: *Providing Details of the Database Connection*

5. **Enter the `SQLAlchemy` Connection String**
    - Superset uses the **SQLAlchemy** library to connect to databases. The connection string follows a specific format:

      `mysql://username:password@host:port/database`
    - For example, if your MySQL instance is running locally with a database named **my_database**, a user root, and password **mypassword**, the connection string will appear as:

      `mysql://root:mypassword@localhost:3306/my_database`

6. **Optional: Advanced Settings and SSL Configuration**

   If the database requires SSL for safe communication or any other advanced setup option, click **`Advanced`** tab. There, you can configure:

   - SSL certificates: Input paths to the SSL certificates.
   - Additional Advanced Parameters Make other adjustments, such as connection pooling or timeouts. These configurations are particularly useful in production environments, which require both strong security and high performance.

7. **Test the Connection**

   Click "**`Test Connection`**."

   Entering all the connection details and then clicking the "**`Test Connection`**" button at the bottom of the page will cause Superset to verify whether it can successfully connect to the MySQL database using those credentials and settings.

8. **Check the Results**

   If everything is correct, it will give a popup message saying "**`Connection looks good!`**." This means that Superset is able to connect with the MySQL database without any issues.

   If it does not pass, check the error message. The most common errors are:

   - Wrong password or wrong username.
   - Hostname or port mismatch.
   - Network/firewall settings blocking access.
   - Incorrect connection string formatting. Review the connection parameters and correct errors if any.

   Also, you may refer to Superset's logs, either via Docker or in your environment, for further details.

9. **Save and Finalize the Connection**

   With the test of the connectivity passing, click **`Save`** to save this connection in Superset. This will save the MySQL database, which will now appear in the list of connected databases.

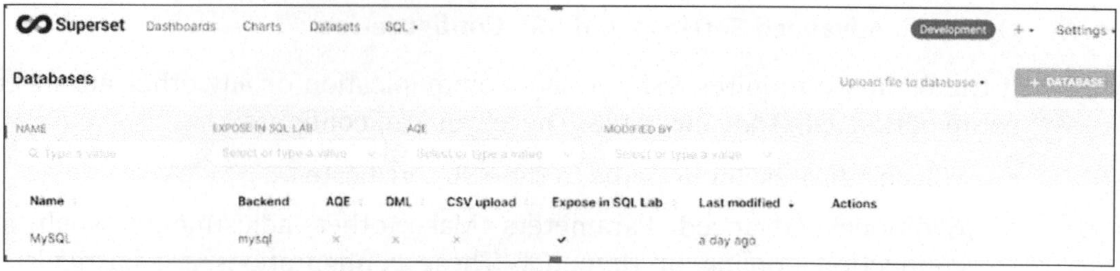

Figure 3.3: *Database Connection Saved*

Creating a Dataset

Here is a step-by-step process for creating a dataset:

Step 1: Attach a Database

In advance of creating a dataset, make sure you are connected to your database in Superset. You can connect from the Database Connections section of Settings if not already done. Once connected, your tables and views will appear there, allowing you to create datasets from them.

Step 2: Accessing Superset

First, access your Superset instance at http://localhost:8088 or your Superset URL.

a. Go to the Data Sets Menu.

b. Click "`Data`" in the navigation bar at the top of Superset.

c. In the dropdown menu, click "`Datasets`." You will now land on the Datasets page, where you can see all the datasets maintained in Superset.

Step 3: Creation of a New Dataset

a. Click "`+DATASET`":

   On the Datasets page, you will see a `+DATASET` button in the top-right corner. Click this button to create a new dataset.

b. **Find a Database:**

   A dialog box appears asking you to select the database for which you require a dataset.

   From the dropdown list, select your connected database where your data is stored-such as MySQL, PostgreSQL, and so on.

c. **Select a Schema**:

   Subsequent to choosing a database, you will be prompted to select a schema. A schema is simply a logical collection of tables and views within the database.

Select the schema in which your target table or view resides. If the schema is not known, consult your database administrator or refer to the database documentation to obtain it.

d. **Select the Table or View:**

Now, subsequent to choosing a schema, a list of tables and views will appear within that schema.

In Select Tables or Views, you can select the table or view upon which to base your dataset.

You can work with various tables or complex queries, but you might preregister a set of complex SQL queries on the database side and then refer to that view in Superset.

e. **Name Your Dataset**:

Selectable tables or views can be assigned meaningful names to clearly identify a dataset when building charts and dashboards.

Fill in all the necessary information, and then click **`Add Dataset`**. Superset will then continue with registering the dataset and preparing it for exploration and visualization.

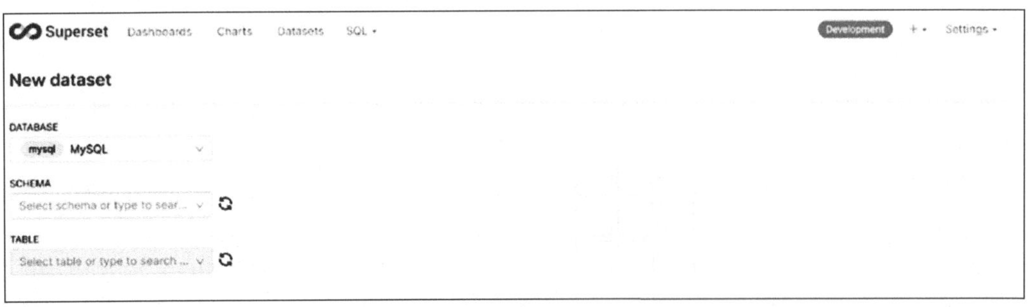

***Figure 3.4:** Creating a Dataset*

Setting the Dataset

Once you create your dataset, you will likely need further configuration to finalize its intended use. This may include metadata definition, metrics, and so on.

Cleaning the Dataset

The dataset will now appear in the list of datasets. Click the name of the newly created dataset to open its configuration page.

Setting Dataset Properties

The dataset's configuration page indicates various properties you can define:

- **Metrics**. Define composite metrics, such as **SUM**, **AVG**, and **COUNT**. They can be illustrated in reports and dashboards.
- **Columns**: Superset automatically picks columns that belong to the table or view you have picked, but if you want to add or even modify columns you can do so. You can also mark them as dimensions or metrics, according to your needs.
- **Column Settings**: Define types of data, default aggregation types, and whether the column can be filtered or grouped.
- **Description**: Add a description to describe more in detail what the dataset is about.

Setting Time Columns (if Necessary)

If your dataset has time-based data, select an appropriate column as a column having type temporal. This is where Superset will be able to handle time-based filtering and visualization, such as in-line charts or time series.

Adding Calculated Columns (Optional)

Superset allows for calculated columns. Calculated columns are derived from existing columns with the help of SQL expressions. You can add a column that computes discounts based on the existing columns' price and **discount_rate** in your table.

Now click the **+ Add** a new column button. Change the name of the column and specify the SQL expression. Once you have configured the dataset, click the Save button to apply the changes. This will save the dataset's metadata and prepare it for use in queries, charts, and dashboards.

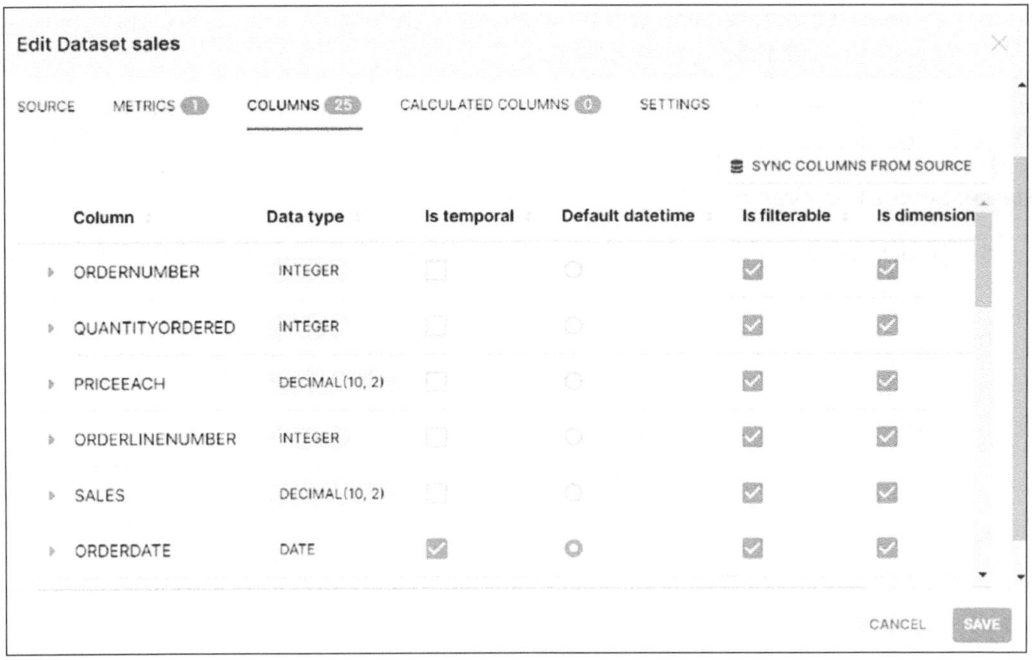

Figure 3.5: *Editing Dataset Columns*

Steps to Create a Chart in Apache Superset

Follow these steps to create the Product-wise Sales Bar Chart:

Step 1: Log in to Superset

a. **Access Superset:** Open a web browser and navigate to your Superset instance (for example, http://localhost:8088).

b. Make sure that your dataset is ready. You should have attached the dataset (`vehicle.sales` in the preceding example) to Superset. If it is not visible there, import it as a new dataset connected to a database.

Step 2: Go to the Charts Section

a. Navigate to the `Charts` tab in the top dropdown menu.

b. On the Charts page, click the **+CHART** button to add a new chart.

Step 3: Choose the Dataset

a. In the dialogue "Create a new chart."

b. Choose the dataset you will be working with for your chart. For this exercise, select the `vehicle.sales` dataset.

c. Subsequent to selecting the dataset, click the button labeled **Create** new chart at the bottom.

Step 4: Select the Type of Chart

a. Subsequent to choosing the dataset, you will be redirected to the chart configuration page.

b. Right above, you will see a dropdown that lets you select the type of chart you want. For this exercise, select **Bar Chart** from the Chart Type drop-down list.

Step 5: Harmonization of Bar Chart

You will now decide how to display your data in the bar chart:

- **Product Code X-Axis:**

  a. Go to the X-Axis and select **PRODUCTCODE** from the dropdown list. This means that for every bar, one product is being profiled, charting by product codes.

  b. To do this, drag the **PRODUCTCODE** field into the X-Axis section or select it from the dropdown.

- **KPIs: Sum of Sales:**

  a. Under Metrics, choose the value that will establish the height of the bars.

  b. If **Sum(SALES)** is selected from the list of accessible measures, the total sales for each product code will be summed.

  c. If the **SALES** metric is not predefined, you can create it manually.

  d. Click **Add** a new metric, select the aggregation function as **SUM**, and choose **SALES** as the column to aggregate.

- **X-Axis Sorting:**

  a. Arrange the X-axis by **SUM(SALES)** in descending order to render the products in order of highest to lowest sales. This way, the best-selling products can be easily identified.

  b. You can use **SUM(SALES)** in the "**X-Axis Sort By**" field and uncheck **X-Axis Sort Ascending** so that the highest sale appears first.

- **Other Optional Settings:**

  a. Finally, in the **FILTERS** section, you can filter the information and view only certain products or a particular time range.

b. You can also switch the type of chart from the dropdown list of available charts, though for this tutorial we will be using a bar chart.

Step 6: Create a Personal Table (Optional)

Under the `Customize` tab, you can modify how the chart appears, including bar colors, chart titles, and legend positions.

- **Chart Titles:** Set the title of the chart as "`Product-wise Sales`," which will appear at the top of your chart.
- **Other Personalization:** You can further personalize settings such as axis labels, tick marks and grid lines if desired.

Step 7: Refresh and View Your Chart

a. Once all fields are filled and the configuration is complete, click the `Update Chart` button. This will display a preview of the chart based on your choices.

b. There ought to be a bar graph where each bar represents a product, and the value of the bar is the sum of sales for that product.

Step 8: Save the Chart

a. Click `Save` on the right-hand side to confirm that the chart looks as it should be.

b. Give a name for the chart, for example: "`Product wise Sales Bar Chart`."

c. You can also add this chart to an existing dashboard or create a new one for easier future access.

Step 9: Add the Chart to a Dashboard (Optional)

If you wish to connect to another graph from this chart, add it to the dashboard:

a. Save your chart. Click any existing dashboard or make a new one under Dashboards.

b. This can help you come up with in-depth views of your sales data with other metrics and charts.

Summary of Activities:

1. Log in to Superset and verify that your dataset is available.
2. To create a new chart, select your dataset and then, under `Charts`, pick `Bar Chart` as the chart type.
3. Configure the chart.
4. X-Axis: Set to `PRODUCTCODE`.

5. Metric: Set to **`SUM(SALES)`**.
6. Sort the X-axis in descending order based on **`SUM(SALES)`**.
7. Modify the chart as needed: title, colors, and so on.
8. Update and view the chart to ensure it displays the bar chart for product-wise sales.
9. Save the chart and, if desired, add it to a dashboard for ready access.

Result: Now, sort each product by total sales in descending order of the amount sold to create a Product-by-Product Sales Bar Chart in Apache Superset. A chart of this type can be used to determine which of the products are most commonly sold; therefore, it can be used for cross-product sales performance analysis.

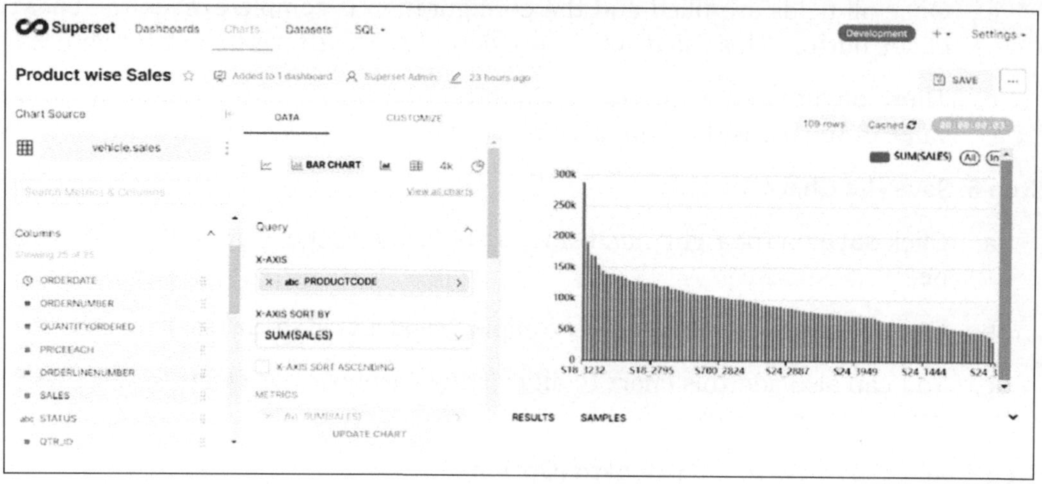

Figure 3.6: *Creating a Chart*

Creating a Dashboard

To create the Vehicle Sales Dashboard using the **`vehicle.sales`** dataset in Apache Superset, follow these detailed steps. Some of the visualization types used on the dashboard are total revenue, total products, and product-wise sales, which is a form of bar chart.

Step 1: Check if the Dataset has been Attached

a. In advance of running this dashboard, ensure that the **`vehicle.sales`** data set is loaded into Apache Superset. If not imported, bring in the data set:

b. Connect the database that contains information about sales on the vehicle.

c. Add the data set. Go to Datasets and click the appropriate table: **`vehicle.sales`**.

Step 2: Build the Necessary Graphs

a. You will need to prepare three different charts for the dashboard:

- Gross Revenue using KPI Visualization
- All Products with KPI Visualization End
- Product-by-Product Sales Bar Chart with the bar chart view

Step 3: Develop Total Revenue KPI

a. **Move to Charts:** Click the top tabs to choose "**`Charts`**" and then click "**`+CHART`**" to add a new chart.

b. Choose a Dataset: Select the **`vehicle.sales`** dataset displayed above, and then click **`Create a new chart`**.

c. Select KPI Chart Type: Select the chart type Big Number with Trendline, also known as a KPI.

d. Define your KPI:

- **Metric:** Set the metric as **`SUM(SALES)`**. This will sum up the sales revenue from the column.
- **Granularity:** You can leave it blank if you want the net amount.

e. Customize the View:

- Under the **`Customize`** tab, add an appropriate title, such as **`Total Revenue`**.
- Remove the trend line if you want only one number to be displayed.

f. Save the Graph:

- Save it under a name such as **`Total Revenue`**. Add it to a new dashboard called **`Vehicle Sales Dashboard`**.

***Figure 3.7:** Creating a KPI*

Step 4: Form the Total Products KPI

a. **Create a NEW Chart:** Click the `Charts` tab. Then click **+CHART** again and select the dataset `vehicle.sales`.

b. **Choose KPI Chart Type**: Just below the chart type selector, choose Big Number with Trendline.

c. **Set the KPI**:

- Metric: Enter the metric as **COUNT DISTINCT(PRODUCTCODE)**. This will give you a count of unique products.
- Granularity: Leave it empty if you are only interested in the overall total count of products.

d. **Personalize the Display**: In the `Customize` tab, provide this chart with a title, such as Total Products.

e. **Save the Chart**: Click `Save`, rename the chart to Total Products, and then attach it to the Vehicle Sales Dashboard created in the previous steps.

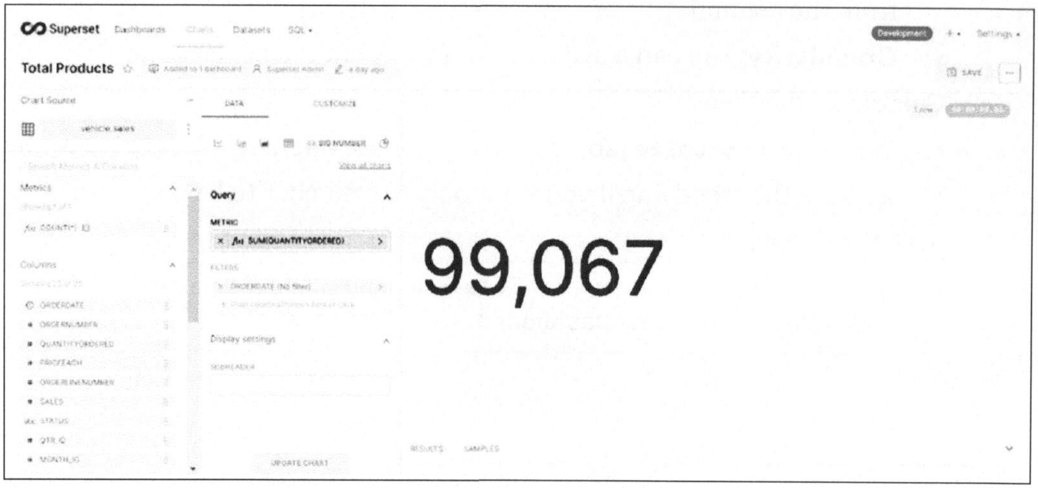

Figure 3.8: *Creating a KPI*

Step 5: Prepare the Bar Graph of Sales Product-Wise

a. Go to Charts: Click **+CHART** to add a new chart and select the `vehicle.sales` dataset.

b. Select Bar Chart: Select the Bar Chart from the list of chart types.

c. Setup the Bar Chart:

- **X-Axis**: Select **PRODUCT CODE**. That way, all sales would be binned by each unique product code available for sale.

- **Metric**: Select the metric as `SUM(SALES)`. It would add up the sales amounts for each product.
- **Sort By**: Order the X-axis by `SUM(SALES)`, so that the highest sales will be the first in the list.

d. **Customize the Graph**: Now go to the `Customize` tab. Enter a title, for example, Product-wise sales.

e. **Save the Chart**: Click `Save`. Assign a name to the chart, Product-wise Sales, and add it to the Vehicle Sales Dashboard.

Step 6: Plotting the Charts into a Dashboard

With all three charts in place – Total Revenue, Total Products, and Product-wise Sales, you can aggregate them into one dashboard.

a. Click on Dashboards:
   - In the left-hand menu, select the Dashboards tab.
   - Find the Vehicle Sales Dashboard that was created when saving the first chart, and double-click to open it.

b. **Edit the Dashboard Layout**: Click the edit dashboard button at the top right.

c. **Rank the Charts**: The dashboard will display three charts: Total Revenue, Total Products, and Product-wise Sales.

d. **Position and Move the Charts to the Following Template**:
   - Position Total Revenue and Total Products as the top KPI. Place the Product-wise Sales bar chart below the KPIs.
   - Restyle the room: You can resize and reposition it in such a way that everything fits in place nicely.

e. **Save the Dashboard**: Click `Save` once you are satisfied with the arrangement to save the layout of the dashboard.

Step 7: Share the Dashboard Exit Edit Mode

Subsequent to saving the layout, exit editing mode by clicking Done or Exit Edit Mode.

Finally, Set the Dashboard Optional: If your dashboard is a draft, you could make the draft final by clicking the Draft button, depending on whether it should be made available to other users or not.

Step 8: Login and Start Operating with the Dashboard

Your Vehicle Sales Dashboard is now ready for use. You can view the total revenue, the number of products, and sales for each product all in one place. Engage with the dashboard by filtering or changing the period to drill down further for more granular information.

Summary

By following these steps, you have successfully created a Vehicle Sales Dashboard in Apache Superset that includes:

- **Total Revenue:** Report the total sales revenue in KPI.
- **Total Products**: The number of unique products appearing in the KPI format.
- **Sales Bar Graph-Product-wise**: It gives a bar graph showing the sales of different products. This dashboard will give you a complete view of sales performance and monitor key metrics in a visually appealing way.

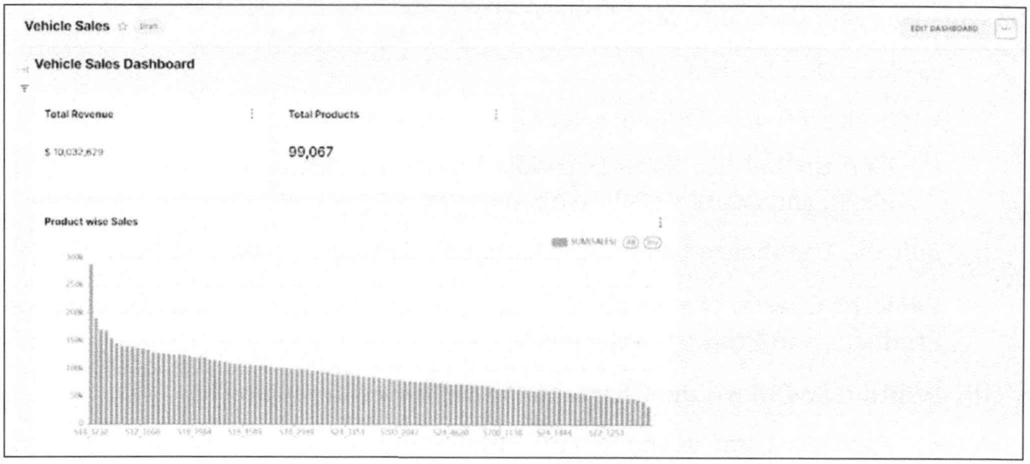

Figure 3.9: *Creating a Dashboard*

Apache Superset is a powerful, open-source platform designed to make data visualization and exploration more accessible and efficient for users with varying technical backgrounds. By becoming more familiar with the basics of working with Superset, connecting to data sources, creating charts, and assembling dashboards, you have gained insights into how raw data can become an actionable visual story.

Accessing Data Sources: Starting Point in Exploring Data

Of course, the first and most important action in using Superset is to connect to a data source. Data sources in Superset represent the building blocks that power your charts and dashboards. Superset supports nearly any type of database, from traditional relational databases such as MySQL or PostgreSQL to modern data warehouses such as Google BigQuery or Amazon Redshift.

It is fairly intuitive to connect to a data source. You attach a data source once you have successfully set up database drivers via the Superset UI. You need to fill in the connection information, for example, the host and port of your database, username, password, and any necessary SSL parameters. Once connected, it lets you work with your database tables or views as datasets that you can directly query and visualize.

It is in this dynamic use of such data connections where the true strength of Superset lies. The tool can present metadata databases with user configurations, dashboards, and chart information. Such data sources can now allow for powerful, interactive visualizations without requiring one to write custom code each time the data changes.

Building Charts Using Superset: Visualizing Your Data

Once connected to a data source, the next step is to build charts. In Superset, creating a chart is intuitive and requires minimal effort, even for non-technical users. The platform offers a wide variety of chart types, including bar charts, line charts, pie charts, scatter plots, maps, and more. Each chart type is fully customizable, allowing users to tailor visualizations to suit their data analysis needs.

In other words, to show sales performance by product, you would use a bar graph that we covered in the preceding example of Product-wise Sales. The X-axis would represent various product codes and the Y-axis would show the consolidated sales of those products. Superset aggregates the sales data on **`SUM(SALES)`** and allows one to view differential performances of products in an easily readable format.

You can start building a chart using a simple dataset. It begins with selecting the right dataset, and chart type, and setting up the necessary fields. The drag-and-drop interface in Superset is rather intuitive, especially when you have mapped your dimension, which is categorizations or product codes, to the X-axis and your measure, such as sales or revenue, to the Y-axis. You then can add filters and groupings as needed or even customizations such as colors, labels, and legends to make it clearer and more presentable.

Superset provides options for more complex configurations, for instance, calculated columns, conditional formatting, and time-series analysis. It proves useful for simple as well as complex views.

Dashboard Building: Aggregation of Charts into Visualization

The real strength of data visualization is seen when multiple individual charts are aggregated in comprehensive dashboards. Superset's dashboards also allow you to combine several charts, KPIs, and other data insights in a single view, giving you a more general view of your main business metrics.

For example, in the Vehicle Sales Dashboard, the components include:

- Total Revenue KPI, which is the total sales from all products.
- Total Products KPI, which provides the total of the unique products sold.
- A product-wise sales bar chart, showing the performance of each product.

With an organizational structure, users can easily see in real-time how the business is performing, quickly pointing out trends, outliers, and opportunities. Superset enables users to filter data on the fly, drill down into specific metrics, or change the time frame for analysis from the dashboard interface. It therefore proves to be flexible and powerful for operational monitoring and strategic decision making.

Dashboards in Superset can also be shared with teams and various stakeholders who participate in collaborative decision-making. You can configure roles and permissions in Superset so that only appropriate users can create or view specific dashboards. This is of great value for any organization seeking to standardize reporting across departments or manage very large datasets with differing access requirements.

Data-Driven Business Decisions

An open-source, scalable architecture design enables growth alongside your data needs and the ability to connect to any database, create more complex visualizations, and build increasingly complex dashboards. It, therefore, connects a data environment with other databases, can handle large datasets for complex queries, and generate accurate and insightful visualizations for real-time pulse checks of business performance.

This gives a platform where firms or analysts can base their decisions on data in one site that encompasses the exploration, visualization, and reporting while centralizing it. Superset enables connections to sources of data, builds meaningful visualizations, and assembles interactive dashboards, making the decision-making process faster and helping organizations unlock the potential of their data.

Closing Reflection

With Apache Superset, you have an end-to-end solution for data visualization, such as connecting data sources, building charts, and assembling dashboards, which can provide you with real-time insights. Whether you are a data analyst or a business leader, with Apache Superset you can escape the circles of spreadsheets or static reports and be able to conduct dynamic analysis of your data, and interactivity. Learning the basics of Superset provides a strong foundation for more advanced data analytics.

Once you move further into the platform, experiment with a variety of charts, more advanced filters, and Superset's SQL Lab, which enables you to run custom queries. Ultimately, Apache Superset gives you an agile environment for transforming raw data into strategic insights, creating smarter, faster, and more effective decision-making. With these foundational skills at your fingertips, you can start leveraging Superset to visualize and analyze your data, making an impact within your organization. The deeper you go and the more customized your exploration is, the more you will realize the flexibility and power of Superset as a data visualization tool.

Conclusion

This chapter gives a practical introduction to the basic features of Apache Superset for data visualization purposes. It starts with guiding readers on how to set up connections with different data sources, making it easier to integrate with their datasets. Once the data source is set up, the chapter guides readers through creating their first chart, focusing on the important steps to ensure successful data visualization.

This gives the audience a wide variety of chart types supported by Superset including bar, line, pie, and scatter charts. This would help them to make the right choice for the visualization of their data. The chapter also talks about how to personalize charts, where the users can change colors, axes, and legends to make it more clear and aligned with their branding or personal taste. To anchor these learnings, the chapter concludes by demonstrating how to assemble a simple dashboard, displaying multiple charts for an all-encompassing data story.

This foundational knowledge enables users to develop strong visualization and dashboard designs but simultaneously lays the groundwork for higher-level analysis techniques. The next chapter shifts the focus to Apache Superset's SQL Lab - a really powerful feature that serves data analysts' and professionals' quest for deeper insights. Learn how to write and execute SQL queries directly in Superset, explore datasets, or create visualizations directly from the query results. Filtering, grouping, aggregation, performing transformations or calculations, and data visualization are some advanced topics that are provided to empower users to use their data to the fullest within the Superset interface.

CHAPTER 4
Data Exploration and SQL Lab

Introduction

Being able to interact with data, either by exploring or finding interesting ways to view data, is essential in today's data-driven world for businesses and organizations looking to make informed decisions. While data visualization platforms offer ways to present data meaningfully, there is a big gap in tools that let analysts dig deeper into the raw data. This is where the power of Apache Superset comes in–SQL Lab, an open-source data exploration and visualization tool. SQL Lab is an interactive environment where the user writes SQL queries to explore data interactively and derive visualizations directly from query results. In this chapter, we will explore what SQL Lab is, how it is different from other SQL interfaces, and why it is a very important tool for data analysts as well as business intelligence professionals.

Structure

In this chapter, we will cover the following topics:

- Overview of SQL Lab
- Use Cases for SQL Lab
- Overview of the SQL Lab Interface
- Writing and Executing SQL Queries in SQL Lab
- Advanced SQL Queries in SQL Lab
- Creating a Chart from SQL Queries in SQL Lab

Overview of SQL Lab

SQL Lab in Apache Superset is a rich, browser-based SQL query editor feature that enables end-users to interactively query and explore data. It is at the heart of raw data and meaningful analysis, providing a complete environment where a user can write SQL queries, inspect results, and generate visualizations.

At its core, SQL Lab is designed to empower users with varying levels of SQL knowledge, enabling them to query the database directly from within Superset. Whether you are looking to perform basic data retrieval or advanced aggregations, SQL Lab supports a wide range of SQL functionalities.

Important Features of SQL Lab

- **SQL Query Editor:** It is a friendly editor in which you can write and execute SQL queries, with syntax highlighting and query history.
- **Schema Browser**: SQL Lab offers a schema browser for easy viewing of the available databases, schemas, tables, and columns without leaving the interface. SQL Lab allows someone to export his or her results of a query in different formats, such as CSV or Excel, to further be analyzed or reported on.
- **Visualizations**: One of the most impressive features of SQL Lab is the direct creation of charts and visualizations from SQL queries without needing to navigate another dashboard or chart-building tool.
- **Query History and Bookmarks**: SQL Lab saves all your past queries to history, which enables the user to recall previous queries, share them, or even schedule for automated execution.
- **Support**: SQL Lab supports multiple databases including PostgreSQL, MySQL, Oracle, Presto, and many others, making it a versatile tool for querying across different database systems.

High-Level Explanation of SQL Lab as a Query Interface within Superset

SQL Lab is a first resort for users who want to directly query their databases from Superset. The workflow initiated in SQL Lab involves the creation of a query in the SQL editor, which is then executed against a connected database. SQL Lab fetches the results, and these can either be examined in the results grid or used to build a visualization on the spot.

The editor itself is intuitive, providing SQL keywords and database object completion for auto-completion, which is designed to allow a minimal amount of mistakes. For users familiar with SQL, it is just like using a standard SQL query tool, only boosted by the additional value of having Superset's in-built charting and visualization capabilities.

Main Characteristics of SQL Lab Interface

- **Query Editor:** It is the heart of SQL Lab where one can type queries, execute them, and retrieve the instant results. This supports multi-line queries and tends to make handling complex SQL logic easier.
- **Schema Browser:** On the left-hand side is a schema browser with the databases, schemas, tables, and views one can access. This enables one to browse each table through the columns and data types available to craft queries.
- **Results Panel:** Succeeding the query is successfully executed, the results are rendered in the results panel as a table. This grid allows the exploration of the data interactively and exportation to import into other tools as needed.
- **Visualization Button:** The results will be transformed into a viewable format instantly with a single click of the visualization button. It directly embeds Superset's visualization tools inside SQL Lab so users can generate a chart or graph right there without switching between multiple interfaces.

One of the strengths of SQL Lab is that users can work on live, raw data. Since most organizations have data spread across multiple databases, SQL Lab can be accessed via countless databases. This means it has the flexibility to be applied to a large number of business applications.

For example, a data analyst can write queries to pull data from a large PostgreSQL dataset, do some aggregations and filtering in SQL Lab, and then draw an insightful visualization using the same tool.

Use Cases for SQL Lab

SQL Lab stands out as an indispensable tool for several use cases, especially for data analysts, business intelligence professionals, and data engineers. Let us explore some key scenarios where SQL Lab shines, starting with:

- **Ad Hoc Data Exploration and Analysis:** Data analysts sometimes have to perform exploratory data analysis to discover insights, trends, and anomalies in the data. SQL Lab offers an excellent means to explore raw data directly. Analysts can easily write SQL queries to filter, group, and aggregate their data within Superset. For instance, a financial analyst may use SQL Lab to filter the date of transactions and then generate reports on revenue trends.
- **Interactive Querying and Visualizations:** SQL Lab is mainly beneficial because it can easily be integrated with Superset's charting capabilities. It becomes possible for users to create visualizations instantaneously, immediately following the execution of a query. Thereby, they can explore the data interactively and derive insights in a much shorter time span. This makes

SQL Lab a perfect tool for business analysts who need to transform raw query results into compelling dashboards for stakeholders.

For example, one can use SQL Lab to pull customer data based on the specific campaign and directly create a bar chart showing the number of conversions. This real-time interaction with the data reduces the time between query execution and insight generation.

- **Advanced SQL Querying for Data Engineers:** SQL Lab may also be used by data engineers to develop more complex SQL logic, such as joins, subqueries, and window functions. SQL Lab is indispensable in data pipeline work because it allows for the validation of transformation and complex joins prior to such code being allowed in the ETL process.
- **Cross-Database Querying:** Many organizations operate using a distributed database. SQL Lab's capability to connect with multiple databases allows for query ability across different data sources without requiring analysts to use different tools. For example, sales data might be in PostgreSQL, while customer support data is in MySQL. An analyst can join these two datasets for deeper analysis in one place with SQL Lab.
- **Team Collaboration and Query Sharing:** Collaboration is highly important in the workflow of data analysis. SQL Lab offers a shared workspace with which team members can save, load, and share queries; this is particularly helpful to business intelligence teams that must ensure consistency in reports or views, such as in weekly sales reports. For instance, an analyst can save a query that produces a weekly sales report, and other members can use it by providing them with the desired modifications.
- **Data Reporting and Scheduling:** Yet this is not where the functionality of SQL Lab ends. SQL Lab also enables users to schedule queries for a specific frequency, including running daily, weekly, or monthly. For reporting purposes, this is very beneficial for companies that require regular reports or want to monitor KPIs without manually running the same queries over and over again.

SQL Lab is a superior feature of Apache Superset that could bridge the gap between raw data and meaningful analysis. Its flexible query interface, rich visualization capabilities, and multi-database support make it an extremely valuable tool for data analysts as well as business intelligence professionals. Integration of both the processes of querying and visualization directly empowers users to reach one place with both exploration and analysis and even visualize data more efficiently than anything until now. Whether you are working on ad-hoc queries, conducting in-depth data analysis, or generating regular reports, SQL Lab is designed to simplify and enhance the process from start to finish.

Overview of the SQL Lab Interface

Users write and execute SQL queries in Superset's SQL Lab within the SQL Editor. This enables interaction directly with their connected databases. It provides an easy-to-use, browser-based environment that caters to users who may have all kinds of levels of SQL experience, which makes it an indispensable tool for querying, data exploration, and analysis.

The SQL Editor is intuitive and efficient. It features syntax highlighting, autocompletion, query history, and error handling. Whether you are executing a very simple **SELECT** to retrieve some rows or building complex joins and aggregations, the SQL Editor makes interactions with your data more streamlined.

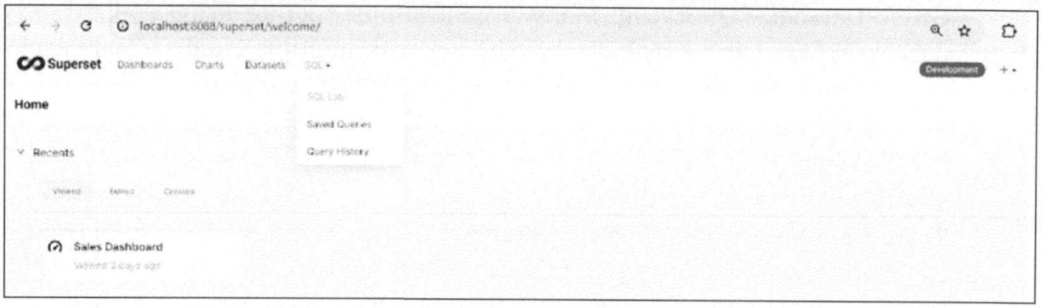

Figure 4.1: *SQL Lab Interface*

Key Features of the SQL Editor

- **Syntax Highlighting:** SQL keywords, table names, and functions are highlighted in different colors to make them more readable and allow easy identification of errors.
- **SQL Autocomplete:** Suggestions by the editor for SQL functions, keywords, table names, and column names are based on the input characters entered; this process is asynchronous with selected database and schema. This saves time writing queries and minimizes a lot of errors.
- **Supports Multi-Line Input:** The editor supports multi-line input. This is very helpful for complex queries that contain multiple clauses, subqueries, or blocks of logic.
- **Limit the Number of Queries Returned:** You can set a limit on the number of rows to return, so large datasets are controlled; as your dataset size grows, queries will run even faster.

Example Query: Basic Data Retrieval

A basic example of retrieving all rows from a table named sales might appear as follows:

```
SELECT * FROM sales;
```

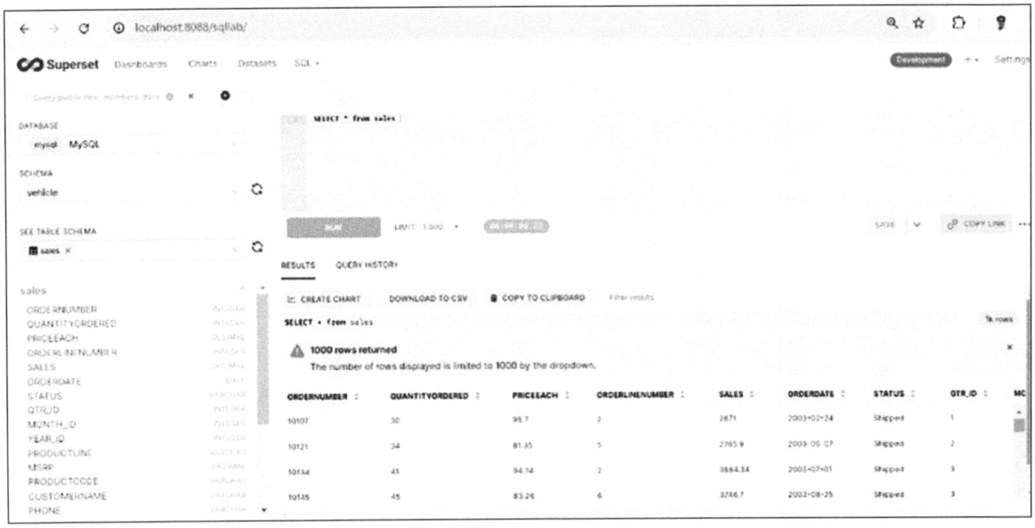

Figure 4.2: *Data Retrieval through SQL Lab*

Here, the query selects all columns from the vehicles table returning each record in the dataset. Although easy to do, this type of query can be useful when quickly checking the data.

Execute Queries

Once you have formulated your SQL query, you can execute it by clicking the Run Query button. The outcome will then be displayed in a Results Panel below the editor. You may also explore further, export, or even create visualizations directly from SQL Lab. The SQL Lab's SQL editor also supports error messaging. If there are syntax errors or if the connection to the database cannot be established, the editor will provide the feedback which will help to quickly debug and correct the query.

Schema Browser: Exploring Tables, Schemas, and Databases via SQL Lab's Interface

The Schema Browser is a SQL Lab component, which lets you explore the structure of databases that are connected without moving from the SQL Editor. It displays databases, schemas, tables, and their respective columns in a hierarchical form for effortless navigation across data sources with which you might be working.

The Schema Browser is located at the left side of the SQL Lab interface and shows an interactive view that is updated according to the currently selected database and schema.

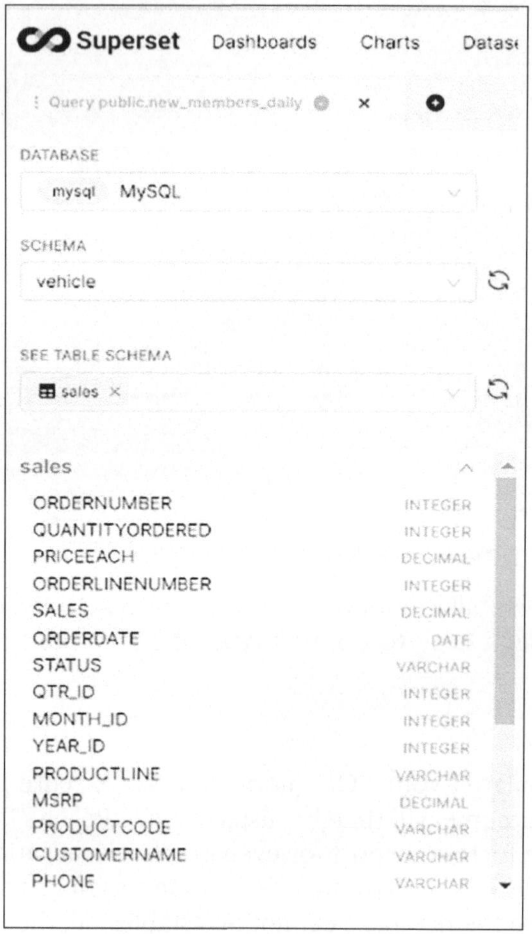

Figure 4.3: *Data Schema View*

Key Features of the Schema Browser

1. **Database and Schema Selection:** A dropdown menu appears above the query editor allowing the user to select which database and schema they want to browse. The Schema Browser will then show the tables and views of that selected schema.

   It lists all the tables and views that are in that schema succeeding it has selected a schema. If the user clicks the name of a table, then he can see columns along with their data types, which makes SQL queries intuitive and more accurate.

2. **Search and Filter:** In working with large datasets or even a large database with many tables, the Schema Browser provides a search function to quickly locate a specific table or column.

Example: Exploring the Sales Table

Once you have explored the table structure, you can begin writing queries to retrieve and analyze the sales data.

```
SELECT * FROM sales;
```

This query will return all columns and rows from the sales table. However, in most cases, you will want to filter or aggregate the data.

Query Example: Total Sales by Customer

Suppose you want to calculate the total sales for each customer. You could write the following query:

```
SELECT CUSTOMERNAME, SUM(SALES) AS total_sales
FROM sales
GROUP BY CUSTOMERNAME
ORDER BY total_sales DESC;
```

The following figure illustrates an SQL query in the SQL lab:

***Figure 4.4**: SQL Query in SQL Lab*

This query pulls in **CUSTOMERNAME** and calculates the sales for each customer using the **SUM()** aggregate function. The result is aggregated by the customer and now ordered by descending **total_sales**, such that the most saleable customers will automatically rank on the first page.

Query Example: Filtering Sales by Date and Status

Let us say you want to see all sales that were completed (**`STATUS = 'Shipped'`**) in the first quarter of the year 2003:

```
SELECT ORDERNUMBER, ORDERDATE, SALES, STATUS
FROM sales
WHERE STATUS = 'Shipped' AND YEAR_ID = 2003 AND QTR_ID = 1
```

The following figure illustrates the SQL query result in the SQL lab:

Figure 4.5: *SQL Query Result in SQL Lab*

This question filters the sales table to include only those orders that have the status of Shipped, were placed in the first quarter of the year (**`QTR_ID = 1`**), and occurred during the year 2003 (**`YEAR_ID = 2003`**).

Query Example: Aggregating Sales by Product Line

To analyze sales performance across different product lines, you could use a query as follows:

```
SELECT PRODUCTLINE, SUM(SALES) AS total_sales
FROM sales
GROUP BY PRODUCTLINE
ORDER BY total_sales DESC;
```

The following figure illustrates the group aggregation in the SQL lab:

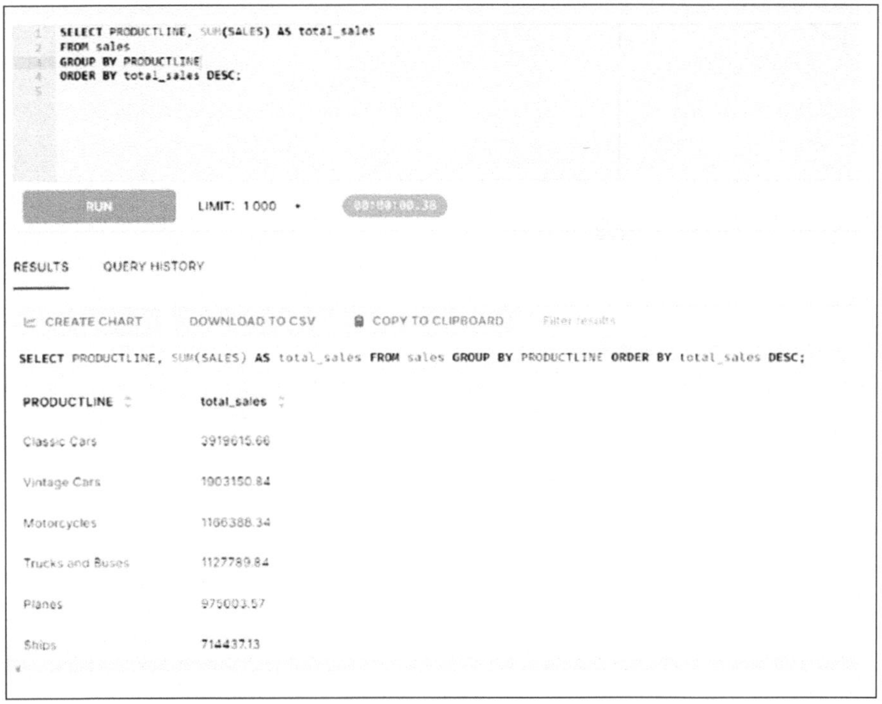

Figure 4.6: *Group Aggregation in SQL Lab*

This type of query displays total sales by product line, allowing for insight into which categories of products are generating the most revenue.

Query Example: Filtering by Deal Size

If you want to analyze large deals only, you could filter by the **DEALSIZE** column:

```
SELECT ORDERNUMBER, CUSTOMERNAME, SALES, DEALSIZE
FROM sales
WHERE DEALSIZE = 'Large';
```

The following figure illustrates filtering in the SQL lab:

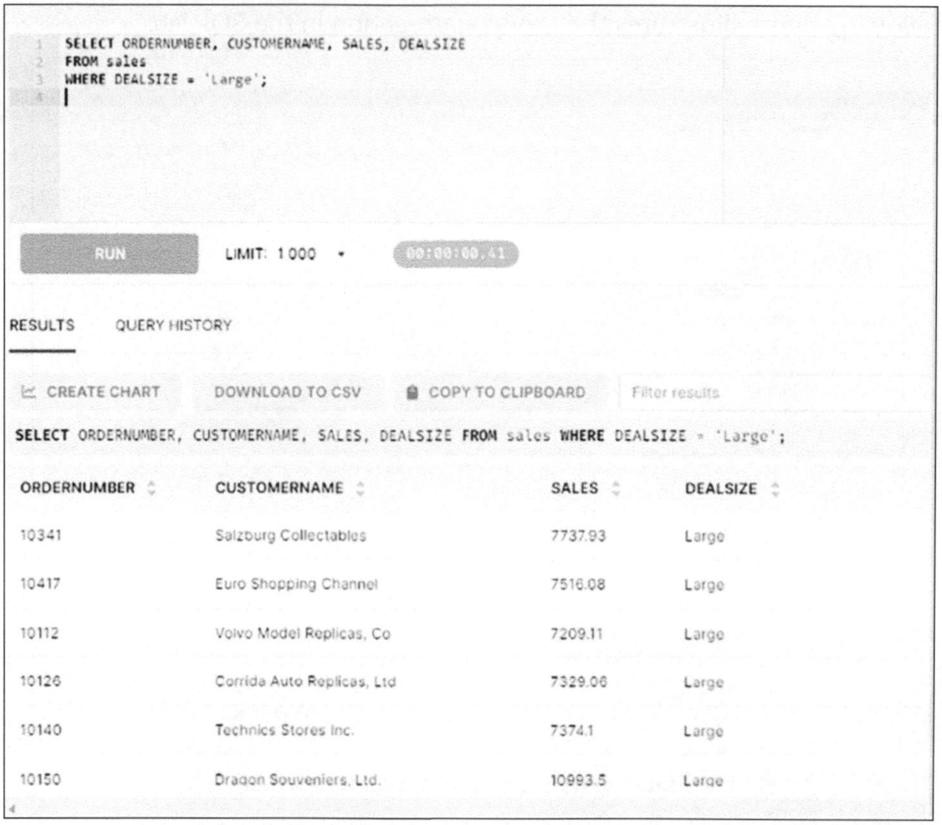

***Figure 4.7:** Filtering in SQL Lab*

The Schema Browser in SQL Lab makes it easy to browse the tables of your connected databases, in this case, the sample sales table. From an examination of columns and their data types, users will quickly begin to appreciate what information they have access to and start to write meaningful SQL queries to analyze it. Whether the goal is to analyze sales data filtered by date, aggregate sales by customer, or drill down into specific deal sizes, the SQL Editor and Schema Browser make up a strong workflow for getting things done.

Saving and Loading Queries

Saving a query in SQL Lab is very painless-you can stash your SQL queries for later use, which turns out to be super handy when you are doing complex data analysis or building a report or anytime later when you would like to revisit the same query in the future.

1. **Click Save Query:** Just above the SQL Editor, you shall notice the **Save query** button. Click this and then open the save query dialog.

2. **Name Your Question:** In the save query dialog, you will be prompted to give a name to your query. Please give a meaningful name to your query referring to the purpose of your query.

   You can also provide an optional description that will be useful in explaining what the query does, in what context, or in further detail.

3. **Save the Question:** Subsequent to naming the query (and optionally adding a description), click **Save**. The query will now be stored in your list of saved queries.

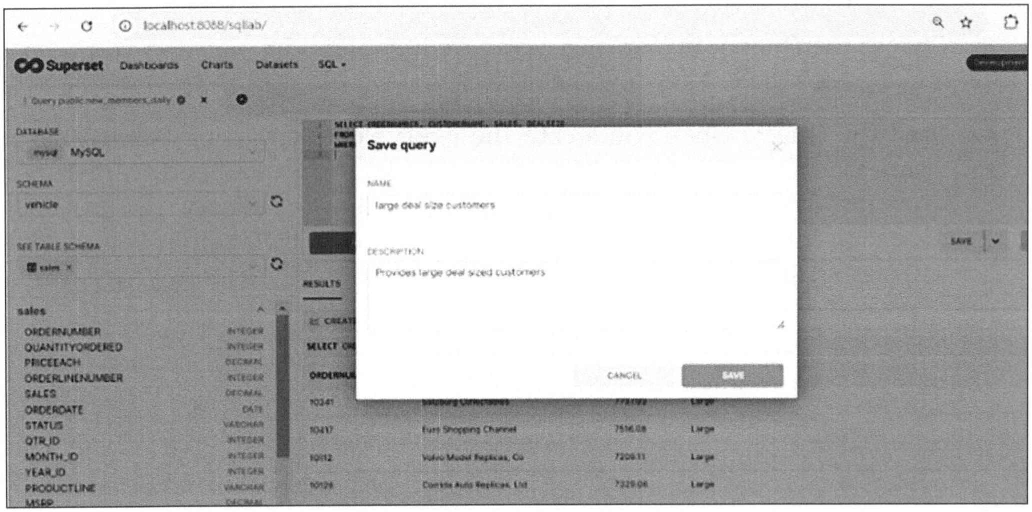

Figure 4.8: *Saving a Query in SQL Lab*

Benefits of Saving Queries

- **Reusability**: Instead of rewriting queries from scratch, you can easily load saved queries and modify them if needed.
- **Collaboration**: Saved queries can be shared across teams, hence making collaboration upon analysis easier.
- **Efficiency**: Routine queries (say, weekly reports or quarterly sales analysis) can be saved and refined and run repeatedly at intervals, saving much time.

Loading a Saved Query in SQL Lab

Once a query is saved, it is easy to use again by simply selecting it from the list of saved queries. This is particularly useful when one has to resume work on an analysis, re-run queries in a frequently repeated task, or refine an analysis, for instance.

Steps to Load a Saved Query

1. **Access Saved Queries:** On the SQL Lab toolbar, there is a Saved Queries button near the SQL Editor. It opens a panel showing all previously saved queries.

2. **Search or Browse for Your Question:** All saved queries appear inside the Saved Queries panel. You either scroll through all of them or use the search bar in order to have any query found by name.

   For instance, you create a saved query for "*Total Sales by Customer* - Q3 2024" - just type any part of the name to search for it.

3. **Choose the Question:** Now that you have identified the question you want to import, click the link to view the details.

4. **Load the Query:** Once you locate the query you want, click Load. This will insert the saved query into SQL Editor and you can then modify, re-run, or work further with the result. Execute or Modify the Query You may then choose to run the query as it stands or edit it in the SQL Editor. For example, you may change the date range or add further filtering to focus your analysis.

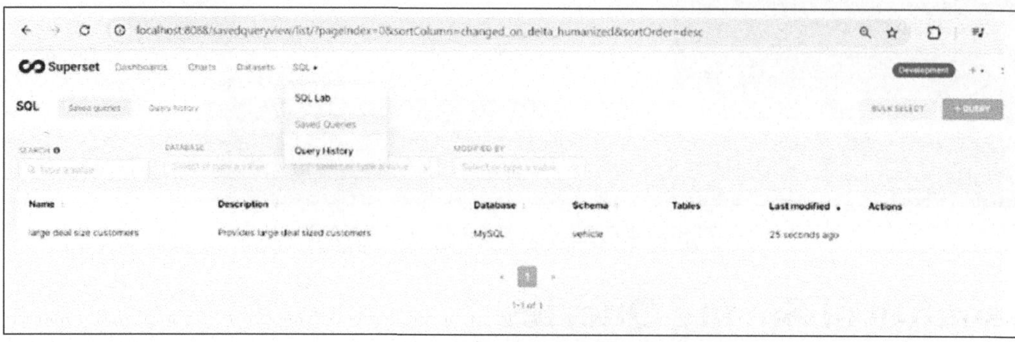

Figure 4.9: *Loading a Query in SQL Lab*

Writing and Executing SQL Queries in SQL Lab

The heart of data exploration through SQL Lab is writing and executing SQL queries. With SQL Lab, users can write SQL directly against connected databases. With SQL Lab, you can write queries that perform simple data retrieval, filtering operations, as well as sorting operations. In this section, we will explore how to write basic SQL queries, execute them, and understand the results. We will also walk through an example query using a sales dataset that illustrates how SQL Lab can help break down how to analyze and explore data well.

Basic SQL Queries

SQL Lab follows standard SQL syntax. Any basic data operation such as selecting data, filtering rows, or sorting results is easy using SQL Lab. Now, we will discuss three primary SQL query operations: **SELECT**, **WHERE**, and **ORDER BY**.

1. **SELECT statements:** Retrieving Information from a Table Data gets retrieved from the database with a SELECT statement. It is the most basic SQL operation in that it lets you select which columns you would like to view.

   Basic SELECT Query Example: `SELECT * FROM sales;`

   It retrieves all columns (*) from the table name sales. Though the * retrieves all possible columns, it is usually best to write the necessary columns explicitly.

Targeted SELECT Query Example:

```
SELECT ORDERNUMBER, CUSTOMERNAME, SALES
FROM sales;
```

This query brings down only the **ORDERNUMBER**, **CUSTOMERNAME**, and **SALES** columns from the sales table, thus eliminating some extraneous data.

2. **Filtering data with WHERE clause:**

   WHERE clause is the one used to filter the rows based on specific conditions. This allows you to narrow data to only those records that meet specific criteria.

Example: Filtering Orders by Status:

```
SELECT ORDERNUMBER, STATUS, SALES
FROM sales
WHERE STATUS = 'Shipped';
```

This query gets only the orders with **STATUS** as **'Shipped**,' thereby filtering out those with pending or canceled order status. This is pretty handy when looking at closed sales.

3. **Sorting Results with ORDER BY:**

   The **ORDER BY** clause allows you to sort the result set by one or more columns. One can specify ascending order by default while descending order is specified by the **DESC** keyword.

Example: Sorting Orders by Sales Amount:

```
SELECT ORDERNUMBER, CUSTOMERNAME, SALES
FROM sales
ORDER BY SALES DESC;
```

This query retrieves the order number, customer name, and sales amount, and sorts the results in descending order of sales. The orders with the highest sales appear first in the results.

Combining `SELECT`, `WHERE`, and `ORDER BY`

We can combine these clauses to write richer queries. For instance, the following query returns all shipped orders sorted by sales in descending order:

```
SELECT ORDERNUMBER, CUSTOMERNAME, SALES, STATUS
FROM sales
WHERE STATUS = 'Shipped'
ORDER BY SALES DESC;
```

Executing Queries in SQL Lab

Executing a query in SQL Lab is easy. Once you write your query in the SQL Editor, you can execute it and view the results in the Results Panel.

Steps to Perform a Query

1. **Write the Query:** Enter your SQL query in the SQL editor. For instance:

   ```
   SELECT ORDERNUMBER, CUSTOMERNAME, SALES
   FROM sales
   WHERE STATUS = 'Shipped'
   ORDER BY SALES DESC;
   ```

2. **Run the Query:** Click the Run Query button above the SQL Editor. SQL Lab executes the query on the database and presents it in a table format below the editor.

3. **View Query Progress:** The SQL Lab has a progress bar during a query run. This is very helpful for lengthy-running queries and large result set pulls.

4. **Cancel the Query (if Necessary):** If your query is running too long or you want to cancel it, you can do so by clicking the Cancel Query button.

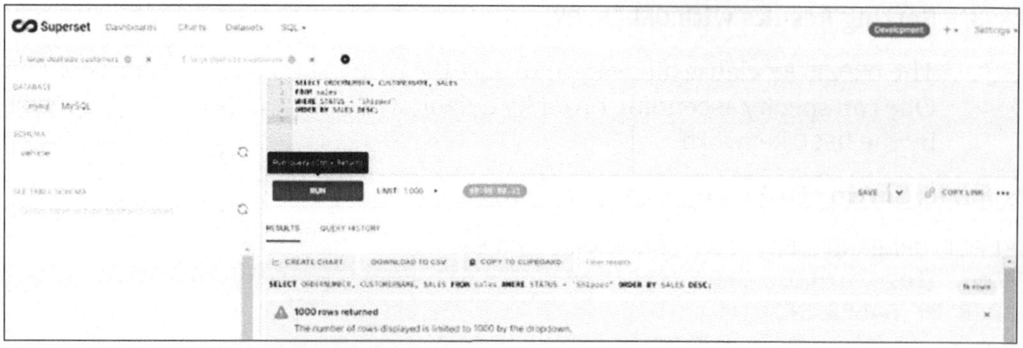

Figure 4.10: *Executing a Query in SQL Lab*

Understanding Query Results

Once you execute your query, SQL Lab displays the result in the grid view below the SQL Editor. You can view and filter as required and export in a suitable format.

- **Results Grid View**
  - **Tabular Format:** Query results are returned in a tabular format comprising rows and columns. For every column there corresponds a field of the dataset and each row represents a record that satisfies the query criteria.
  - **Interactive Exploration:** You can scroll through results or pages through very large datasets. This allows you to more easily scan the output of your query to make sure it is what you had in mind.
- **Exporting Query Results:** SQL Lab provides several options to export results, enabling you to download your query results to use them again outside the system.
  - **Export as CSV:** You can export the results of your query in CSV format, which can be opened in spreadsheet applications such as Excel or Google Sheets for further analysis or reporting.

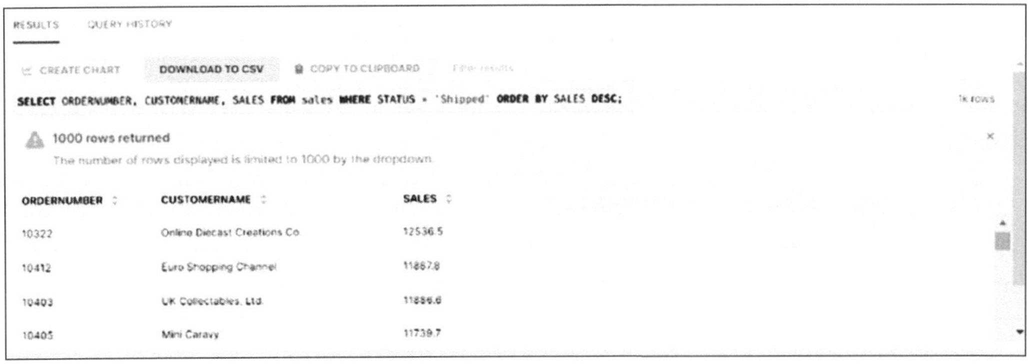

***Figure 4.11**: Exporting Data in SQL Lab*

SQL Lab is a great place to learn how to write and execute SQL queries for efficient data exploration and analysis. Basic SQL commands, such as SELECT, WHERE, and ORDER BY, help you retrieve the specific data you need. Executing your queries in SQL Lab is easy, where results can be shown in a grid format and you have export options for further analysis. We have demonstrated, using some examples from a sample sales dataset, how easy it is to obtain and interpret data using SQL Lab, allowing you to gain insights and drive business decisions based on your data.

Advanced SQL Queries in SQL Lab

As you become more comfortable with SQL, more advanced techniques include self-joins and window functions, which you can use more deeply to explore data and analyze it. We will go through how to use these powerful SQL operations with the sales dataset to discover richer insights. In this section, we will focus on how to use self-joins and advanced window functions such as LEAD and LAG to make calculations over ordered sets of data.

Self Joins in SQL: Working with Related Orders

Sometimes you may need to join a table with itself. This can be helpful for comparing rows within a table or for viewing relationships between rows; in the case of a sales table, you may want to identify all orders made by a customer on different dates.

Finding customers who placed multiple orders. Suppose we are interested in finding customers who have ordered more than once and want to compare the order dates of their first and second orders. We can do a self-join on the sales table, this time joining it on CUSTOMERNAME but comparing different **ORDERDATE** values.

```
SELECT
    a.CUSTOMERNAME AS customer_name,
    a.ORDERNUMBER AS first_order,
    a.ORDERDATE AS first_order_date,
    b.ORDERNUMBER AS second_order,
    b.ORDERDATE AS second_order_date
FROM sales a
JOIN sales b
    ON a.CUSTOMERNAME = b.CUSTOMERNAME
    AND a.ORDERDATE < b.ORDERDATE
ORDER BY customer_name, first_order_date;
```

The following figure illustrates the process of joining data in the SQL lab:

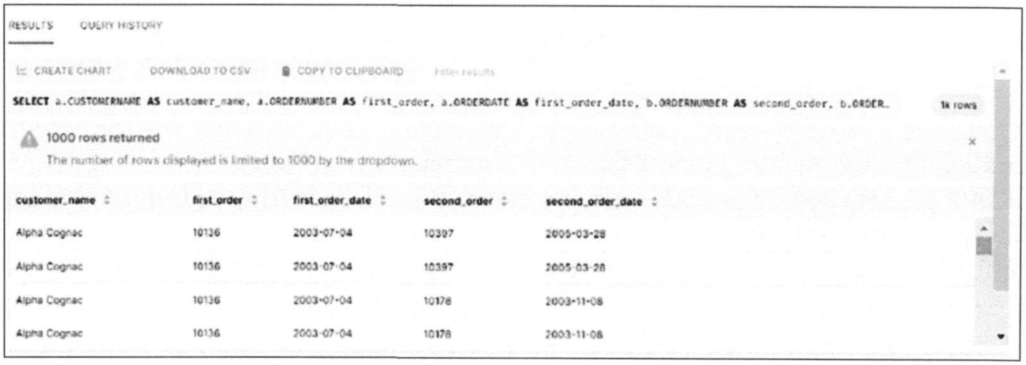

Figure 4.12: *Joining Data in SQL Lab*

Explanation

a and b: These are aliases representing two different instances of the same table.

Self-Join Logic: We join the sales table with itself on customer name (**`CUSTOMERNAME`**), but we only join rows where the first order date is earlier (**`a.ORDERDATE < b.ORDERDATE`**).

Result: This query gives the customer orders who have made more than one. It also gives the first and the second orders from the customer.

Window Functions: LEAD and LAG for Time-Based Analysis

Window functions allow you to perform aggregation or computation across a number of rows that are related to the current row without needing to aggregate the data. They are very powerful for time-based analytics as well as comparisons. Some of the most common window functions you will use are LEAD and LAG.

- **LEAD:** Draws value from the row succeeding the current row in your dataset.
- **LAG:** Returns the value from the previous row in the dataset.

These types of functions are particularly useful when one needs to compare sales between consecutive orders or determine the difference between two time periods.

Example

Comparing Sales Between Consecutive Orders (Using LAG): This question will enable us to compare sales amounts for each customer's orders with their previous order to be able to track sales growth or decline over time.

```
SELECT
    CUSTOMERNAME,
    ORDERNUMBER,
    ORDERDATE,
    SALES,
    LAG(SALES, 1) OVER (PARTITION BY CUSTOMERNAME ORDER BY ORDERDATE) AS
previous_order_sales,
    SALES - LAG(SALES, 1) OVER (PARTITION BY CUSTOMERNAME ORDER BY OR-
DERDATE) AS sales_difference
FROM sales
ORDER BY CUSTOMERNAME, ORDERDATE;
```

The following figure illustrates the window functions in the SQL lab:

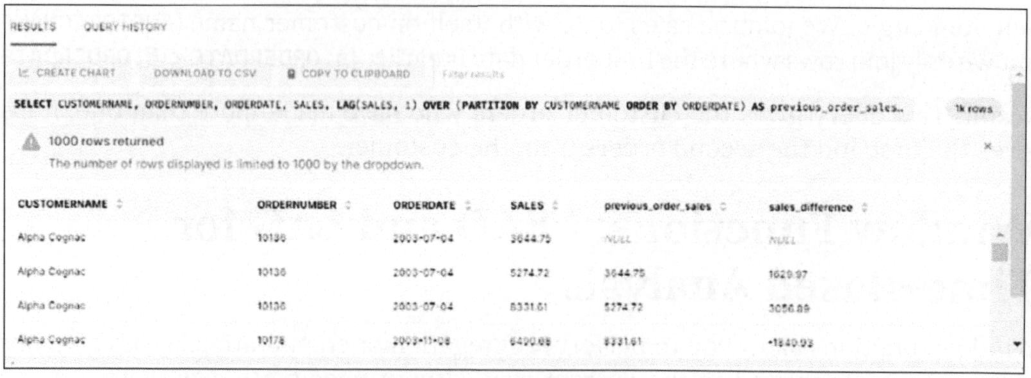

Figure 4.13: *Window Functions in SQL Lab*

Explanation

1. **`PARTITION BY CUSTOMERNAME`:** This ensures the window function works within each customer's set of orders.
2. **`ORDER BY ORDERDATE`:** Orders the rows in ascending date of order to compare sequential orders.
3. **`LAG(SALES, 1)`:** Retrieves the sales value from the previous order for each customer.

   `sales_difference`: This computes the difference between the current order's sales and the previous order's sales.

Result:

The aforementioned query will show the orders by each customer along with their previous order sales and the difference in sales. This can help determine the trend whether sales increase or decrease for each customer.

Example: Finding the Next Order Date for Each Customer (Using LEAD)

The LEAD function can also be used in finding future values in the dataset. Here, we can use LEAD to find the next order date for each customer, which may help in understanding patterns in customer buying.

```
SELECT
    CUSTOMERNAME,
    ORDERNUMBER,
    ORDERDATE,
   LEAD(ORDERDATE, 1) OVER (PARTITION BY CUSTOMERNAME ORDER BY ORDERDATE)
AS next_order_date
FROM sales
ORDER BY CUSTOMERNAME, ORDERDATE;
```

The following figure illustrates the LEAD function in the SQL lab:

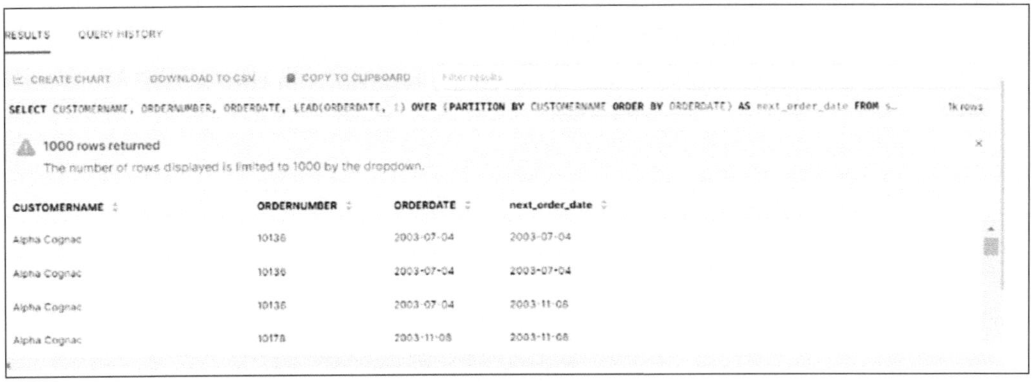

Figure 4.14: *Window Functions- LEAD in SQL Lab*

Explanation

1. **`LEAD(ORDERDATE, 1)`:** This will give the next order date for the same customer.
2. **`PARTITION BY CUSTOMERNAME`:** It groups the result by the customer and ensures the window function is being applied within each customer's order.

Result:

This query returns each order with the date of the customer's next order, it gives you an idea of purchase patterns.

Conditional Aggregations Using SUM with CASE

In other cases, you might be required to do some conditional aggregations. Here you calculate the totals based on a specific condition. The most common way of obtaining this is by using the CASE statement inside an aggregation function, such as SUM. This allows you to sum values based on certain criteria, such as summing sales only for shipped orders or orders coming from a particular country.

Example

Total Sales Shipped versus Canceled Orders: Suppose you want to compare the total sales, for orders that were shipped versus for orders that were canceled. You can do this by using a CASE statement inside the SUM() function to create conditional sums based on the STATUS of the order.

```
SELECT
    CUSTOMERNAME,
    SUM(CASE WHEN STATUS = 'Shipped' THEN SALES ELSE 0 END) AS total_
shipped_sales,
    SUM(CASE WHEN STATUS = 'Cancelled' THEN SALES ELSE 0 END) AS total_
cancelled_sales
```

```
FROM sales
GROUP BY CUSTOMERNAME
ORDER BY total_shipped_sales DESC;
```

The following figure illustrates the conditional aggregations in the SQL lab:

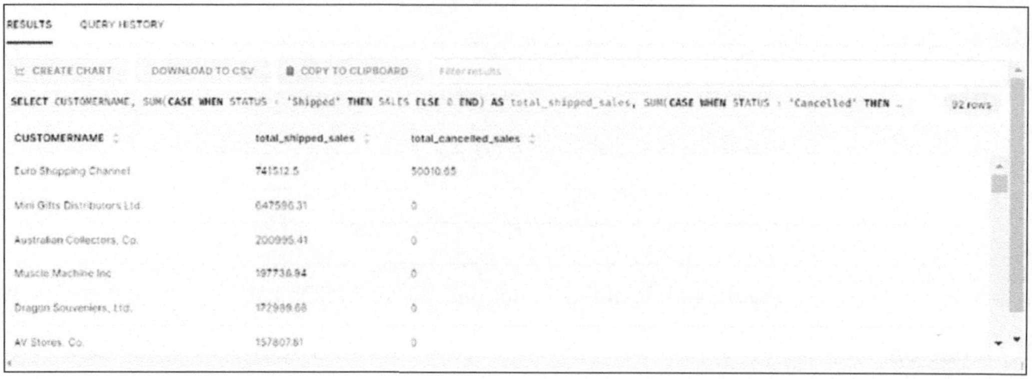

Figure 4.15: *Conditional Aggregations in SQL Lab*

Explanation:

1. **`CASE WHEN STATUS = 'Shipped' THEN SALES ELSE 0 END`:** This part of the query checks if the **`STATUS`** of the order is **`'Shipped`**.' If it is, the sales value for that order is added to the total; otherwise, a zero is returned.
2. **`SUM()`**: This aggregate function adds all the values returned by the CASE statement, which computes the total sales of shipped orders.

The same logic is applied to calculate the total sales for **`'Cancelled'`** orders.

1. **`GROUP BY CUSTOMERNAME`**: it computes the total per customer.
2. **`ORDER BY total_shipped_sales DESC`**: This returns the results ordered by total shipped sales in descending, so the customer with the highest shipped sales appears first.

Result:

The returned query gives back the total shipped sales and total canceled sales for every customer, and this way you can easily compare how much value was generated from shipped orders and how much potential sales were lost due to cancellations.

Creating a Chart from SQL Queries in SQL Lab

Here is a step-by-step process of creating a chart from SQL queries in the SQL lab:

Step 1: Write and Run SQL Query

Start by creating your SQL query in SQL Lab's Query Editor. It returns the total sales by country.

Step 2: Execute the Query

```
SELECT COUNTRY, SUM(SALES) AS total_sales
FROM sales
GROUP BY COUNTRY
ORDER BY total_sales DESC;
```

a. **Enter the Query:** Paste or type the aforementioned query into the SQL Lab Query Editor.

b. **Click "`Run Query`":** Once the query is ready, click the **`Run Query`** button to execute it. SQL Lab will retrieve the results and display them in the Results Panel below.

View Results: The query returns a table with two columns: **`COUNTRY`** (listing each country) and **`total_sales`** (the sum of sales for each country, ordered by descending sales).

Step 3: Click "`Create Chart`"

With the query running successfully:

a. Click the "**`Create Chart`**" button In the Results panel, sometimes labeled as "**`Explore`**."

b. Click it to open the chart creation interface.

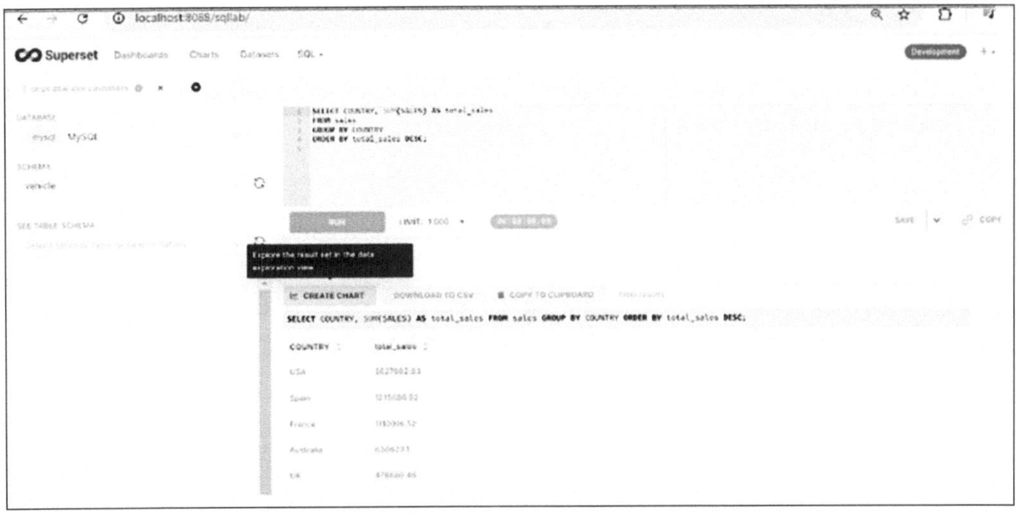

Figure 4.16: *Creating Charts through SQL Lab*

Step 4: Configure the Bar Chart

Now, that you have entered the chart config interface:

Select Chart Type:

From the **`Chart Type`**, choose **`Bar Chart`**. This type of chart will be appropriate for comparing values; for example, here it is sales-across several categories, whereas here it is countries.

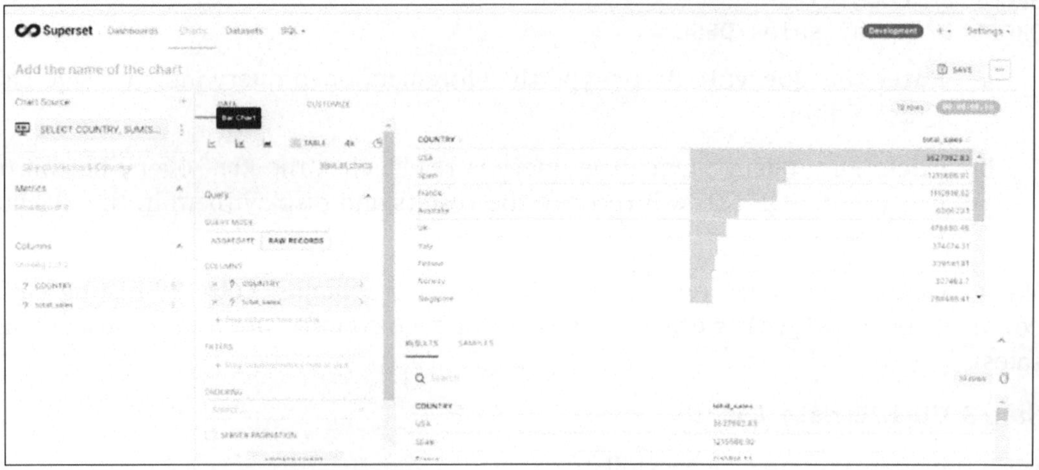

Figure 4.17: *Selecting Chart Types*

Set the X-Axis and Metrics as follows:

a. **X-Axis (Dimension):** Assign the x-axis to be **`COUNTRY`**. This way, every country will be placed on the x-axis.

b. **Y-Axis (Metric):** Choose **`SUM(SALES)`** from the metrics to automatically label that as **`total_sales`** in the query. This will appear as the total sales for each country on the y-axis.

Figure 4.18: *Setting Chart Axis*

Customize the Chart:

Change sort options if needed. The query already orders, by default, in descending order by total sales, so you probably do not need any added sorts.

Add Labels: Use data labels to display sales figure values on each bar if you intend to enhance the clarity of each bar.

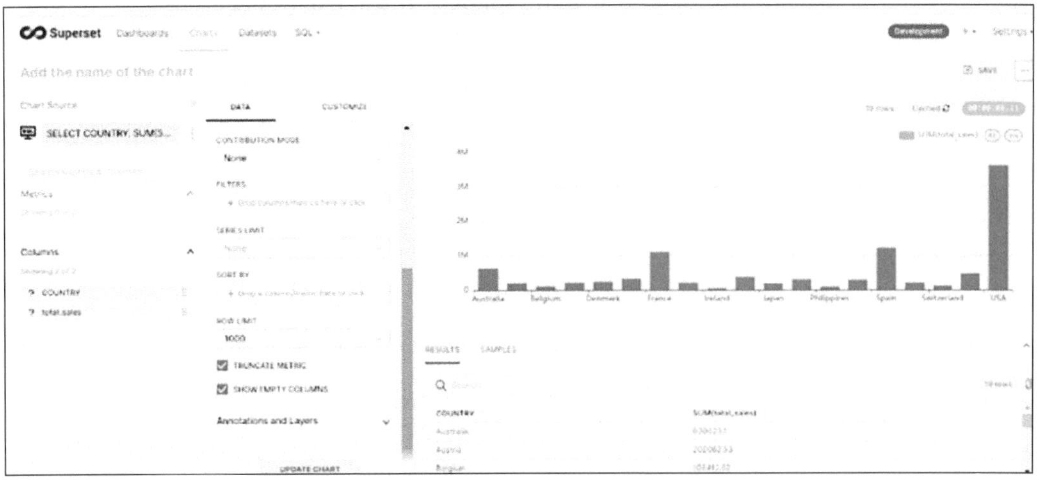

Figure 4.19: *Adding Labels*

Step 5: Save and Update the Chart

a. **Update the Chart:** Set the x-axis to country and the metric to sum of sales, then click `Update Chart` for your preview to update.

b. **Save the Chart:** Subsequent to reading the table, click `Save` in the top-right corner. Give your chart a descriptive name, such as "`Total Sales by Countries`."

c. **Add to a Dashboard**: You may opt to add this chart to an already created dashboard or build a new dashboard from scratch. Dashboards help you group various visualizations for easy sharing and presentation.

Figure 4.20: *Updating the Chart*

The following figure shows the chart being loaded in the Dashboard:

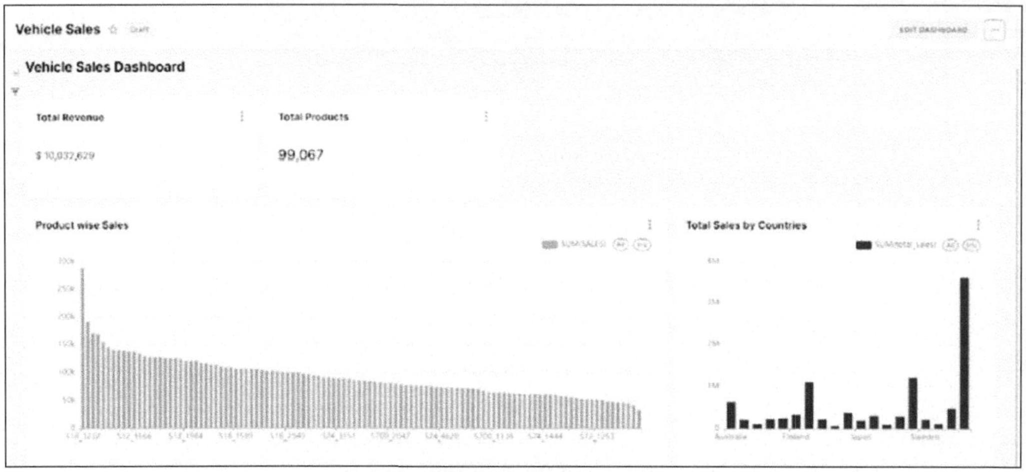

Figure 4.21: *Loading Chart in Dashboard*

By following these steps, you have successfully run a query in SQL Lab and created a bar chart that visualizes total sales by country. The x-axis (dimension) is set to the country, and the y-axis (metric) displays the sum of sales for each country. Once you have customized the chart, saving it and adding it to a dashboard makes it easy to share and revisit for ongoing analysis.

Conclusion

SQL Lab in Apache Superset is a powerful browser-based interface for writing SQL queries, exploring datasets, and creating data visualizations. It provides a very intuitive environment where users can work directly with their own data by writing SQL queries, executing them against connected databases, and transforming the results into meaningful visualizations.

SQL Lab in Superset is a querying environment for executing SQL queries directly. Whether the task requires the retrieval of simple data or complex analytical work, SQL Lab lets users dig deeper into their data in real-time.

The most critical functionalities include an SQL Editor, through which queries can be easily written with syntax highlighting and autocompletion, thus greater accuracy and usability. Another functionality is a Schema Browser that provides a structured representation of databases, schemas, tables, and columns, which enables users to navigate and write queries more conveniently. The Query Results component also includes an interactive grid interface for data exploration, with the ability to sort, filter, and export results in different formats like CSV and Excel, thus making the data analysis and reporting process easier.

The SQL Lab is the most crucial application for business analysts, data engineers, and other kinds of data professionals who are exploring their data, testing hypotheses, or preparing datasets for more in-depth analysis and visualization.

We also learned how to make charts using the SQL Lab. SQL Lab is a complete, flexible tool for querying, exploring, and visualizing data in Apache Superset. It simplifies the workflow by offering one place to write your SQL query, retrieve results, and create visualizations all from that one query. Whether basic data retrieval or advanced SQL techniques with window functions, SQL Lab enables both technical and nontechnical users to take raw data to meaningful insights easily.

The next chapter will explain how further development of the visualization capabilities in Apache Superset can be done by using custom plugins. It starts with a general overview of the currently offered visualization plugins and their capabilities, followed by practical work on how to build, extend, and install custom plugins for specific visualization requirements.

The upcoming chapter is built with help from JavaScript frameworks such as D3.js to support complex, interactive visualizations with excellent customization opportunities. The last part of the chapter exhibits best practices for developing and keeping custom plugins compatible, scalable, and usable. By the end of the next chapter, readers will be equipped to use Superset, customizing their unique requirements for analytics purposes.

Chapter 5
Custom Visualizations and Plugins

Introduction

Data visualization stands out as the core of good data storytelling and the whole process of decision-making. Apache Superset is an advanced business intelligence solution offering a long list of visualization plugins. It allows people to turn complex datasets into useful insights. There are also bundled plugins covering a wide spectrum of chart types and configurations for every business need. This starts from simple bar charts up to complex geospatial visualizations. Superset has powerful instruments for any form of data analysis or presentation.

However, one-size-fits-all solutions hardly work in today's fast-changing data context. Organizations face different challenges and opportunities that demand special visualizations. This is where custom visualization plugins become essential. Building these custom plugins enables businesses to make visualizations tailored to specific analytic needs, ensures brand consistency, and gains a competitive edge.

Structure

In this chapter, we will cover the following:

- Overview of Available Visualization Plugins
    - Types of Built-In Visualization Plugins in Superset
- Building and Installing Custom Visualization Plugins
- JavaScript Integration with Superset
- Using D3.js for Advanced Charts
- Best Practices for Custom Plugins

Overview of Available Visualization Plugins

Though the default visualizations that Superset offers are pretty robust, they are less likely to meet specific niche demands or specializations consistently. With custom plugins, organizations can innovate and create visualizations according to their very peculiar data narratives.

For instance, custom plugins allow developers to:

- **Introduce New Visualization Types:** Create charts and graphics that are not part of Superset's default library, such as Sankey diagrams, radar charts, or specialized KPIs.
- **Enhance Interactivity**: Incorporate advanced interactivity, animations, or drill-down capabilities that improve user experience.
- **Handle Specific Data Formats**: Customize data handling and rendering to support unconventional or proprietary formats.

The new generation data exploration and visualization platform Apache Superset has an extensive set of in-built plugins. While it will certainly form the core of your presentation, users can present data in multiple formats, from simple charts to complex, interactive dashboards.

A visualization plugin in Apache Superset is a module that defines the rendering process of a specific category of charts or graphs within the system. It serves as an intermediary between processed data in Superset and the final visual form presented to a user. Each plugin therefore includes mechanisms for converting the data into visual elements together with settings to tailor how it is displayed as well as its level of interactivity.

Plugins in Superset are designed to be:

- **Reusable**: Each plugin can be used across multiple dashboards and datasets.
- **Configurable**: Plugins often come with options for adjusting visual elements such as colors, scales, legends, and tooltips.
- **Extensible**: Developers can modify or create plugins to extend the platform's visualization capabilities.

Types of Built-In Visualization Plugins in Superset

Superset comes with a variety of pre-installed plugins to meet diverse data visualization needs. Here is an overview of some of the most commonly used plugins:

Bar Chart

- **Description**: Represents categorical data with rectangular bars, where the length of each bar is proportional to the data value.
- **Use Cases**: Comparing sales across regions, analyzing category-wise performance, and so on.
- **Customizations**: Adjust bar orientation (horizontal/vertical), stack values, or group categories.

Line Chart

- **Description**: Visualizes trends over time by connecting data points with a line.
- **Use Cases**: Tracking stock prices, monitoring website traffic, and analyzing time-series data.
- **Customizations**: Configure axes, add markers, or enable smoothing for a more polished look.

Pie Chart

- **Description**: Displays proportions of a whole as slices of a circular graph.
- **Use Cases**: Showing market share, distribution of survey responses, and so on.
- **Customizations**: Modify slice colors, add labels, or enable a donut-style view.

Table

- **Description**: Presents data in a tabular format, ideal for precise, row-level information.
- **Use Cases**: Viewing detailed transaction data, customer profiles, or financial statements.
- **Customizations**: Format columns, add sorting and filtering, or apply conditional formatting.

Heatmap

- **Description**: Represents data intensity or frequency using color gradients on a grid.
- **Use Cases**: Analyzing website traffic by hour, understanding seasonality in sales.
- **Customizations**: Define gradient scales, customize axes, or add tooltips.

Scatter Plot

- **Description**: Plots data points on two axes to reveal relationships or clusters.
- **Use Cases**: Exploring correlations between variables, and identifying outliers in datasets.

- **Customizations**: Add trend lines, adjust point sizes, or enable grouping by categories.

Time-Series Chart

- **Description**: Designed specifically for time-series data, with options for line, area, or bar styles.
- **Use Cases**: Visualizing revenue growth over months, and analyzing user activity trends.
- **Customizations**: Apply rolling averages, configure date ranges, or enable annotations.

Box Plot

- **Description**: Displays statistical summaries of data, including median, quartiles, and outliers.
- **Use Cases**: Comparing performance metrics across teams, and analyzing distribution of values.
- **Customizations**: Adjust whisker lengths, and enable tooltips for detailed insights.

Geospatial Plugins

- **Examples**: Mapbox, Deck.gl
- **Description**: Visualize geospatial data using layers, markers, and regions.
- **Use Cases**: Tracking shipments, plotting store locations, or visualizing population density.
- **Customizations**: Add custom map layers, define color scales for regions, or adjust zoom levels.

Word Cloud

- **Description**: Represents text data visually by sizing words based on their frequency or importance.
- **Use Cases**: Analyzing survey responses, and summarizing customer feedback.
- **Customizations**: Change font styles, adjust color palettes, or set minimum word frequencies.

Sunburst Chart

- **Description**: Visualizes hierarchical data as concentric circles.
- **Use Cases**: Breaking down revenue by category and sub-category, visualizing organizational structures.
- **Customizations**: Configure levels, adjust colors, or add interactivity for drill-downs.

Treemap

- **Description**: Represents hierarchical data as nested rectangles, with size proportional to values.
- **Use Cases**: Visualizing resource allocation, and showing category contributions.
- **Customizations**: Adjust nesting depth, define color schemes, or add labels.

Big Number with Trendline

- **Description**: Highlights key metrics with optional trendline visualization.
- **Use Cases**: Displaying KPIs such as total revenue, conversion rate, or active users.
- **Customizations**: Set thresholds, define colors for positive/negative trends, or adjust layouts.

Features Common Across Plugins:

- **Customization Options**: Each plugin allows users to modify elements such as colors, labels, scales, and interactivity.
- **Interactive Capabilities**: Plugins support features such as tooltips, zooming, filtering, and drill-downs.
- **Extensibility**: Developers can modify existing plugins or build new ones to meet specific requirements.
- **Seamless Integration**: All plugins integrate smoothly with Superset's dashboard builder, enabling dynamic layouts and interactions.

Building and Installing Custom Visualization Plugins

Development and Installation of Custom Visualization Plugins lets users add to the visualization capabilities of Apache Superset based on their needs. This chapter walks through the step-by-step design, installation, and implementation of custom plugins.

Step 1: Plugin Boilerplate Setup

To begin, you need to set up a boilerplate for your custom plugin. Superset provides a structured framework for creating visualization plugins, typically using Node.js and JavaScript.

a. Clone the Superset repository and navigate to the plugin directory.

```
git clone https://github.com/apache/superset.git
cd superset/superset-frontend/plugins
```

b. Use the provided template to generate a new plugin scaffold.

```
npx @superset-ui/cli create-plugin-visualization bubble-chart
```

c. Navigate to the newly created plugin directory.

```
cd plugin-chart-bubble-chart
```

Step 2: Configure the Plugin

a. **Define Metadata:** Open the **src/plugin/index.js** file and update the metadata for your plugin.

```
import { ChartPlugin } from '@superset-ui/core';
import transformProps from './transformProps';
import controlPanel from './controlPanel';

export default class BubbleChartPlugin extends ChartPlugin {
  constructor() {
    super({
      metadata: {
        name: 'Bubble Chart',
        description: 'A customizable bubble chart for data
visualization.',
        thumbnail: 'thumbnail.png', // Add a relevant thumbnail
for the chart
      },
      loadChart: () => import('./BubbleChart'),
      transformProps,
      controlPanel,
    });
  }
}
```

b. **Set Control Panel Options:** Define the control panel options users will configure in the **src/plugin/controlPanel.js** file.

```
export default {
  controlPanelSections: [
    {
      label: 'Bubble Chart Configuration',
      controlSetRows: [
        ['x_axis'], // X-axis metric
        ['y_axis'], // Y-axis metric
        ['bubble_size'], // Size of the bubbles
        ['color_scheme'], // Color scheme
      ],
    },
  ],
};
```

Step 3: Implement the Visualization Logic

a. **Data Transformation:** Create a **`transformProps.js`** file to process raw data from Superset and prepare it for rendering.

```
export default function transformProps(chartProps) {
try {
const { width, height, formData, queriesData } = chartProps;

if (!queriesData?.[0]?.data) {
throw new Error('No data available');
}

const data = queriesData[0].data;

return {
width,
height,
data,
x: formData.x_axis,
y: formData.y_axis,
size: formData.bubble_size,
colorScheme: formData.color_scheme,
};
} catch (error) {
console.error('Error transforming props:', error);
return {
width: 0,
height: 0,
data: [],
error: true,
};
}
}
```

b. **Bubble Chart Rendering Logic:** Use D3.js in the **`BubbleChart.jsx`** file to render the chart.

```
import React, { useEffect, useRef } from 'react';
import * as d3 from 'd3';

const BubbleChart = ({ width, height, data, x, y, size,
colorScheme }) => {
  const ref = useRef();

  useEffect(() => {
    const svg = d3.select(ref.current)
```

```
      .attr('width', width)
      .attr('height', height);

    const color = d3.scaleOrdinal(d3.schemeCategory10);

    const xScale = d3.scaleLinear()
      .domain([0, d3.max(data, d => d[x])])
      .range([50, width - 50]);

    const yScale = d3.scaleLinear()
      .domain([0, d3.max(data, d => d[y])])
      .range([height - 50, 50]);

    const sizeScale = d3.scaleSqrt()
      .domain([0, d3.max(data, d => d[size])])
      .range([5, 20]);

    svg.selectAll('circle')
      .data(data)
      .join('circle')
      .attr('cx', d => xScale(d[x]))
      .attr('cy', d => yScale(d[y]))
      .attr('r', d => sizeScale(d[size]))
      .attr('fill', d => color(d.category))
      .attr('opacity', 0.7);
  }, [data, width, height, x, y, size]);

  return <svg ref={ref}></svg>;
};

export default BubbleChart;
```

Step 4: Build and Install the Plugin

a. **Build the Plugin:** Compile your plugin to prepare it for deployment.

```
npm run build
```

b. **Register the Plugin:** Add your plugin to the visualization registry in Superset's superset-**frontend/src/setup/setupPlugins.js** file.

```
import BubbleChartPlugin from 'plugins/plugin-chart-bubble-chart';

new BubbleChartPlugin().configure({ key: 'bubble-chart' }).
register();
```

c. **Start Superset:** Run the Superset server to see your custom chart in action.

```
superset run -d
```

Step 5: Test and Debug

a. **Load the Plugin:** In the Superset Explore interface, choose "`Bubble Chart`" as the visualization type and configure the control panel options.

b. **Verify Functionality:**

   Ensure that:

   - Bubbles are sized, positioned, and colored correctly.
   - The chart is responsive and interactive.

c. **Debugging:** Use browser developer tools and D3 debugging techniques to resolve any issues.

   Once you have checked the functionalities of your Bubble Chart it is a good time to get into more advanced features and add tooltips, animations, and drill-down interactions in your interface.

d. **Add the Plugin:** Make your production instance of Superset and add this up to other users in your company.

JavaScript Integration with Superset

JavaScript serves as the base architecture to complement the visualization strengths of Apache Superset by allowing developers to create customized views and high-level user interfaces. The frontend architecture of Superset is built with the latest JavaScript technologies that are mostly React, which enables developers to create dynamic, interactive, and user-centric visualizations. Developers also use JavaScript libraries such as D3.js or Chart.js, which can help create customized solutions and enhance the functionalities and aesthetic appeal of Superset dashboards.

The greatest strength of JavaScript lies in its adaptability by nature. Superset, therefore, enables developers to generate visualization plugins with customized rendering logic. A couple of special plugins can even be quite specifically arranged or can have interactions beyond the ones possible for defaults designed inside the platform. Thus, it is now conceivable to take advantage of D3.js's capabilities for rendering intricate graphics such as bubble charts, heatmaps, and geospatial views. Therefore, adequate tool sets are provided for addressing the analytical needs.

JavaScript is also an important data transformation part for visualizations. The **`transformProps`** JavaScript function, through which Superset query results get passed, transforms the data prior to rendering. This assures, for example, that the code of visualization will not need to wait for data already formatted; thus, integration of frontend and backend gets eased out. It adds richness to the feature of user interaction; thus, hover tooltips, drill-downs, and others make possible transitions by which the changes animate themselves.

The frontend is built on React, so it inherently includes React components and allows it to work with the visualization lifecycle; in addition, it requires Superset-UI, an accumulated library of precompiled JavaScript utilities and components geared for building and customizing plugins. This, by itself, means that by using those tools, developers package and transpile their code into JavaScript, which is facilitated by being supported across multiple browsers by Webpack and Babel.

Multi-staged example of how one can make D3.js integrate within a Superset visualization. The first is to use the function **transformProps** to process raw data to determine relevant fields applicable to use in the visualization then the rest of D3.js goes within the React component to draw either an SVG or a canvas construct such as bubbles or nodes, adding any further interactivity such as hovering effects or interactive components allows for increased involvement from viewers. With the strong features of D3.js and the Superset plugin framework, developers can design custom visualizations that allow for interactivity while being aesthetically pleasing.

Best practices must be followed to ensure effective integration of JavaScript. Methods of rendering huge datasets must be efficient so that it does not become a bottleneck. The Superset-UI library can be utilized in order to maintain the same consistency with other visualizations that already exist on the platform and maintain the design standards. Debugging tools, such as browser developer tools, can also be used to sort out rendering or data transformation issues to ensure the plugin works correctly.

It concludes that because of including JavaScript in Apache Superset, it is possible for the developers to stretch the boundary of data visualization. Modern libraries and frameworks allow developers to create personalized, interactive, and visually appealing dashboards as per analytics requirements. It has enhanced functionalities within Superset and optimized the user experience.

Using D3.js for Advanced Charts

D3.js is a powerful JavaScript library for creating advanced, interactive data visualizations. Its ability to modify the DOM along with its use of Scalable Vector Graphics makes it an excellent tool for creating customized charts in Apache Superset. This means that if D3.js is included in the plugin framework of Superset, developers are able to generate extremely dynamic and graphically complex visualizations that extend beyond traditional categories of charts.

One of the main advantages of D3.js is that it can easily manipulate complex data structures into meaningful visual representations. It enables developers to bind data to DOM elements and apply custom scales, axes, and styles. For instance, when one creates a Bubble Chart, D3.js will size the bubbles according to some metric, position them dynamically with the X and Y axes, color them according to some categorical variable, and much more. Such capabilities offer unprecedented flexibility, and thus charts can be fit into specific business requirements.

Traditionally, developers begin the entire process by processing data using a **`transformProps`** function in an integration of D3.js with Superset. Normally, such a function refines a dataset that identifies relevant metrics and dimensions and then aligns with the necessary input format for the chart inside this system of transformations, which finally renders the chart inside a React component. The plugin system used in Superset makes integration easy and allows a developer to merge D3.js with React to find a modern and responsive way toward visualization.

One of the most common use cases of D3.js in Superset is to implement interactive elements such as tooltips, hover effects, and animations. Such features add much to the user experience by offering secondary information and making the interface much more dynamic. For example, in a Bubble Chart, category, size, or growth rate can be offered when hovered over a bubble. In the same way, animations easily offer smoother transitions between datasets, enhancing the visual quality and functionality of the visualization.

D3.js, though, supports much more complicated chart types, such as Sankey diagrams, radial charts, and hierarchical visualizations which are not in the standard library of Superset. Such graphics are especially useful for checking complicated relationships, hierarchical structures, or multi-dimensional data sets. The ability to produce such custom charts ensures that Superset is very flexible and applicable in a wide variety of domains and uses.

Here is an example of a D3.js-powered Bubble Chart implemented in a custom Superset plugin:

```
import React, { useEffect, useRef } from 'react';
import * as d3 from 'd3';

const BubbleChart = ({ width, height, data, x, y, size,
colorScheme }) => {
  const ref = useRef();

  useEffect(() => {
    // Clear any existing elements
    const svg = d3.select(ref.current).html("").append("svg")
      .attr("width", width)
      .attr("height", height);

    const xScale = d3.scaleLinear()
      .domain([0, d3.max(data, d => d[x])])
      .range([50, width - 50]);
```

```
    const yScale = d3.scaleLinear()
      .domain([0, d3.max(data, d => d[y])])
      .range([height - 50, 50]);

    const sizeScale = d3.scaleSqrt()
      .domain([0, d3.max(data, d => d[size])])
      .range([5, 30]);

    const color = d3.scaleOrdinal(d3.schemeCategory10);

    svg.selectAll("circle")
      .data(data)
      .enter()
      .append("circle")
      .attr("cx", d => xScale(d[x]))
      .attr("cy", d => yScale(d[y]))
      .attr("r", d => sizeScale(d[size]))
      .attr("fill", d => color(d.category))
      .attr("opacity", 0.7)
      .on("mouseover", (event, d) => {
        d3.select(event.currentTarget).attr("stroke", "black").
attr("stroke-width", 2);
      })
      .on("mouseout", (event) => {
        d3.select(event.currentTarget).attr("stroke", null);
      });

  }, [data, width, height, x, y, size]);

  return <div ref={ref}></div>;
};

export default BubbleChart;
```

This example displays how D3.js is used to produce an on-the-fly interactive Bubble Chart. The chart scales its position and sizing with a color code by category along with hover effects that allow the user a little bit better experience. When the application demands it, developers may use D3.js in similar advanced visualizations as needed.

The best practices must be followed to leverage the full potential of D3.js in Superset. Optimize data transformations so that there is no processing overhead, charts are responsive, and they render well on different devices. Also, thoroughly test with varied datasets so that edge cases are taken care of. If properly implemented, D3.js can take visualization in Superset to a whole new level.

Best Practices for Custom Plugins

By developing a customized plugin on Apache Superset, you can add functionality and further personalize the visualizations as needed in your organization. Yet good and maintainable plugins require thoughtful planning and some best practices.

These are the key best practices in designing, developing, and deploying custom plugins in Superset:

- **Principle for Visual Design:** The visualization should clearly depict the insights. It should not make use of complicated designs that confuse the user. Visualize with the needs of the target audience in mind. Select the graph that best fits your data and tell its story the best.
- **Obey the Codified Standards:** Divide the code into reusable elements even further. It makes your plugin more understandable and maintainable. Make your code full of comments that explain complicated reasoning. Produce documentation for other developers or users.
- **Optimize Plugins Performance:** Transform the data such that the chart only receives what it needs. Avoid transmitting large datasets to the client. Instead, preprocess as much as possible on the server side. Render using lightweight libraries and frameworks, such as D3.js. Minimize DOM updates using virtual DOM techniques or efficient data binding. Use lazy load to get dependencies and render charts. The rendering should not block the initial loading of the dashboards.
- **Better User Experience:** Add tooltips with hover effects and drill down to make visualizations more engaging and informative. Your plugin will respond to different screen sizes and resolutions, making it more usable on desktops and mobile devices. Allow users to customize and personalize the look of their control panels by changing colors, scales, labels, and other visual properties according to one's preference or branding requirement.
- **Ensure Scalability:** Use an enormous data set to test if the plug-in runs without any delay, so it will not crash the system. The asynchronous operations manage data processing and rendering without blocking the user interface. Best practices in memory management to prevent, at least minimize leaks, especially with huge datasets.
- **Testing and Debugging:** Test for significant components `transformProps` to ensure proper data transformation–how seamless integration is with the larger Superset ecosystem and how well it plays with dashboards and filters. The plugin should be cross-browser-compatible on modern browsers, such as Chrome, Firefox, and Edge.

  Tool stack: Chrome DevTools, React DevTools, and D3.js debugging utilities are used in debugging and isolated problem identification.

- **Maintainability:** Use Git or another versioning system to make tracking changes to code and tracking updates on plugins easier. It should offer backward compatibility; the updates of the plugin shall not break the existing dashboards or configurations. Maintain dependencies up-to-date in order to avoid such security vulnerabilities as well as compatibility issues.
- **Security Issues:**

  Input Validation: Validate all user inputs. Prevents injection attacks, but ensures corrupted data does not affect the plugin. If libraries such as D3.js are used, sanitize the outputs to avoid rendering malicious code.
- **Documentation and Training:** User guides for the end users would provide instructions on how to use the plugin, customize it, and its special features, if any. Techno documentation of its architecture, setup process, and code base for developers is a must.
- **Iterative Development:** Gather user and stakeholder feedback for iterative improvement of the plugin. Introduce updates incrementally, more in small, manageable quantities to provide stability and swift resolution. Monitor plugin usage and performance for areas of improvement.

Conclusion

Lock the door to a world of extension possibilities for Apache Superset–custom visualization plugins. Using these plugins, developers can create highly customized dynamic, and visually appealing charts related to specific business needs. This chapter has covered in detail how to work with visualization plugins, from familiarity with built-in options to designing and installing custom plugins. The developers advance the visualizations by utilizing JavaScript frameworks such as D3.js. Sophisticated interactivity, animations, and complicated data representations are from this.

We also walked through best practices in how to build maintainable and scalable plugins, meaning that your customizations bring powerful insights but stay robust and secure as your data visualization needs to evolve. Being able to customize and extend Superset is awesome proof of its flexibility and modern design, and it adds a lot of value for organizations looking to gain deeper insight from their data.

Continue reading while remembering that visualization is only one part of the picture. Security is an extremely important component of any BI platform, and the next chapter covers Security and Access Control in Superset. You will learn about the robust security features of the platform, such as Role-Based Access Control (RBAC), user authentication management, and permissions on datasets, dashboards, and visualizations. Because ensuring the security of your data while keeping user accessibility in mind is just as important as effectively transmitting it.

Chapter 6
Security and Access Control

Introduction

Business Intelligence (BI) platforms play an important role in rendering organizations capable of making well-informed decisions in the current information-intensive environment. However, since these platforms collect and analyze large quantities of sensitive information, they become attractive targets for a wide range of security threats. One of the widely used open-source BI applications is Apache Superset. It is necessary to secure the data kept within Superset not only against unwanted access but also in order to meet compliance requirements and the need to maintain the reputation of the organization.

Fully developed mechanisms serve as the security measures available through Superset, including strategies for data protection and the management of access to the platform. Topics such as role-based access control (RBAC), techniques for user authentication, dataset protection, and permission management are discussed. In addition, we also go into depth about the tools and best practices necessary for the security of the business intelligence ecosystem. With this in mind, understanding and thus implementing these security measures will ensure that sensitive data remains protected and therefore available only to authorized users to facilitate safe data analysis.

Structure

In this chapter, we will cover the following topics:

- Role-Based Access Control in Superset
- Importance of RBAC in BI Security
- Setting Up and Managing Roles in Superset: A Step-By-Step Guide
- Adding a User and Assigning a Role in Superset: A Step-By-Step Guide
- Admin User in Superset

- Creating Row-Level Security Rule: A Step-By-Step Guide
- Superset Authentication Using OAuth
- Securing Datasets and Dashboards
- Best Practices for Security in Apache Superset

Role-Based Access Control in Superset

Role-based access control (RBAC) is an integral part of any Business Intelligence (BI) solution, and Apache Superset applies this concept. The application of RBAC provides organizations with the capability to enforce access control based on user roles for certain data and features. Through this approach, users will only be given permission for those actions necessary to fulfill their task and, in turn, reduce the propensity for unwarranted access that jeopardizes the security of sensitive information.

Importance of RBAC in BI Security

In BI tools such as Superset, users interact with multiple data sources, dashboards, and visualizations containing sensitive information. RBAC gives a way of handling interactions in an organized manner, thus making it easy to enforce security policies and maintain the standards' compliance with governance on data. With the help of RBAC, an administrator will be in a position to assign roles according to job responsibilities to the users for accessing data, not to those who do not need it. This avoids potential security vulnerabilities since each user has the minimum access needed for the tasks that they will perform and is referred to by the principle of least privilege.

Overview of Roles in Superset

Superset includes a few predefined roles for different classes of users. Additionally, there is an option to define special, project-specific roles based on specific needs. Some of the roles include:

This administrative role has ultimate access to all Superset features and configurations—the ability to manage users, roles, and data connections down to every possible configuration. Additionally, administrative users have the ability to set security configurations within the platform.

- **Alpha** users have access to every functionality in Superset. They have the ability to add and delete dashboards, charts, and datasets. However, the users cannot manage other users of the system or have access to global configurations.
- **Gamma**: This is for the users of data and reports. Gamma users can see dashboards and charts but cannot edit them. It is a role suitable for business

users or stakeholders who will require insights from the data without the need to edit at all.

- **Public**: The role is assigned to users who are not authenticated against the system. This usually includes the most basic access privileges, normally limited to reading public resources. It is also typically disabled or used in scenarios where a resource is intended to be open to the public.
- **Custom Roles:** Superset allows custom roles to be set up based on the access needs of an organization. The following types of granular permissions can be created by combining the predefined standard roles or access to specific resources and actions.

How Roles Determine User Permissions and Access

In Superset, each type of user role is assigned a specific set of permissions that determines the activities the users are empowered to perform. Such permissions are defined across multiple resources such as datasets, dashboards, and charts. For instance, the Admin role includes permissions to create, edit, and delete dashboards, but the Gamma role will typically consist of only permissions to view them. This way, linking users to their relevant roles, Superset automatically enforces permissions such that access is uniformly controlled anywhere in the product.

Setting Up and Managing Roles in Superset: A Step-By-Step Guide

Creating and managing roles can be done directly through the interface of the tool. The following is a step-by-step process on how to configure and manage roles.

1. **Access the Security Menu**

    a. **Log in to Superset**: Open your Superset dashboard and log in with an account that has administrative privileges.

    b. **Navigate to Security**: From the top navigation bar, select `Security`. A dropdown menu will appear.

    c. **Manage Roles**:

        i. Click `List Roles` to view existing roles in your Superset environment.

        ii. Click `Add a Role` to create a new role if you need to define specific permissions for a new group of users.

2. **Add a New Role (for example, `usrole`)**

   a. **Add Role**: In the **`List Roles`** page, click **`+ Add a new Role`**.

   b. **Configure Role Details**:

      - **Role Name**: Enter the name of the role. For this example, let us name the role **`usrole`**.
      - **Permissions**: After naming the role, you will need to assign specific permissions to control what users with this role can access.

3. **Grant Access to a SQL Table**

   To give the **`usrole`** role access to a specific SQL table, follow these steps:

   a. **Access Permissions Section**: On the **`Edit Role`** page for **`usrole`**, scroll down to the **Permissions** section. Here, you can define what this role can do.

   b. **Assign Database/Table Access**:

      - Look for permissions that start with **`database access`** or **`data source access`**.
      - Select **`database access on [Database_Name]`** if you want to grant broader access to the entire database.
      - For table-specific access, locate and select **`data source access on [Table_Name] (schema_name)`** from the permissions list. This grants the **`usrole`** access to only the specified table within the database.

   c. **Save Changes**: Once the appropriate permissions are selected, click **`Save`** at the bottom of the page.

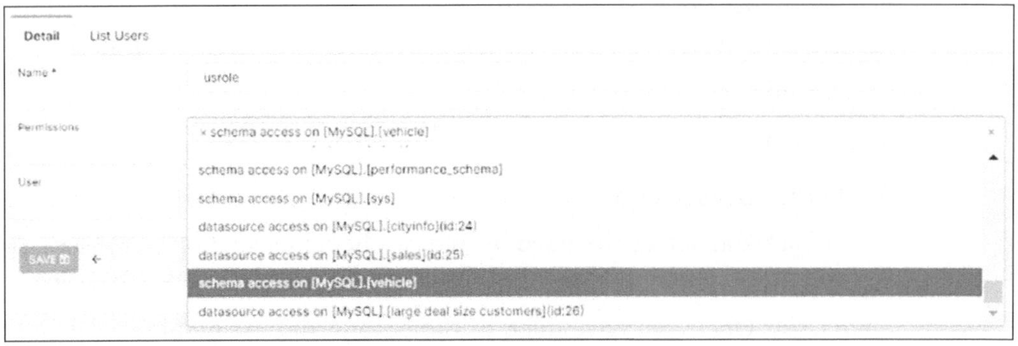

***Figure 6.1:** Permissions to Users*

Adding a User and Assigning a Role in Superset: A Step-By-Step Guide

Adding a user in Apache Superset and assigning them to a role involves a few straightforward steps. In this case, we will create a new user called `ususer` and assign them to the previously created role, `usrole`.

1. **Access the Security Menu**
    a. **Log in to Superset**: Go to your Superset dashboard and log in with administrative credentials.
    b. **Navigate to Security**: From the top navigation bar, select `Security`. A dropdown menu will appear with various options.
    c. **Manage Users**: Click `List Users` to see a list of existing users. Here, you will also have the option to add a new user.
2. **Add a New User (for example, `ususer`)**
    a. **Add User**: On the `List Users` page, click `+ Add a new User`.
    b. **Fill in User Details**:
        - **Username**: Enter the username for the new user; in this case, `ususer`.
        - **First Name** and **Last Name**: Enter the user's first and last name for identification purposes.
        - **Email**: Enter the user's email address. This is important for communication and password recovery.
        - **Password**: Set a password for `ususer`. You may also have the option to require the user to reset this password upon their first login.
3. **Assign the `usrole` Role to `ususer`**
    a. **Assign Role**:
        - In the `Roles` section, you will see a list of available roles.
        - Locate and select the `usrole` role by checking the box next to it. This will grant `ususer` all permissions associated with the `usrole` role.
    b. **Save User**: Once you have filled in the details and assigned the role, click `Save` at the bottom of the page to create a new user and apply the role.

4. **Verify User Access**

   After creating **`ususer`** and assigning them to **`usrole`**, it is a good practice to confirm that the user has the intended access:

   a. **Log in as `ususer`**: Log out of your admin account and log in as **`ususer`** using the credentials you just set up.

   b. **Confirm Access Permissions**: Ensure that **`ususer`** has the expected access to data resources, such as the specific SQL table or other resources defined in the **`usrole`**.

By following these steps, you can successfully add a new user in Apache Superset and assign them the necessary permissions through their role. This setup ensures that each user has appropriate access aligned with their responsibilities, supporting secure and efficient data management.

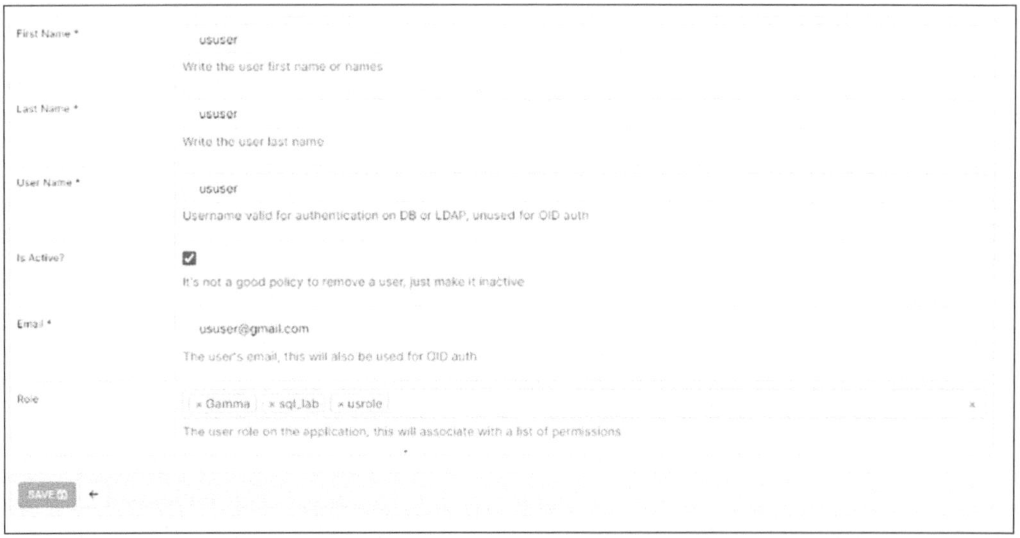

Figure 6.2: *Verification of User Access*

Admin User in Superset

When you log in using the **`admin`** profile in Apache Superset, you will have full access to all tables and schemas within the **MySQL** database. This is because the admin role in Superset typically has comprehensive permissions, allowing it to manage and view all data sources, databases, schemas, and tables.

1. **Access to All Databases**: Upon logging in as an admin, navigate to the **`Datasets`** section from the main menu. Here, you will be able to see all the datasets that exist across various databases, including MySQL.

2. **View All Tables and Schemas**: Since the admin profile has unrestricted access, you will have visibility into all tables and schemas within the MySQL database. This allows you to:
    a. Browse and query data across any table or schema.
    b. View metadata associated with these tables, such as column names, data types, and any constraints or relationships.
3. **Manage Database Connections**: With admin privileges, you can also add, edit, or delete connections to different databases, including MySQL. This means you have full control over data source configurations and permissions.

By leveraging your admin privileges, you can effortlessly oversee and manage the MySQL data landscape in Superset, ensuring you have the tools to support data governance, access control, and overall data management for your organization.

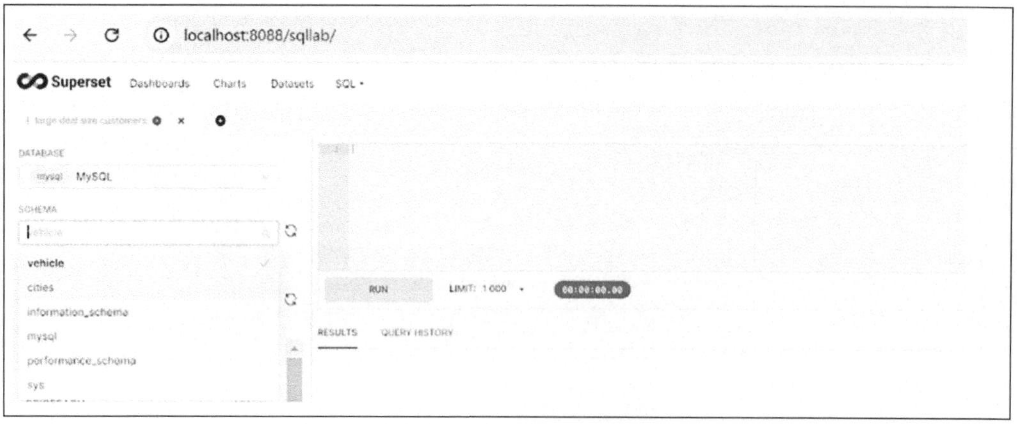

Figure 6.3: *Admin User in Superset*

When you log in to Apache Superset using an admin account and navigate to the SQL Lab, you can easily run a query to find the distinct countries present in the **`vehicle.sales`** dataset. Here is how the process generally works:

1. **Log in as `Admin`**: Start by logging into your Superset instance with your admin credentials. This ensures you have full access to all datasets and can execute queries without permission issues.
2. **Navigate to SQL Lab**: Once logged in, go to the **`SQL Lab`** tab, where you can directly interact with the underlying database using SQL queries.
3. **Select the Appropriate Database and Schema**: Make sure you select the database and schema where the **`vehicle.sales`** dataset is located. This step ensures your query runs against the correct dataset.

4. **Run the Query**: To find the distinct countries, type and execute a query similar to the following:

```
SELECT DISTINCT country

FROM vehicle.sales;
```

View the Results: After executing the query, the result table will display all unique country names present in the **`vehicle.sales`** dataset. This gives you a comprehensive list of countries where vehicle sales data has been recorded.

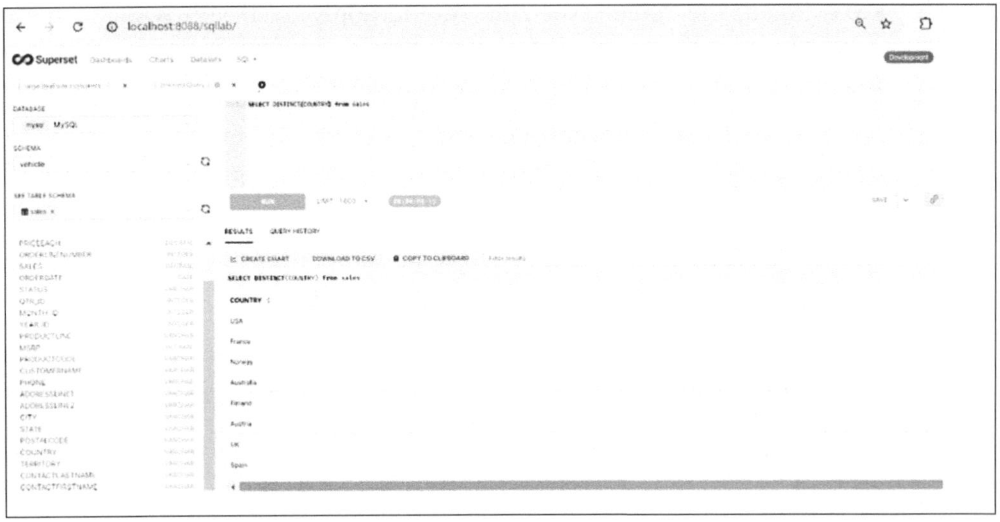

Figure 6.4: *Admin User SQL Result in Superset*

Creating Row-Level Security Rule: A Step-By-Step Guide

To create a row-level security rule in Apache Superset that filters for only USA-related rows in the **`vehicle.sales`** dataset, follow these steps. This will help you enforce a restriction that limits visibility to records specific to the United States when accessing a dashboard.

Creating row-level security rule "`usrule`"

1. **Log in as `Admin`**: Make sure you are logged into Superset with admin credentials, as creating and managing row-level security rules requires admin permissions.

2. **Navigate to `Security` > `Row Level Security`**:

   a. In the main navigation menu, go to **`Security`**, then select **`Row Level Security`**.

   b. This will bring you to the interface where you can define and manage row-level security filters.

3. **Create a New Rule**:

   a. Click **`+ Add Rule`** to create a new row-level security rule.

4. **Configure the Rule**:

   a. **`Rule Name`**: Enter a name for your rule, such as "**`usrule`**."

   b. **`Role`**: Select the role(s) this rule should apply to. If you want to restrict access for specific user roles, select those roles here. If you want this rule to apply globally, select the **`Public`** role as well.

   c. **`Data Source`**: Choose the data source corresponding to your **`vehicle.sales`** dataset. You will need to find the database, schema, and table (**`vehicle.sales`**) where the data is stored.

   d. **`Filter Clause`**: In the **`Filter Clause`** field, enter the condition to filter for USA-related rows only:

   ```
   country = 'USA'
   ```

   Group Key (optional): If you are managing more complex security rules, you can use group keys to define overlapping permissions. However, for this simple filter, this field can be left blank.

5. **Save the Rule:**

- After configuring the rule, click **`Save`** to apply it.

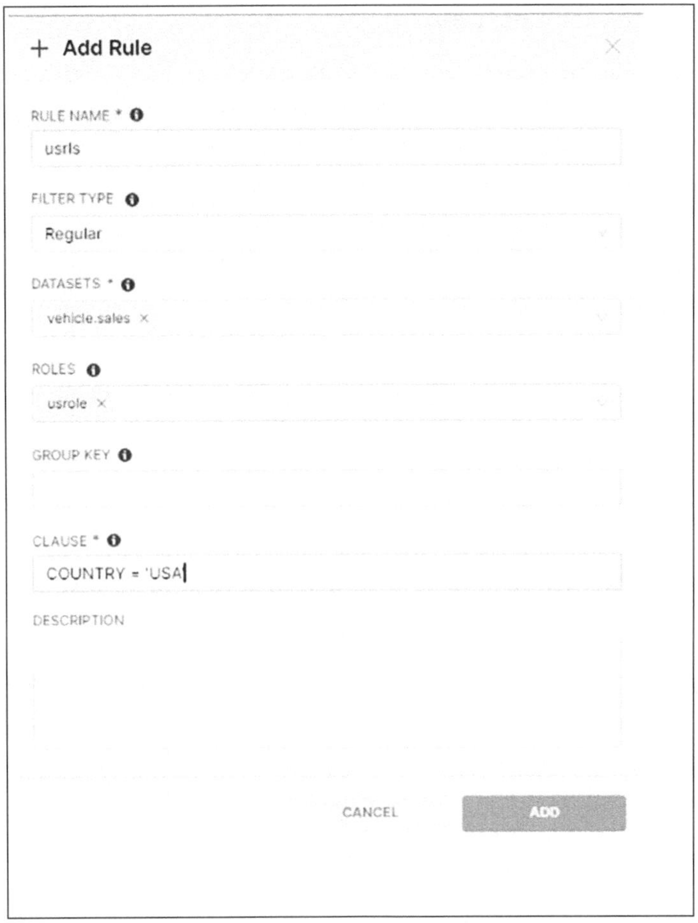

Figure 6.5: *Creating Rules in Superset*

When you log in as the user associated with the "**usrule**" (let us call this user **ususer**), and then navigate to the **Explore** section in Superset to build charts, you will only have access to data rows related to the USA.

Here is how it works in practice:

1. **Log in as ususer**: Start by logging into Superset using the **ususer** account. This user account is subject to the row-level security rule "**usrule**," which you created, and which filters data to only include rows where the **country** column is "**USA**."

2. **Go to Explore to Build Charts**:

    a. After logging in, go to **Explore** (or **Charts**) to begin building your visualizations.

    b. Select the **vehicle.sales** dataset as the source for your chart.

3. **Data Visibility for Chart Building**:

    a. While building charts, you will notice that only rows with **`country = 'USA'`** are available. This restriction ensures that all charts and visualizations created under this user profile will exclusively display data pertaining to the USA.

    b. Whether you are creating bar charts, line charts, or other types of visualizations, only USA-specific data will be represented, and data from other countries will not be accessible.

This setup is particularly useful for user-based data segmentation, allowing the **`ususer`** to focus solely on the USA data without needing to manually filter out other regions. The row-level security rule automatically applies to all queries that the **`ususer`** runs, providing a seamless experience tailored to their specific data access requirements.

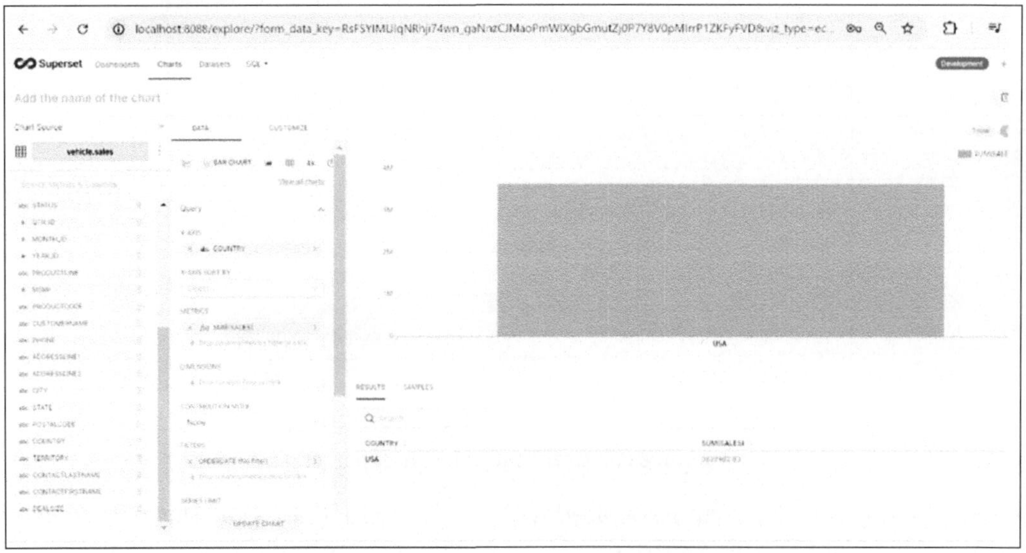

Figure 6.6: *Filtered Data Based on Rules*

Superset Authentication Using OAuth

To make OAuth 2.0 authentication work with Google in Apache Superset, you would first need to configure your Google Cloud Console and then your Superset. Here is how you can do it step-by-step:

Step 1: Set up OAuth credentials in the Google Cloud Console

a. Go to **`Google Cloud Console`**: Navigate to the **`Google Cloud Console`**.

b. **`Create a New Project`**: If you have not already, create a new project or select an existing one. You can do this by clicking the project dropdown at the top and selecting **New Project**.

c. **Enable `OAuth Consent Screen`**:

   i. Go to **`APIs & Services`** > **`OAuth consent screen`**.

   ii. Choose **`External`** for user type if you plan to allow any user with a Google account to authenticate. Click **`Create`**.

   iii. Fill in the **`App name`**, **`User support email`**, and other required details, then save and continue.

   iv. In the **`Scopes`** section, you can add any scopes you need. For a basic setup, you do not need to add additional scopes beyond the default.

d. **Create OAuth 2.0 Credentials**:

   i. Go to **`APIs & Services`** > **`Credentials`** and click **`+ CREATE CREDENTIALS`**. Select **`OAuth client ID`**.

   ii. Under **`Application type`**, select **`Web application`**.

   iii. Name your credentials and set the **`Authorized redirect URIs`**. Add the following redirect URI for Superset:

   http://<your-superset-domain>/oauth-authorized/google

e. Click **`Create`**, and Google will generate a **`Client ID`** and **`Client Secret`**. Copy these for later use.

Step 2: Configure Superset to use Google OAuth

a. **Edit the Superset Configuration File**:

   i. Open your **`superset_config.py`** file. This file is typically located in the Superset configuration directory.

   ii. Add the following settings to enable **`Google OAuth`**:

```
AUTH_TYPE = AUTH_OAUTH
OAUTH_PROVIDERS = [
    {
        'name': 'google',
        'icon': 'fa-google',
        'token_key': 'access_token',
        'remote_app': {
            'client_id': '<your-client-id>',
            'client_secret': '<your-client-secret>',
            'api_base_url': 'https://www.googleapis.com/
oauth2/v2/',
```

```
                'client_kwargs': {
                    'scope': 'email profile'
                },
                'authorize_url': 'https://accounts.google.com/o/
oauth2/auth',
                'access_token_url': 'https://accounts.google.
com/o/oauth2/token',
                'authorize_params': None,
                'access_token_params': None,
                'jwks_uri': 'https://www.googleapis.com/oauth2/v3/
certs'
            }
        }
]
```

Replace **`<your-client-id>`** and **`<your-client-secret>`** with the values you obtained from Google Cloud Console.

b. **Enable Secure Headers**:

   i. Ensure that Superset is configured with **`ENABLE_CORS`** and **`ENABLE_PROXY_FIX`** in the configuration file to avoid potential issues with CORS and proxy headers:

   ii. `ENABLE_CORS = True`

   iii. `ENABLE_PROXY_FIX = True`

c. **Set Up OAuth Redirect URL in Superset**:

   i. Update the **`REDIRECT_URI`** setting in **`superset_config.py`**:

   ii. `GOOGLE_REDIRECT_URI = "http://<your-superset-domain>/oauth-authorized/google"`

d. **Restart Superset**:

   1. Once all configurations are updated, restart Superset to apply the changes:

   ii superset **`run`**

Step 3: Test Google OAuth authentication

a. **Access the Superset Login Page**: Navigate to your Superset instance (for example, **`http://<your-superset-domain>/login`**).

b. **Login with Google**: You should see a **`Sign in with Google`** button. Click it, and you will be redirected to Google for authentication.

c. **Authorize Access**: On the **`Google consent screen`**, authorize access to your application. After successful authentication, you should be redirected back to Superset, where you will be logged in.

Optional: Configure User Roles and Permissions in Superset

After the activation of OAuth, it may be necessary to establish user roles and permissions within Superset corresponding to the authenticated individuals. Superset provides the capability to delineate roles, including Admin, Gamma, and Alpha, to regulate access and functionality within the application.

Securing Datasets and Dashboards

Apache Superset is a powerful, open-source tool for exploring and visualizing data, allowing users to build, share, and collaborate on dashboards. As organizations rely on Superset for data-informed decision-making, the protection of datasets and dashboards becomes essential.

Next, we will go through a series of methods to lock down data within Superset so sensitive information stays protected and access can be reasonably managed.

Understanding Superset's Role-Based Access Control

Superset uses a framework called Role-Based Access Control to control access. In this framework, users are assigned roles, which each contain a set of permissions that specify the actions they can undertake.

Key Default Roles in Superset

- **Administrator**: Comprehensive access to all resources and configuration settings.
- **Alpha**: Fully access most functions but has no authority controls.
- **Gamma**: Primarily an onlooker of the data; can only see but not make or edit dashboards and datasets.

The public access configuration will be set to allow unknown people to view certain viewpoints; however, it is usually turned off in secure environments.

Custom roles may also be implemented to tailor permissions in line with specific organizational needs. These roles can be tailored to limit only a couple of datasets, dashboards, or functionalities to be accessed.

Protecting Datasets

Datasets in Superset are basically raw data feeding into visualizations. Security over these datasets ensures that only authorized users have access to query sensitive data.

- **Configuring Dataset Permissions:**
    - **Assigning Permissions to Roles**: Superset facilitates the assignment of particular datasets to designated roles, thereby permitting or restricting access according to the user's role. To safeguard a dataset:
    - **Navigate to Datasets in the Superset UI**: Right-click your chosen dataset's menu and click Edit Dataset. In the Permissions section, decide which roles need to access the dataset.
- **Limit Data Access through User Attributes:** RLS filters should be part of security measures in order to limit data access by means of user attributes. Therefore, data can be managed as per the view of user roles, departments, or geographical areas.
    - Go to `Security > Row Level Security Filters`.
    - Develop a filter to reduce the view of data depending on criteria such as "`country = assigned country`."
    - Implement this filter into a dataset and use it for relevant roles.
- **Access Secure SQL Lab:** The SQL Lab feature of Superset lets a user write and run SQL queries on data sources. To help prevent unauthorized access or accidental data exposures:
    - Access to SQL Lab is limited to trusted roles, namely Admin or Alpha.
    - Restrict access to designated databases or schemas within SQL Lab to mitigate the risk of querying sensitive tables.

Dashboard Access Control

Dashboards in Superset are collections of charts and visualizations. The concept of having control over who gets to view, edit, or share dashboards matters for sensitive insights.

Set Dashboard Permissions

- **Role-Based Access to Dashboards**: Just like for datasets, access to dashboards can be controlled by setting permissions on roles. For every dashboard, define which roles are allowed to:
- **Read**: View the dashboard.
- **Refresh**, or do the dashboard.

- **Menu Accessibility**: Regulate the visibility of the dashboard in the navigation menu for specific roles.

Implement RLS filters at the dataset level for dashboards containing sensitive data. This way, even if the user is able to see a dashboard, they will only be allowed to view the data they are authorized to access.

Configure Access Control to Embedded Dashboards: In the case of integrating Superset dashboards into third-party apps or websites, it is advisable to use JSON Web Tokens for authentication. Superset supports iFrame embedding, but access management should be done in terms of permissions to such embedded dashboards.

Use Superset's Advanced Security Features

Beyond role-based access control, Superset provides auxiliary security functions to protect datasets and dashboards.

- **Data Masking and Anonymization:** For sensitive data sets, consider masking or anonymizing data before it is imported into Superset. Masking techniques include:
    - **Redaction:** Masking sensitive fields, such as Social Security Numbers or credit card information.
    - **Tokenization**: Here, sensitive data is replaced with tokens stored in a safe location, which are not accessible by Superset.
- **Safe Interconnections Promotion:** Ensuring proper connections to your data sources and the Superset instance itself is also important:
    - **Use SSL/TLS**: Encrypt all data connections by applying SSL/TLS. This will be important to prevent interception of data in transit.
    - **Enable Database Authentication**: Configure Superset to use LDAP or OAuth 2.0 protocols for authentication purposes. This configuration supports the implementation of secure login policies, possibly extending up to multi-factor authentication and integration with existing organizational identity providers.
- **Logging and Auditing Configuration:** Superset does offer built-in logging features about what users do. You should be monitoring logs for unauthorized access attempts and so on. Let us implement the action logging and track user engagements such that it captures activities such as login attempts, query executions, and changes in permissions through Superset.
- **Regularly Review Access Logs:** Access logs should be frequently reviewed to ensure there is no suspicious activity or pattern. This is important for ensuring ongoing security and adherence to data regulations.

Best Practices for Security in Apache Superset

Apache Superset is a robust tool for data visualization and exploration, yet securing it adequately is essential to protect sensitive information. Following best practices for security in Superset can help prevent unauthorized access and data leaks. This guide provides key practices to enhance the security of your Superset environment.

- **Utilize RBAC:** Administrators can assign permissions based on roles that define exactly what users can access and even modify. Using default roles such as Admin, Alpha, and Gamma, or creating your own custom roles, ensures that control over datasets, dashboards, and specific Superset features is maintained. Grant trusted users access to sensitive data and assign read-only roles where needed to mitigate the risk of data modification or accidental leaks through exposure such as SQL Lab.
- **Establish Filters for Row-Level Security (RLS):** Row-Level Security filters restrict data visibility based on user attributes, ensuring that users can only see the data relevant to them. For example, you can limit access to regional sales data based on a user's location or department. By applying RLS filters to datasets, you can protect sensitive data from unauthorized users, even if they have access to the dataset or dashboard.
- **Secure Data Connections and Activate HTTPS:** Data connections should be encrypted to protect against unauthorized access when transferring data. All your connections between Superset and your data sources should use SSL/TLS. Your Superset instance also needs to be configured with HTTPS, which encrypts all traffic that flows from the users to the server. This serves as a critical protection for intercepting login credentials as well as sensitive data.
- **Organize and Conduct Action Logging Events:** Superset logging allows administrators to track user activities, such as login attempts, execution of queries, and changes in permissions. Action logging can be enabled to audit the behavior of users to detect suspicious activities. Logs can be accessed by you to analyze unauthorized access attempts and identify potential violations of security policies.
- **Implement Robust Authentication Techniques:** Add integration with single sign-on providers of your choice (such as LDAP or OAuth 2.0) to include additional layers of authentication for security purposes. These include MFA capabilities and reliance on your organization's existing security infrastructure. Use non-simple, shared passwords and ask users to generate strong, unique passwords if using local authentication.
- **Data Exposure Minimization:** Import only the required datasets into Superset and do not expose entire databases to minimize the risk of leakage. Use views

or subsets of particular data rather than importing the whole table when dealing with sensitive information. This enhances security while optimizing performance.

- **Keep the Superset Updated and Patched:** Stay abreast of what Superset is releasing—security patches and features—with regular updates that mitigate vulnerabilities in your environment. Also, make sure all dependencies are up-to-date; older libraries can introduce security risks to your instance.

The deployment of these best security practices will significantly improve the protection of your data inside of Superset. A properly secured Superset is mostly based on role-based access control, row-level security filters, secure connections, and complete logging. In combination with effective authentication mechanisms, minimized exposure of data, and timely updates, these practices can help maintain a secure and compliant Superset environment.

Conclusion

In conclusion, securing Apache Superset involves multiple layers of protection, all made to secure the data and control access very effectively. Role-Based Access Control (RBAC) helps manage permissions by defining user roles so that only authorized users can access certain datasets and dashboards. Implementing Row-Level Security (RLS) further refines visibility by restricting access based on user attributes. The integration of Superset with OAuth 2.0 for authentication purposes significantly improves security by facilitating multi-factor authentication and centralized identity management. Adhering to established best practices—such as utilizing HTTPS for securing data connections, enabling logging mechanisms, and ensuring the system remains up-to-date—can establish a strong security framework for your Superset environment, thereby safeguarding sensitive information and promoting a secure data culture.

The next chapter will talk about how dashboards can be engaging and high-performing using Apache Superset. This reader will find best practices in designing dashboards for optimum performance and seamless interactivity, proper usage of filters and parameters in creating dynamic user experiences, and techniques on the responsiveness of dashboards when rendered across different devices. It ends with how one can improve user experience and performance optimization ideas on how to make one a delivery powerhouse of impactful, effective dashboards.

CHAPTER 7

Building and Optimizing Dashboards

Introduction

This chapter will be guiding readers to create high-performance and interactive dashboards using Apache Superset. The best practice for designing a dashboard for optimized performance and fluid interactivity is covered in this chapter. Readers will also understand how filters and parameters can be applied effectively towards supporting dynamic user-centric experiences and how dashboards can be developed responsively to support multiple devices. The discussion concludes by recommending improvements to the user experience and the application of performance optimization techniques, thereby enabling readers with resources to create effective and efficient dashboards.

By the end of this chapter, you will learn how to do justice to the construction and improvement of a dashboard that is beautiful but very functional and thus can become an indispensable tool for making data-driven decisions.

Structure

In this chapter, we will cover the following topics:

- Understanding Dashboards
- Structuring Dashboards for Performance
- Designing Responsive Dashboards
- Using Filters and Parameters
- Best Practices for User Experience (UX)
- Performance Optimization Techniques

Understanding Dashboards

Dashboards are now an important tool for any organization, irrespective of the size, that describes complex information in graphical form easily. Dashboards include sales performance, evaluating operational efficiency, and an analysis of customer behavior, in which users can clearly understand trends and make the appropriate decisions based on the data. This preface introduces the purpose of dashboards, explores the types of dashboards that are commonly applied, and describes the organization of this chapter.

Purpose of Dashboards

The core functionality of dashboards is to represent information in a way that is understandable and actionable. Dashboards are quite different from the usual reports, supporting interactivity, better performance, and often changing according to the demands of users and devices.

The following describes how these three core features empower dashboards:

- **Interactivity**: Interactive dashboards allow a user to interact immediately with data. With the use of filters, parameters, and drill-down functionalities, a user can tailor the presentation of data in order to answer specific questions or research trends. Such interactivity makes dashboards from static reports into a dynamic tool for greater understanding.
- **Optimization**: Good dashboard optimization ensures that users have the best experience. Optimization basically includes data structure, reduction of loads, and designing visuals that speed up the appropriation of information. Poorly optimized dashboards can readily cause a great deal of frustration and delays in decision-making.
- **Responsiveness:** With the increasing trend of a multi-device world, the dashboards have to be responsive on various devices, be it desktops, tablets, or smartphones. Responsive dashboards automatically rescale based on the varied sizes of each screen, so the user experience remains constant regardless of the device being used. This is particularly important for distributed teams that work from home or access information on the go.

This chapter explores how dashboards can be built based on distinguishing interactivity, optimization, and responsiveness qualities, making the decision-making process swift and well-informed for the users.

Types of Dashboards

Dashboards are not universally applicable; they differ based on their intended function and target audience. The following is a concise summary of the four primary categories of dashboards:

- **Operational Dashboards:** These dashboards focus on real-time information, often monitoring the daily happenings. Examples include metrics dashboards of customer-support-related issues and manufacturing operations. Operational dashboards can be highly interactive; for example, users can drill down as needed into specifics.
- **Analytics Dashboard:** An analytical dashboard is there to analyze data in large volumes and often allows a more graphical representation and interaction. Typically, data analysts and business strategists use them because the results help find trends, correlations, and insights that impact strategic planning.
- **Strategic Dashboards**: Strategic dashboards are high-level views of the performance of an organization over time. They are not as interactive but will generally be used for tracking KPIs that assist in achieving long- term goals. These dashboards help leaders monitor the health of the organization and make strategic decisions.
- **Tactical Dashboards:** Situated between the operational and strategic dashboards, tactical dashboards give insight that enables mid-level managers to build decisions toward short-term goals. They may track progress either on a weekly or monthly basis, showing progress on specific projects or department performance.

Understanding what category the built dashboard falls under is important because different categories involve different considerations with regard to interactivity, optimization, and responsiveness. The methods covered in this chapter are relevant to all categories and will guide you through the building of dashboards that meet different needs.

Structuring Dashboards for Performance

In data visualization, the most important feature that significantly affects user satisfaction and the overall efficiency of decision-making processes is the performance of dashboards. That means more than good looks; it is responsive, loads quickly, and is interactive. Poor performance can even make the most insightful dashboard nearly unusable and cause delays, missed opportunities, and ultimately a very bad user experience. This section addresses the concept of performance within the context of dashboards, investigating the impacts of performance on user experience and decision-making processes.

Defining Performance in the Context of Dashboards

There are three primary aspects that characterize dashboards, namely, loading time, responsiveness, and interactivity. Together, these ensure that users can retrieve, browse through, and interact with data in a quick manner. This module is to be performed with the intricacy analysis of each of these components.

- **Loading Time**: The number of times it will take to fully load the dashboard and become ready for use is very crucial. A fast loading time dashboard is supposed to improve user experience, allowing one to retrieve data faster, which aids in taking some extra time to make the necessary decisions. Among the many things that contribute towards the loading time are the size of the dataset, the quantity of visual elements, and how effective data queries are.
- **Responsiveness:** Responsiveness pertains to the effectiveness with which a dashboard accommodates varying devices and screen dimensions. An effective responsive dashboard preserves its functionality regardless of whether it is accessed via a desktop, tablet, or smartphone, modifying its layout and content in real-time. This flexibility is essential given that contemporary users anticipate dashboards to be reachable across multiple devices, particularly within mobile-first contexts.
- **Interactivity**: Interactivity is the ability of a dashboard to respond to a user's inputs, such as selections across various filters, modifications made to parameters, or drills down. Interactivity at an optimized level allows users to explore data, customize their view, and find insights relevant to their specific needs. An optimally interactive dashboard should respond in real time with no noticeable delay to sustain user engagement and increase productivity.

Collectively, these elements define the extensive performance of a dashboard. Emphasizing these factors ensures that users experience little friction when accessing and interacting with data, which is crucial for the effectiveness of the dashboard.

Impact of Slow Dashboards on User Experience and Decision-Making

A slow or unresponsive dashboard can significantly hinder the user experience and, as a result, affect decision-making in several ways:

- **Frustration and Reduced Engagement**: Slow loading or response time of a dashboard is probably going to annoy the user. This frustration can lead to low engagement wherein users might avoid using the dashboard completely or try alternative methods to access the required information. If the users lose confidence in the dashboard's ability to provide timely insights, it greatly affects the usability and functionality that the tool was designed for.

- **Delayed Decision-Making**: It is for many of these dashboards that timing is crucial with real-time or near real-time decision-making. For example, an operational dashboard may be used to monitor call center activities, and agents need to access information quickly to enable effective and quick decisions. A slow dashboard necessarily slows down the otherwise rapid decision-making process, giving way to lost opportunities, inefficiencies, and possibly financial losses.
- **Cognitive Load and Information Overload**: Inefficient dashboards often bring about user frustration due to lengthy time delays to load data, thus losing the users' focus and increasing cognitive loads. Such interruptions might cause users to not focus on the relevant information available, thereby increasing the chances of misinterpretation or wrong conclusions drawn from the data viewable. Slowness in applying filters or in drill-down functionalities would discourage users from further study of the data presented and thus minimize overall utility derived from the dashboard.
- **Negative Perception of Data Accuracy**: If the dashboard is slow or slow to respond, users can start questioning the accuracy and reliability of the figures that the dashboard will be presenting. In a nutshell, sometimes by having a slow or sluggish performance, data may appear outdated or flawed without being inherently so.

To get around these issues, dashboards need to be built with performance as a consideration from the start. Highlighting speed, responsiveness, and interactivity within a tool leaves one building something that meets user expectations while contributing substantially to their ability to make quick, well-informed decisions. In the following sections, we will take a closer look at specific approaches for organizing, designing, and fine-tuning dashboards in order to attain maximum performance so that users have an uninterrupted, satisfying, and productive experience.

Organizing Data Sources for Dashboard Performance

Data sources interconnectedness and structuring are critical influences on the performance of a dashboard. Well-structured data also has a tendency to decrease loading times, data retrieval, and overall user satisfaction by drastic amounts. Optimal linking and structuring techniques involving sources of data are explored in this section, focusing primarily on minimizing load times using methods such as data extracts, caching mechanisms, and fewer database queries for direct access.

Connecting and Organizing Data Sources to Minimize Load Time

Data sources interconnectedness and structuring are critical influences on the performance of a dashboard. Well-structured data also has a tendency to decrease loading times, data retrieval, and overall user satisfaction by drastic amounts. Optimal linking and structuring techniques involving sources of data are explored in this section, focusing primarily on minimizing load times using methods such as data extracts, caching mechanisms, and fewer database queries for direct access.

- **Consolidate Data Sources**:
  - Pre-aggregate data into fewer sources or views before loading it into the dashboard, if possible. This will reduce the quantity of queries that need to happen and simplify the joins required for the data, thus improving load times.
  - Using data integration tools (such as ETL platforms) to pre-process and combine data into a single source can streamline data handling and improve performance.
- **Use Selective Querying**:
  - Limit the data fetched to only what is needed for the dashboard. Avoid loading full datasets when only a subset is necessary. The use of filters or executing SQL queries that would specify the particular columns and rows being transferred can greatly reduce the data transferred.
  - By setting refreshing protocols for data at uniform intervals as specified for dashboards, an immediate transactional dashboard could require refreshing more frequently than a strategic one set to refresh on a daily or weekly basis.
- **Optimize Data Joins and Aggregations**:
  - Avoid complex joins and aggregations directly within the dashboard tool itself–these often increase the load time; perform these operations where possible within the database, as databases are generally better optimized for these types of tasks.
  - Another approach could be to create materialized views or even indexed tables in the database that aggregate pre-summarized data. This way, the dashboard can fetch the already summarized data, hence reducing processing times on the dashboard side.

Tips on Using Extracts, Caching, and Reducing Direct Database Queries

The direct querying of databases each time a dashboard is loaded can significantly impact performance, especially when large or complex data sets are concerned. Using extracts and implementing caching are effective ways to mitigate this issue:

- **Data Extracts**: Data extracts are snapshots that have been captured at a point in time and are held either locally or in-memory within the dashboard application. These extracts eliminate the need for real-time connections and can be refreshed at specified intervals depending upon the needs of the dashboard.

  Advantages of Extracts: Extracts comprise stored data. Thus, they made the dashboard load much faster than a real-time database query. Extracts also impose less load on the source database, which will be updated less often, since data needs to be retrieved only once for each update of the extract.

  Executing Data Extracts: Identify components of the dashboard that do not require real-time data to work. For example, historical datasets or fixed reference tables could be good candidates for extraction. Establish a consistent refresh interval so the extracts will be up-to-date with the latest data.

- **Caching**: Caching involves the temporary storage of frequently accessed information in memory, enabling the dashboard to swiftly retrieve data without the necessity of executing a new query with each request.

  Types of Caching: Caching varies with the kind of dashboard tool, usually occurring at multiple levels—you could have your browser, server-side, and in-memory caching within the dashboard application. This typically depends on where the most frequent bottlenecks occur.

  Best practices: Identify the views that users access most frequently and enable caching for those views; subsequent loads will become faster. Propagate appropriate expiration values in the cache to attempt to balance performance versus the last updated piece of information.

- **Minimizing Direct Database Queries:**
  - **Batch Data Requests**: Instead of sending many single queries, batch requests should be used when possible to reduce database connection overhead. This batching minimizes round trips to the database, reducing how long it takes for the page to be loaded.
  - **Leverage Aggregation and Pre-processing**: Pre-process data before it is sent to the dashboard by using database procedures or ETL processes.

For example, aggregation of data into pre-calculated summaries enables the dashboard to query smaller datasets, leading to faster response times.

- **Utilization of Connection Pools:** Employing a connection pool for active database interactions can enhance operational efficiency by facilitating the reuse of pre-existing database connections instead of generating new connections for every individual query. This practice minimizes the duration required to establish connections and may result in expedited data retrieval.

Such optimization significantly cuts down on loading times, reduces server load, improves user experience, and lets the user gain insights rather than waiting interminable amounts of time to be served the data. Thoughtful integration and structuring of sources of data along with effective strategies to apply extracts and caching can, in fact, significantly enhance the performance of dashboarding.

Designing Data Architecture for Dashboard Performance

The effective way to lay down high-performance dashboards that handle big data efficiently is through proper data architecture. Using data hierarchies, aggregations, and filters thoughtfully and techniques such as indexing and partitioning will ensure that it loads quickly, responds to user interaction seamlessly, and finally delivers insights on relevant stuff. This section will move on with the best practices to design a proper data architecture that balances performance with usability.

Using Data Hierarchies, Aggregations, and Filters Efficiently

Data Hierarchies: Data hierarchies organize information into structured form in tiers such as Year → Quarter → Month → Day that allow the user to drill-down and explore details in depth. Additionally, they save time; data can be found at different levels of granularity according to the requests submitted by the user.

Build hierarchies that capture the natural order of your data, as well as the usual drill-down paths that users will want to explore. For example, in a sales dashboard, a hierarchy of Region → Country → State/Province → City can provide geographic context.

- **Performance Advantages**: It only fetches data of the required detail level for any view. Therefore, hierarchies cut down on the volume of data being loaded at one time, which then improves load times and enables much faster explorations of data at aggregated levels before necessarily zooming into specifics.

Aggregations: Aggregations summarize data by summing up totals, averages, or counts at a higher level than the original data. For example, instead of loading every single transaction, you might aggregate sales data by day or product category.

- **Aggregations to Improve Efficiency:** Pre-aggregate data for dashboard visualizations that do not need deep granularity. The pre-aggregation can take place at the database tier, thus reducing the volume of data the dashboard needs to handle in real-time.
- **Dynamic Aggregations:** When users are allowed to browse through different detail levels on a given dashboard, dynamic aggregations based on the choice of filters or parameters available can be used. This reduces data processing because data only loads in the required amount at every level.

Filters: Filters refine datasets by narrowing down records based on user-defined criteria, improving data relevance and dashboard performance.

- **Smart Filtering:** It filters the dataset to relevant records according to user criteria, such as date ranges, product categories, or geographies. Real-time querying reduces the volume of data in dashboards and makes them more responsive.
- **Cascading Filters:** Cascading filters can be implemented to show an option to dynamically reduce available options based on previous selections. Selecting a country could dynamically adjust the options that are available in the state filter. This would eliminate unnecessary data loading and improve user experience by limiting the choices.
- **Reducing Infiltration of Filters:** Add filters at front stages so that unnecessary data is not drawn into the dashboard. For SQL-based sources, add filters in the query itself, which will reduce the amount of data that gets pulled from the database.

Leveraging Indexing and Partitioning for Large Datasets

Indexing and partitioning are the techniques that are vitally important for the improvement of data retrieval efficiency and overall performance of big datasets. These enable fast processing with millions of records, thus allowing the dashboard to maintain loading times while possessing interactivity.

Indexing

The indexing function deals with the establishment of database structures that increase the efficiency of data retrieval by providing expedited access routes to records. Proofs of indexes are quite helpful for columns that are frequently used in the processes of filtering, joining, and sorting.

- **Types of Indexes**
    - **Single-Column Indexes** These are indexes on individual columns, which are particularly useful for common filter fields, such as dates or unique identifiers.
    - **Composite Indexes:** Composite indexes encompass multiple columns and are advantageous for queries that filter on several fields. For instance, a composite index comprising Region and Product Category can enhance performance when both fields are commonly subjected to simultaneous filtering.
- **Indexing Best Practice:** Identify the most frequently accessed columns and create an index on those. Avoid over-indexing, as multiple indexes slow the insertion of data and grow the storage requirements. Routine review and optimization of indexes based on query patterns.

Partitioning

Partitioning divides a large table into smaller, manageable chunks based upon the provided criterion. The criteria may be a time interval or even classes. This enables the database to only scan the relevant partition, thus enhancing query performance.

Types of Partitioning

- **Range Partitioning:** Data is split into predefined ranges, such as a list of monthly or annual sales figures. This type of partitioning is suitable when time-series datasets or large tables are added over time.
- **List Partitioning:** Distributes data by specific criteria, including geographical areas or categories of products.
- **Hash Partitioning:** It distributes data evenly across partitions using a hash function, thus being suitable for large datasets without inherent ranges or categories.
- **Partitioning Best Practices:** Choose partitioning criteria that, based on how users interact with the dashboard, make sense. If users commonly want to filter on date, for example, range partitioning in a date field can be helpful. Be proactive about watching partition sizes and performance to ensure that partitioning remains efficient as data grows.

It reduces data load by enriching user interaction with user hierarchies, aggregations, and filters. Meanwhile, indexing and partitioning also enhance faster querying through higher performance when using large data volumes. All these approaches work towards creating data architecture that ensures quick load time, seamless interaction, and the best user experience on the dashboard.

Designing Responsive Dashboards

In the contemporary mobile-oriented environment, users anticipate that dashboards will function effectively across a range of devices, whether they are being utilized on a desktop computer, tablet, or smartphone. Responsive design constitutes a strategy that guarantees dashboards automatically adjust to differing screen dimensions and orientations, thereby preserving usability and legibility irrespective of the device in use. By adopting the principles of responsive design, dashboards can improve accessibility and provide a uniform user experience, rendering data more available and actionable at any time and from any location.

A methodology in web and application development, responsive design allows for automatic adaptation of content to the dimensions, resolution, and orientation of the viewing device's screen. Under the dashboard framework, responsive design ensures that data visualizations, filters, navigation menus, and other interface elements are presented accurately with systematic arrangement regardless of the device or screen size used.

Responsive design is crucial for dashboards because:

It allows the user to work with dashboards on any device of their choice without sacrificing readability or functionality, thereby providing a more intuitive and enjoyable experience for the user.

- **Accessibility**: The dashboard is accessible on any device, making it handy for those using mobile devices but also for those who switch between devices a lot.
- **Engagements and Productivity**: A user-friendly interface with dashboards on mobile devices allows users to stay connected to all these pieces of information while on the go, encouraging quicker decisions and greater productivity.

Principles of Responsive Dashboard Design

The fundamentals of a sound responsive design are based on a few fundamental principles, namely, fluid grids, elastic images, and media queries. These elements will ensure that a dashboard remains effective in terms of functionality and highly attractive on various devices.

Fluid Grids: Fluid grids are the layout structures, which do not rely on fixed units (such as pixels) but use relative units (such as percentages) to define the size of the elements. This way, the elements proportionally adapt to the width of the screen.

The Significance of Fluid Grids in Dashboards: Fluid grids help to scale up the contents of the dashboard, including charts, tables, and filters. They ensure that their arrangement and clarity are maintained regardless of the screen size. For example, a three-column configuration desktop may change to a single column on the mobile device, allowing content to flow without forcing the user to process too much information at one time.

Flexible Images: In responsive design, images are declared with relative sizing or maximum-width constraints so that they scale proportionally and do not overflow their containers when the screen is smaller.

In dashboards, images and graphical elements, including charts and graphs, need to be resized at times without losing the specific information or clarity. This flexible image incorporation is important in ensuring that these elements remain easily viewable and interactive on numerous devices. For example, a chart placed next to a table on a larger screen can be sized down and placed above or below the table when viewed on a smaller screen.

Media Queries: Media queries are, in fact, CSS rules that match specific styling based on the characteristics of a device–screen width, height, resolution, or orientation.

The use of media queries with dashboards allows for the specification of specific styles tailored to different screen sizes so that layouts, typography, and color schemes are responsive and ensure a good view. For instance, one might apply media queries to alter font size and hide non-critical elements on smaller-sized displays in order to improve user experience.

Using Breakpoints for Different Screen Sizes

Breakpoints refer to the specific screen widths where the layout changes to accommodate a new form factor, namely, desktop, tablet, or mobile. Some common breakpoints include 1024px for tablets and 768px for smartphones.

Applying breakpoints in dashboards means that dashboards will adapt their layout based on how it makes reading more efficient and accessible. For example, a dashboard can display three charts horizontally on a desktop for better readability while displaying those three charts vertically on a mobile for a longer and less cluttered screen area.

Designing for Different Devices

Responsive design requires not only adaptable layouts but also user interface components that cater to the unique needs of different devices, particularly with respect to users of mobile phones and tablets.

Creating dashboards that adapt to different screen sizes:

- **Layout Adjustments:** In a desktop environment, dashboards can be more complexly designed and contain many graphical elements at once. In a mobile context, it is often mandatory to simplify or stack elements vertically in order to fit the screen. Technologies such as CSS Grid and Flexbox allow for dynamic rearrangement of layout.

- **Element Scaling**: Use relative sizing to ensure that text, icons, and graphics scale appropriately across the range of devices. Using a mobile-first approach means starting with the smallest screen and scaling up for each larger screen, ensuring that every device still enjoys a coherent design experience.

Touch-Friendly Elements for Mobile and Tablet Users

Significance of Touch-Optimized Design: People using mobile devices and tablets rely on touch interactions, so there is a need for producing buttons, filters, and other interactive elements that can easily be tapped and scrolled through by touch.

Best Practices for Touch Interactions

- **Touch Targets**: Buttons and any other kind of interactive elements have to be big enough so that users can comfortably tap them. Typically, this is 44×44 pixels to avoid accidental hits and enhance usability.
- **Spacing and Padding**: It is essential to incorporate sufficient spacing between interactive components to prevent overlap and inadvertent touches. This consideration is particularly critical for filters and navigation menus.
- **Streamlined Navigation**: For compact displays, it may be beneficial to implement expandable menus or icons that obscure non-essential navigation elements, thereby maintaining a clean interface that prioritizes the data.

Responsive design is one of the core elements in modern dashboard development to effortlessly access and interact with data from different devices. The implementation of fluid grids, adaptable images, and even media queries coupled with touch-friendly components ensures the dashboard will not only be pleasing to the eye but also work properly in any case. It is with careful planning and design that responsive dashboards become strong tools that meet the needs of a heterogeneous and mobile user demographic.

Using Filters and Parameters for Interactivity

Filters and parameters form the basic tools of the dashboard design; they give users the capability to interact with the data and tailor their visualization to meet specific needs. Filters enable the user to narrow down their data based on specific criteria, which could be temporal considerations, categories, or geographically factors, while parameters allow for a much greater level of personalization by allowing users to change parts of the dashboard, such as metrics, or swap calculations on the fly.

Together, filters and parameters turn dashboards dynamic and interactive, where users can drill down into the data to better understand it.

Roles of Filters and Parameters in Making Dashboards Interactive

Filters control the visibility of data on the dashboard by allowing users to set specific parameters and filter the database to achieve the required presentation. They are normally used to display subsets of the data relevant to specific questions, such as choosing a date range or focusing on a preferred product category. This enables the management of information overload and helps users zero in on the data relevant to their needs.

Parameters are control variables that can be set to change the appearance or calculations displayed in a dashboard. Unlike filters, which usually reduce the number of rows presented, parameters can dictate exactly what metric is used, the methods of calculation, or which dimensions are included. A typical example for a parameter would be an option that lets the user toggle between visualizing sales by revenue or by units sold.

The engagement of the users is greatly improved through the interactivity offered by filters and parameters. Users often get a deeper insight and a uniquely customized experience when interacting with a dashboard that has been customized to meet their individual requirements. Interaction also encourages exploration and allows users to quickly review different scenarios and probe the data in ways that static reports cannot facilitate.

Effective Use of Filters

Filters are essential tools, and through them, users can explore their data meaningfully; however, this requires careful consideration to ensure that their use adds to rather than detracts from the experience of the user. The following is a discussion of the different kinds of filters commonly used in dashboards along with best practices in regards to their positioning.

Types of Filters

- **Time Filters:** Let users input a time scale of days, weeks, months, years, or the like. Time-based filters are necessary in any dashboard that utilizes historical data so that users can analyze trends over time.
- **Category Filters**: These filters serve to refine data according to categorical variables, including product categories, customer segments, or departments. Such filtering mechanisms are especially beneficial when users aim to concentrate on a particular facet of the data.

- **Range Filters**: This enables easy setting of the upper and lower limits for the quantitative data, such as defining an age, income, or sales range. The range filters enable users to analyze data within fixed limits instead of being tied to preconceived categories.
- **Geographic Filters**: Allows users to filter by location-related information such as country, state, or city, which is very useful for geographically distributed data. Such filters allow users to understand regional performance or trends.
- **Custom Filters:** Refer to user-defined parameters that can integrate various criteria or facilitate more intricate queries. These filters prove advantageous when conventional filter types fail to address particular user requirements, enabling highly customized data presentations.

Best Practices for Filter Placement and Performance

- **Placement**: Position filters in areas of the dashboard that are easily accessible and user-friendly, usually in the top or side regions of the dashboard. Group similar filters together for easier use by users.
- **Limiting Filter Options:** Limit filter options to those that are totally relevant as multiple filters can confuse a user and slow down the dashboard due to increased data queries.
- **Minimize Load:** Filters should be applied at the database level or as early as possible in the data processing pipeline. This means that only relevant data is loaded, thereby improving dashboard performance.
- **Default Values**: Choose default filtering values that represent common views of the data. This not only helps in reducing time to load but also provides a natural default for most users.

Using Parameters for Customization

Parameters offer enhanced flexibility by enabling users to modify the data representation or computations on the dashboard without the need to directly filter the data. Grasping the differences between filters and parameters is crucial for the effective utilization of each instrument.

Understanding Parameters and their Differences from Filters

Filters help shrink the dataset into a focused subset by removing unwanted records based on specific criteria. For example, a filter may limit the data to a given time frame or category.

Conversely, parameters do not omit data; instead, they alter the manner in which information is presented or computed. For instance, a parameter may allow for the selection between various metrics, such as revenue and profit, or transition a dashboard display from monthly to quarterly information.

Using Parameters to Dynamically Adjust Dashboard Elements

- **Switching Between Metrics:** Set parameters so that the user can toggle the display between "`Sales Revenue`" and "`Profit Margin`." This maintains the clean and simple nature of the dashboard and allows the user to have full control over what they are measuring.
- **Adjusting Calculation Logic:** Some parameters may control different dimensions of the computations, such as changing discount rates or currency type. This functionality is particularly handy in financial dashboards wherein one may have to examine different scenarios under different conditions.
- **Changing Visualizations**: Parameters can also facilitate changing between different types of visualization. A parameter could be used to toggle a chart between a bar graph display and a line graph display, based on the user's preference for the best way to see data.

Implementing Cascading Filters

Cascaded filters, also referred to as dependent filters, use a successive refinement of filter choice based on the earlier selections. It is used for letting users step through data, making the process easier and more user-friendly.

Benefits of Cascading Filters

It improves the user experience by limiting filter options based on previous choices, prevents the irrelevant from popping up, and thus makes any interface easier to navigate and less cognitively demanding.

Effective Data Retrieval: Because the cascading filters progressively refine information, they eliminate the quantity of data loaded at each level and thus potentially optimize performance by reducing the amount of data to be processed.

Step-by-Step Guide to Setting Up Cascading Filters

1. **Identify Filter Dependencies:** Define an order of operations for your filters. So, in the context of a sales dashboard, the user would select a "`Region`" filter, which in turn updates the possible choices in the "`Country`" filter as a function of the region selected.

2. **Set up the First Filter**: Create the first filter that will guide all the other filters that follow. Create this filter with the broadest scope, such as by selecting a particular region in an area-based hierarchy filter.
3. **Configure the Dependent Filters:** Tie the subsequent filters to the main filter so that they change accordingly when the selected choice is made. In most dashboard tools, it is all about setting up a relation or dependency among the filters. For example, if a region is chosen, then the countries in that region would be the options listed in the "`Country`" filter.
4. **Test the Cascading Filters:** Ensure the filters update as expected and that selections properly narrow down the options. Calibrate any settings so that they will be seamless and predictable for the user.
5. **Optimize for Performance:** Cascading filters should be used at the database level if possible and only on large datasets because they reduce the load on data and make interaction faster, as they fetch only essential data at every stage of the filter.

Filters and parameters are the key to interactive and personalized dashboards that will finally captivate the users and provide insights custom-fit to their requirements. In this case, improved user experience is when these tools are appropriately used with an apt application of advanced techniques such as cascading filters, and people can intuitively explore data.

Best Practices for User Experience (UX)

Good dashboard creation is more than grouping data; it is about building something that provides value to users with a thoughtful UX design approach. It involves interaction with the UX interface in dashboard design in a way that is intuitive, accessible, and engaging. Clarity, consistency, and accessibility form the foundation on which dashboards are designed to be not only useful but also enjoyable to use. This section discusses basic UX principles and the best practices to create dashboards that satisfy the needs of users by providing a great user experience.

Foundations of UX in Dashboard Design

UX stands for the combined experience that an individual develops in his or her interaction with a product. Such experience encompasses navigational ease and the emotional responses the product elicits. In dashboard design, UX is very critical since it defines how well the user will interpret the presented information and make sufficiently informed choices. A well-crafted UX ensures that one quickly derives the information needed with minimal feelings of confusion or frustration.

Core UX Principles for Dashboards

- **Clarity:** A well-designed dashboard minimizes cognitive overload and ensures users understand the data being shown rather than the interface. A good dashboard will use simple language, clear images, and organized content.
- **Consistency**: Consistency in all the design elements—that is, font, color scheme, and icon—also enables intuitive navigation of the dashboards for users. Users quickly learn to use the dashboard if the elements behave predictively.
- **Accessibility:** It should allow access and use to everyone, including persons with disabilities, since access and usability should be the considerations; readable fonts, high-contrast colors, and assistive technology such as screen readers for the visually impaired.

These principles can therefore be applied in different dimensions of design to create dashboards that are both user-accessible, engaging, and effective.

Designing with the User in Mind

- **Understanding User Personas**: User personas are hypothetical constructions designed to represent various types of users along with their goals, challenges, and preferences. Designing personas helps in tailoring the overall experience of a dashboard to meet the needs of different user groups.
- **Applicability of Personas to Dashboard Development** In such a case, for example, a financial analyst would focus on rich data and dynamically filtering capabilities, whereas the senior executive might focus on high-level KPIs, simplifying the visualizations. Defining personas ensures that the design meets the exact needs and expectations of each user group.

User-Friendly Navigation and Intuitive Layouts

- **Navigation Design:** The user can easily navigate the dashboard. Use familiar navigation patterns, such as a top or side menu, to put things where users expect to find things. Keep the depth of the navigation limited to prevent users from getting lost.
- **Formulate Intuitive Layouts:** Arrange dashboard elements based on importance, usage frequency, and coherent flow. Important metrics must always be located centrally; ancillary information along with filters should be on one side. Use grid patterns systematically to align items and make the visualization more attractive.
- **Visual Hierarchy and Information Clarity:** The presentation of information is just as important as the information itself in the world of data visualization. The backbone for ensuring that dashboards and charts are communicating with their audience effectively involves a visual hierarchy and clear information.

This part discusses the art of combining visuals such that the viewer's focus follows intuitively. If core metrics are emphasized and the content ordered in a logical fashion, then it is ensured that key insights are well-centered. We will also cover techniques for simplifying complex data, using appropriate graphical cues, and reducing extraneous information to enhance overall understandability.

Acquiring competence in these principles will enable the development of visualizations that look professional and also come equipped with the ability to quickly and confidently gain insights by users.

Prioritizing Content with Size, Color, and Placement

- **Use Size to Convey Value**: Big items draw attention. Use size to focus attention on important information or metrics. Headlines and main information are differentiated from ancillary information.
- **Appropriate Use of Color**: Color can be used to draw attention to important statistics or separate functional areas. Avoid extensive color use; it only distracts, besides creating inconsistencies in meaning across the dashboard.
- **Strategic Placement of Elements**: Place the most critical information in the top-left quadrant, where the user's eyes are likely to first enter. Place ancillary information in groups so that users may easily find more information while remaining focused on key information.

The Role of Whitespace and Alignment

- **Adding Whitespace Improves Readability**: Whitespace or negative space avoids clutter and brings ease to the processing of information. It is visually less noisy; the eye captures what is relevant to bring it into focus with well-spaced elements.
- **Grid-Alignment for Consistent Design**: To align elements to a grid that would ensure a structured, uniform layout. Alignment is more readable and cleaner when consistent.

Color Theory and Accessibility: Colors are essential toward making data visualizations more informative, but only if implemented appropriately. This chapter is able to take the foundation of color theory and apply this to help select palettes that are informative while aesthetically pleasing.

Accessibility is equally important—ensuring your visualizations are usable and inclusive for all audiences, including those with color vision deficiencies. We will cover best practices for selecting accessible color schemes, leveraging contrast effectively, and designing visuals that prioritize clarity and usability.

Being that with this knowledge of color theory and principles of accessibility, one will be equipped to create effective and accessible designs.

Basics of Color Theory in Dashboards

- **Selection of Color Scheme**: Select a color scheme that will contrast the purposes of the dashboard. Consider colors such as shades of blue to represent confidence and professionalism, and tones of red or orange to represent urgency or warnings.
- **Using Color in Data Points to Distinguish**: Give different colors to various kinds of data so that the data points can be distinguished easily. However, do not include too much color because it may get confusing and lower the clearness.

Maintaining Accessibility Standards

- **High contrast for readability**: The text must have enough contrast with the background so that one can read. WCAG lets you test your conformance and pass the contrast criteria.
- **Color-Blind-Friendly Palettes**: About 8 percent of all males and 0.5 percent of all females are colorblind. Besides using red and green as indicators for different data points, it is better to use palettes that are more color-blind friendly or add text labels.

Prototyping and User Testing

It takes more than good design to create an effective data visualization or dashboard. One would need to iterate on design and incorporate user feedback before landing on the final product, which meets the needs and expectations of its users.

This chapter introduces building prototypes in order to previsualize a concept and test layouts before full implementation. Techniques for actionable feedback are also discussed, such as user testing for usability, functionality, and clarity. In this way, prototyping and user testing enable the delivery of solutions not only aesthetically pleasing but also built around user needs and are effective.

Importance of Prototyping and Feedback

- **Prototyping for Early Insight**: Prototyping gives you a preview of the layout and functionalities before you finalize your design. This way, early usability issues are discovered, and the dashboard is refined based on real user interactions.
- **Gather What Works**: To determine if your dashboard effectively meets users' needs, it is crucial to gather feedback directly from users. It might be able to identify confusion points, inefficiencies, or missing elements within the dashboard.
- **Using Prototyping Tools and Conducting User Testing**: Some of the popular

prototyping tools where designers can create interactive prototypes and simulate real user experiences include Figma, Sketch, and Adobe XD. In such tools, the feature of collaboration is often available to easily facilitate gathering feedback from stakeholder levels and end-users.

- **Conduct user testing**: From that, pick a different set of users and choose the personas for demo purposes. Observe their behavior with the dashboard, list down problems, and ask clarifying questions about what they experienced. Iterate based on insights drawn from sessions to refine the design.

Dashboards are based more on the usability of dashboards–how intuitive and accessible they are. It all relates to understanding the needs of the user here. These time-saving steps, visual hierarchy in designing, judicious use of color, and testing before a launch are the very same steps that create value in dashboards and enhance user experience.

Performance Optimization Techniques

From dashboards, improvement in performance is very crucial for a smooth and efficient user experience. Easy accessibility and interaction with information occur through fast and responsive dashboards that are reflected in much better decision-making and much higher engagement rates. Poor performance culminates in frustration of users, low productivity, and minimal engagement. This chapter will be talking about some basic strategies that optimize dashboard performance, such as reducing loads, database queries, and monitoring.

Dashboard performance optimization is all the things done to make dashboards load and respond as fast as possible so that latency at the time of load, filtering time, and interaction time can be minimized. It seeks to make a smooth experience for the user in which the data loads readily and correctly without wide delay or interruption. Performance is highly considered when dashboards are implicated while handling large datasets or when many users access their contents on various devices and bandwidths.

Importance of Performance Optimization

- **User Satisfaction**: Such dashboards that are quick and interactive increase users' satisfaction and retention. Users will get frustrated and leave the dashboard when their time to load is high.
- **Engagement and Productivity Involvement**: A dynamic dashboard encourages deeper data exploration, enables easy testing of various scenarios, and improves efficiency in acquiring insights. More succinctly, it helps decision-makers respond more quickly and, therefore, enhances productivity.
- **Scalability**: A good dashboard can take more traffic and larger datasets without

deteriorating its performance; it will thus be much more scalable toward growing user bases or expanding data needs.

Techniques for Reducing Load Times

High-performance loading is highly critical because a slow load time might discourage users from continuing to explore their data visualizations and dashboards. The following best practices highlight minimizing the load times, even for larger datasets or more complex visualizations.

- **Managing Data Volume:** Probably among the most efficient approaches to improve data loading times is data aggregation to load pre-aggregated data before it is displayed. Then, while showing huge detailed data, there is an advantage in summarizing that data into meaningful categories. For example, summing up daily sales totals into weekly or monthly summaries reduces the data sizes that must be retrieved and processed by many folds.
- **Data Sampling**: In some very large datasets, sampling really helps. Load only a representative subset of the data instead of all of them. Sampling is helpful, particularly when sacrificing precision for speed is acceptable, as in trend analysis or exploratory work in early stages.
- **Data Filtering**: Implement filters at the earliest opportunity to reduce data volume retrieved for the dashboard. Any place where users would frequently want access to data for specific regions or certain time ranges is a good place to define default filters so that the dataset only contains pertinent information. This removes unwanted processing of data, thus accelerating loading time.
- **Limiting the Number of Visual Elements**: Reduce visual clutter; do not overcrowd the dashboard with too many charts, graphs, and tables. Each visual asset loads data and increases rendering time. Include only the important information, portrayed in a clean format and ready to drill into additional details, either as needed or through secondary dashboards.
- **Critical Metrics**: Identify the most important metrics of interest in the scope of a dashboard and emphasize those. This approach not only increases performance but also helps one to concentrate attention on key insights, thereby decreasing the problem of cognitive overload.

Efficient Use of Calculations and Scripts

Efficient calculations and scripts are the backbone of high-performing dashboards and data visualizations. Mismanaged scripts or excessive calculations can lead to sluggish performance and hinder user experience.

- **Managing Complex Calculations**: Pre-Compute Calculations: Heavy computations to be done at the point of origin of data rather than at the dashboard's location. Using such calculations at the database level reduces the load on the dashboard tool, which increases performance. Instead of computing year-over-year growth at the dashboard level, one can compute it at the database level and then pass the result to the dashboard.

- **Asynchronous Computations**: For most of the real-time computations, it is better to try to utilize asynchronous approaches that maintain the dashboard's interactivity while the actual computations run in the background.
- **Server-Side versus Client-Side Calculations**: It is probably faster to handle big datasets on the server side because servers are more powerful in computing and are set to read the entire dataset; hence, no transfer of data is done between the database and the dashboard, thus improving the scalability and speed of the application.

  Side calculations on a client should be used with caution and, in the first instance, for conditions of smaller data sets or real-time updating scenarios. Because client-side calculations do allow for flexibility, they may make a dashboard less responsive when working with large data sets or when accessed by users with less powerful tools.

Optimizing Database Queries

Efficient database queries are crucial for powering fast and reliable dashboards. Poorly optimized queries can lead to slow load times, increased server load, and a diminished user experience.

- **Techniques for Optimizing Database Queries:** Index those columns on your tables that frequently appear in your queries, such as filter and join columns. Indexing improves query performance since retrieval of data is faster for the database in locating the desired data. For instance, indexing columns such as "`Date`," "`Region`," or "`Product Category`" can improve query performance significantly.

  Partitioning separates large tables into smaller bits based on a judicious criterion that could be date or region. This method enables the queries to access only the relevant pieces of information so that time and resources spent in fetching the results are lessened.
- **Query optimization**: There could be inefficient SQL queries with superfluous joins or that rely on complex conditions. Use `EXPLAIN` or its equivalent tool to evaluate the execution plan of your queries and determine bottlenecks. Optimize your queries to retrieve only the necessary data for the dashboard.
- **Query Scheduling and Caching**
  - **Scheduled Queries on Dashboards without Real-Time Data**: These run the queries at scheduled intervals. The results are cached to prevent most

live queries in order to reduce the database load and increase dashboard speed.

- **Data Caching**: Caches frequently accessed data to avoid repeated query calls to the database. It provides caching at multiple tiers–server-side or in-memory–to store the most recent results and serve them immediately without querying the data source again.

Monitoring and Maintenance

This is just the starting point; functionality and validity over time are issues of ongoing monitoring and maintenance. Periodically reviewing it will identify performance bottlenecks or outdated data sources and shifts in user needs.

- **Tools for Monitoring Dashboard Performance:** Use the following performance monitoring tools: Google Analytics, New Relic, or Datadog for monitoring dashboards' performance metric load times, the data on user interaction, and any resource utilization. The tool signals a possible choke point as well as what to improve in one's work.
- **Dashboard Analytics**: This would analyze the usage of a dashboard with user interactions on how extensively filters are used and which pages are frequently hit. This type of analysis would help recognize areas for enhancement, mainly high-traffic sections, for some performance optimization.

Best Practices for Maintenance

- **Updating Data Connections**: It is one of the aspects that ensure data connections are always at their best. For instance, it could be a simple switch to a more efficient data source or query method.
- **Remove Irrelevant Data**: Delete all unused data sources and connections to not create any extra burden on the dashboard. Handling a data pipeline regularly could ensure that only relevant and current data is dealt with.
- **Review Dashboard Design**: As the volume of information grows and user needs change, review your dashboard design periodically to ensure it still meets all performance goals. Consider redesigning complex arrangements or reducing the number of visual elements for best performance.

Optimization of the performance of the dashboard continuously requires proper consideration in terms of data management, processing calculation, and database query efficiency. All these approaches will reduce in volume, enhance the method-based calculations, improve the execution of database queries, and provide a periodical maintenance of dashboards for rapid loading, responsive interaction, and excellent user experience. Continued surveillance keeps the dashboard up-to-date with shifting performance benchmarks due to increased usage and changing requirements of data.

Conclusion

Building and fine-tuning dashboards involves much more than simply exposing information–it is way beyond careful consideration of performance, interactivity, responsiveness, and user experience. The practice reflected here follows the guidelines of this chapter so you can build dashboards not just to report information but to facilitate data exploration toward important decisions and responses.

Dashboards are powerful decision-making tools but may only contribute toward that end based on a functional and user-experience-oriented approach to their design. In the event that outlined best practices in this chapter–that take performance, interactivity, responsiveness, and user experience into consideration–develop dashboards from aesthetic ones to functioning and effective ones. The optimally designed, well-crafted dashboard enables users to meaningfully interact with data, thereby resulting in better insights, faster decision-making, and better results.

Yet, by continually refining one's methodology and keeping up with new tools and methodologies, one can ensure that dashboards are technologically sophisticated but profoundly centered on user needs. Exemplary dashboard design improves not only the experience for individual users but also contributes to the overall efficiency and efficacy of data-informed decision-making throughout the organization.

The next chapter will show how to integrate Superset into existing workflows, starting with modern data warehouses for dynamic access to large datasets. It will cover data refreshing, ETL tools such as Airflow and Talend, and real-time dashboards for timely insights. Readers will learn to manage data pipelines effectively, making Superset a key part of their data infrastructure.

CHAPTER 8
Integrating Superset into Data Pipelines

Introduction

In this landscape of data, the interplay between data visualization platforms and data infrastructure will be crucial for deriving insights efficiently. Although Apache Superset excels at creating interactive dashboards, its strength lies in its data pipeline integration. Let us use Superset with a data warehouse, automate refreshing, or integrate it with tools such as Airflow or Talend, and Superset will give you dynamic, real-time insights.

Structure

This chapter will guide you through integrating Apache Superset into your existing data pipelines, covering topics such as:

- Connecting Superset to Data Warehouses
- Automating Data Refreshes
- Integrating with ETL Tools
- Building Real-Time Dashboards
- Monitoring Data Pipelines

Connecting Superset to Data Warehouses

A data warehouse is basically that contemporary component in the ecosystem of data in which a considerable amount of structured data gets derived from multiple sources. Apache Superset connects to such warehouses, thus enabling efficient querying and visualization of data.

Superset supports a wide variety of databases and data warehouses, including:

- **Amazon Redshift**
- **Google BigQuery**
- **Snowflake**
- **PostgreSQL**
- **MySQL**
- **Presto**
- **ClickHouse**
- **Oracle**

To use Apache Superset for business intelligence and analytics, one has to establish a connection to all relevant data sources. This chapter talks about installing database drivers, connection settings configuration, and specific considerations about cloud data warehouses such as Amazon Redshift, Google BigQuery, and Snowflake.

PostgreSQL/MySQL: Installing Drivers, SQLAlchemy URIs, and Connection Configuration

PostgreSQL and MySQL are among the most widely used relational databases today in various data environments, along with other choices such as Google BigQuery or Presto. To connect Apache Superset to any of these relational databases, one needs to download the relevant driver, set up the connection using the SQLAlchemy URI, and then change performance settings according to that step.

Installing Drivers

- **PostgreSQL:** Superset relies on **`SQLAlchemy`** to manage database connections, which in turn requires a **`psycopg2`** driver for PostgreSQL.

  Install the driver using **`pip`**: **`pip install psycopg2`**

- **MySQL**: It will use mysqlclient for MySQL driver.

  Install it using pip: **`pip install mysqlclient`**

Note: *You need to have PostGreSQL or MYSQL installed on your computer or you can use Docker Image for the same.*

Generate SQLAlchemy URIs: Superset connects to databases using SQLAlchemy URIs, the standard format for connection strings. This is how you configure them for PostgreSQL and MySQL:

- **PostgreSQL SQLAlchemy URI**

  `postgresql+psycopg2://username:password@host:port/database`

  Example

  `postgresql+psycopg2://admin:secret@localhost:5432/mydatabase`

- **MySQL SQLAlchemy URI**

  `mysql+mysqlclient://username:password@host:port/database`

  Example

  `mysql+mysqlclient://admin:secret@localhost:3306/mydatabase`

The **Database Connection** is integrated inside Superset. Go to **Data** > **Databases**.

Click **+ Database**.

- Fill in the details to include the SQLAlchemy URI.
- Review the relation to affirm that it works.

Best Practices for PostgreSQL/MySQL

- **Connection Pooling:** Both PostgreSQL and MySQL provide connection pooling, so you could handle an extremely large number of concurrent connections. SQLAlchemy supports this, using pooling options such as:

  ```
  SQLALCHEMY_ENGINE_OPTIONS = {END 'pool_size': 10, 'max_overflow': 20, 'pool_timeout': 30}
  ```

- **Read replicas**: If you run PostgreSQL or MySQL in production at high query loads, then you use read replicas for offloading read-heavy operations to improve the performance of queries.

Amazon Redshift: Setting Up the Connection and Optimizing Performance

Amazon Redshift is a popular, cloud-based data warehouse that is ideal for large-scale data analytics. Connecting Superset to Redshift is straightforward but requires certain optimizations to handle large datasets efficiently.

- **Installing the Redshift Driver:** You will also need psycopg2 because Redshift is natively compatible with PostgreSQL-based connectors to connect to Redshift.

  Use **pip** to install the driver: `pip install psycopg2`

- **Creating the SQLAlchemy URI for Redshift:** The SQLAlchemy URI follows the same syntax as PostgreSQL, but is specifically designed for Amazon Redshift.

```
redshift+psycopg2://user:pass@redshift-cluster-address:5439/data-
base_name
```

Example:

```
redshift+psycopg2://admin:secret@redshift-cluster-1.abc123xyz.
redshift.amazonaws.com:5439/mydatabase
```

Google BigQuery/Snowflake: Special Considerations for Cloud Data Warehouses

Cloud-based data warehousing solutions, such as Google BigQuery and Snowflake, are gaining substantial traction attributable to their enhanced scalability, superior performance, and capacity to manage extensive datasets. Nevertheless, establishing a connection between Superset and these platforms necessitates specific considerations to optimize cost-efficiency and performance outcomes.

Google BigQuery

BigQuery is a serverless service with very high scalability from Google Cloud and, therefore, is well-suited for data analytics as well as real-time reporting but does require careful cost management because it operates on pay-per-query terms.

Install the BigQuery Driver

To connect Superset to Google BigQuery, install the **`pybigquery`** package:

```
pip install pybigquery
```

Configuration of the SQLAlchemy URI for BigQuery

Here is how the SQLAlchemy URI for BigQuery looks:

```
bigquery://project_id
```

Example:

```
bigquery://my-GCP-project
```

Your Google Cloud credentials should be configured either using a service account or using user credentials, usually from environment variables **`GOOGLE_APPLICATION_CREDENTIALS`**.

Snowflake

Snowflake is a cloud-based general-purpose data platform that distinguishes between storage and computations to allow flexible and scalable management of data.

Superset is compatible with Snowflake, but to fully exploit its functionalities, further configurations are required.

Installing the Snowflake Driver

To start a connection with Snowflake, the following package should be installed first:

```
pip install snowflake-connector-python
```

Configure the SQLAlchemy URI for Snowflake

The SQLAlchemy URI for Snowflake looks like this:

```
snowflake://username:password@account.region.snowflakecomputing.
com/database/schema
```

Example:

```
snowflake://admin:secret@myaccount.us-east-1.snowflakecomputing.
com/mydb/public
```

Setting up Apache Superset with any number of databases and cloud-based data warehouses calls for careful setup and configuration. Subsequently, it is possible to have your data visualization tools integrated nicely as you enhance their performance by ensuring the installation of proper drivers and setting suitable SQLAlchemy URIs along with database-specific optimizations. With PostgreSQL, MySQL, Amazon Redshift, Google BigQuery, and Snowflake, there will be careful configuration so that your team will extract more insights into the data more promptly and efficiently.

Automating Data Refreshes

Given today's fast-paced, fast-changing business environment, immediate, accurate information is a tool to guide effective decisions. Indeed, whether related to sales or customer behavior, or even assessing the efficiency of operations, having up-to-date information allows organizations to quickly respond to both opportunities and problems. Outdated data—that is, information that is no longer relevant or true—can cause misguided insights and less-than-optimal decisions, with potentially far reaching consequences.

One popular solution for handling real-time data and analytics is **Apache Druid**, an open-source distributed data store designed for ingesting large amounts of event data quickly. Its architecture and real-time streaming capabilities enable fast query performance and immediate insights, making it a powerful choice for organizations aiming to harness continuously updated information for more informed, timely decisions.

Timely Data is Crucial

The most important thing in today's fast-paced world is that information be timely so that the decision is both informed and impactful. Whether it is real-time sales tracking, system performance monitoring, or response to market changes, updated data enables organizations to act quickly.

This section discusses the urgency for real-time data. Then it covers various methodologies on how one would effectively generate these outputs in real time, along with the techniques for keeping dashboards and reports updated in real time at all times.

Timely data will unlock truly valuable analytics and enable smarter, faster decision-making to be central.

- **Adaptive Decision-Making:** Fields such as finance, e-commerce, and logistics compete on real-time or near-real-time data, with the margin sometimes being the difference between grasping a market opportunity and losing it. Leadership in such markets depends on fresh data for time-sensitive decisions related to pricing, resource allocation, and managing risk.

  For instance, an e-retailer that tracks its inventory needs to know the current on-hand stock. If a restocking decision is made based on obsolete data, then the organization might overorder or run out of some items, and hence sales might decline along with customer services.

- **Operational Efficiency:** Timely data is also essential for operational teams monitoring processes, equipment, or production lines. Systems such as IoT sensors, logistics tracking, and performance monitoring require live data to optimize operations in real time.

  A manufacturing company can use data from its production lines to determine potential bottlenecks or equipment failures. Old or incorrect data can translate into long periods of idleness, wasteful use of resources, or failure to achieve intended production results.

- **Adaptability in Dynamic Markets:** Markets can fluctuate in an instant due to various factors–customer preferences, competitor actions, or economic conditions. Organizations that possess the most up-to-date information can change their strategies immediately. Whether changing marketing campaigns based on feedback received from customers or shifting focus to inventory items when trends are shifting, timely insights afford the agility to adapt. Organizations that have real-time data can adjust investments, orders, or even operations during volatile periods, such as a stock market crash or supply chain disruption, to minimize losses or even gain a competitive edge.

Improving Performance Through Query Caching

The intrinsic caching mechanism of Apache Superset is the heart of dashboard performance, storing the results of database queries. This mechanism reduces the requirement for costly, repeated execution of expensive database queries and thus enhances speed and efficiency while presenting visualizations or dashboards. This chapter will explain the query caching functionality in Superset, which enables configuration for setting cache intervals. It will also describe the methods for invalidating the cache.

In many data-driven applications, querying large datasets could be very resource-intensive, and there is a delay in response times—particularly for users with a tendency to refresh dashboards or multiple users querying the same set of data at the same time. By caching query results, Superset can serve pre-computed results quickly, which drastically lowers database load and enhances the user experience.

Caching in Superset: How it works

This Superset, however, uses an asynchronous mechanism that stores the results of database queries temporarily. Whenever a user requests a dashboard or a chart, it checks whether the query result is in the cache first.

- If the result is cached and has not expired, the data is retrieved from the cache, bypassing the database query.
- If the result is neither cached nor valid because it has expired, Superset will execute the query against the database, retrieve its result, and cache it for future use.

Superset uses Redis or Memcached as a caching backend. The results of queries are, by default, cached in the configured system, but it is possible to change the length of time they remain available before expiring.

Advantages of Query Caching

- **Diminished Database Load:** Frequent queries do not access the database, thereby decreasing the total load and enhancing the scalability of the system.
- **Faster Dashboards:** Cached queries return data faster, making the user experience more responsive.
- **Lower Costs**: In cloud-based databases, such as Google BigQuery, Snowflake, and so on, caching reduces the number of billable queries for better cost savings.

Configuring Cache Intervals

Before configuring cache intervals, you must have caching installed and configured as Redis or Memcached.

- **Illustration of Redis Configuration:** In Redis, one can use Redis as a caching backend by running the installation for the required package and setting up the connection in **superset_config.py**.
- **Implement Redis and the Python client for Redis:** `pip install redis`
- **Configure Superset for use with Redis**

  Add the following to your **superset_config.py**:

```
from cachelib.redis import RedisCache

CACHE_CONFIG = {
    'CACHE_TYPE': 'RedisCache',
    'CACHE_DEFAULT_TIMEOUT': 60 * 60,  # Default timeout in
seconds (1 hour)
    'CACHE_KEY_PREFIX': 'superset_',
    'CACHE_REDIS_HOST': 'localhost',
    'CACHE_REDIS_PORT': 6379,
    'CACHE_REDIS_DB': 1,
}

RESULTS_BACKEND = RedisCache(
    host='localhost',
    port=6379,
    key_prefix='superset_results'
)
```

  This particular configuration will instruct Superset to use Redis both for general-purpose caching (**CACHE_CONFIG**) and results caching (**RESULTS_BACKEND**).

- **Define Cache Lifetimes:** Once the caching backend is configured, you can configure the cache intervals for different components. The default configuration of Superset caches the query results for a period of 1 hour, but it can always depend upon your requirement.

  Global Cache Timeout: You can set a global timeout for cached results changing the **CACHE_DEFAULT_TIMEOUT** parameter in the **superset_config.py** configuration file.

```
CACHE_DEFAULT_TIMEOUT = 60 * 10  # Cache timeout in seconds (10
minutes)
```

It is established that an expiration period for all queries is 10 minutes. When that time is consumed, any results from cached queries are stale, so another query has to reach the database.

- **Dataset-specific cache configuration:** In Superset, you can also cache at the dataset level for finer-grained control. This gives you control over the cache for individual datasets, which is particularly useful because you might be creating some datasets that are very dynamic, while others do not change as frequently.
- **Go to Datasets:**
  1. Go to **`Data`** > **`Datasets`** in Superset, select a dataset you would like to configure.
  2. **Set a Cache Timeout for the dataset**: Navigate to the **`Advanced`** section and adjust the cache timeout settings for the particular dataset.

  For example, if your dataset updates every 15 minutes, you can set the cache timeout to match this frequency:

  ```
  CACHE_TIMEOUT = 60 * 15  # 15 minutes
  ```

  This results in the fact that the cached results for that dataset become invalidated every 15 minutes.

Scheduling Data Refreshes Using Superset's API

Apache Superset is a useful business intelligence and data visualization tool; however, for dashboards to always point to the latest figures, periodic or event-driven refreshes must be enabled. Fortunately, the REST API from Superset enables automatic refreshes of data, making it possible to interact with various tools, such as cron jobs, task schedulers, or orchestration frameworks such as Apache Airflow. In this section, we will explore methods for configuring automated refreshes as well as methods for turning them on upon certain events or workflows.

Explanation of Superset's REST API

The REST API of Superset provides a means of programmatically interacting with the platform and automates tasks such as refreshes of datasets, dashboard updates, and more. Dataset and dashboard refreshes are performed by the main API endpoints, which invalidate the cached queries and start loading new data.

Key API Endpoints for Refreshing Data

- **Dataset Refresh Endpoint**: This endpoint invalidates the cache for a specific dataset, triggering a fresh query on the next dashboard load.
  - Method: `POST`
  - Endpoint: `/api/v1/dataset/<dataset_id>/refresh`
  - Purpose: Invalidate the dataset's cache, ensuring that fresh data is queried.
- **Dashboard Refresh Endpoint**: This endpoint triggers a refresh of a specific dashboard.
  - Method: `POST`
  - Endpoint: `/api/v1/dashboard/<dashboard_id>/refresh`
  - Purpose: Triggers the dashboard to query new data from the database.

Authentication

To get to the Superset API, you start by authenticating in order to obtain a JWT or API token. For security's sake, ensure your API calls are authenticated and tokens are kept secure.

Example of Generating an API Token

```
curl -X POST "http://your-superset-url/api/v1/security/login" \
    -H "Content-Type: application/json" \
    -d '{"username": "admin", "password": "yourpassword"}'
```

This will return an API token that can be used in subsequent API requests:

```
{
  "access_token": "YOUR_API_TOKEN"
}
```

You can then use this token in the **`Authorization`** header for the subsequent refresh API calls:

```
curl -X POST "http://your-superset-url/api/v1/dataset/1/refresh" \
     -H "Authorization: Bearer YOUR_API_TOKEN"
```

Setting Up Periodic Refreshes via API Calls Using Cron Jobs or Task Schedulers

For most use cases, you will want to set up a periodic data refresh to ensure your dashboards are displaying up-to-date information. This can be achieved using cron jobs or other task schedulers to periodically trigger API calls to the Superset endpoints for dataset or dashboard refreshes.

To refresh the data, let us create a cron job. Cron is a Unix utility that can be used to schedule the running of scripts or commands at specific times. Using cron will generate periodic API requests that refresh datasets or dashboards in Superset.

Step 1: Write a Refresh Script

Create a simple shell script that makes an API call to Superset's refresh endpoint. Here is an example:

```
#!/bin/bash

# Superset API Token (replace with your actual token)
API_TOKEN="YOUR_API_TOKEN"

# API call to refresh dataset (replace <dataset_id> with your actual
dataset ID)
curl -X POST "http://your-superset-url/api/v1/dataset/<dataset_id>/
refresh" \
     -H "Authorization: Bearer $API_TOKEN"
```

Step 2: Schedule the Cron Job

Edit the crontab file to set up the periodic refresh. For example, to run the refresh script every hour:

```
crontab -e
```

Add the following line:

0 * * * * /path/to/your/refresh_script.sh

This cron job will trigger the script every hour, on the hour, refreshing the dataset in Superset.

Windows Task Scheduler

If you are using a Windows environment, you can use `Task Scheduler` to automate refreshes instead of cron. The same script can be executed periodically based on a scheduled task you define.

Triggering Automatic Refreshes Based on Events

In many scenarios, you will want to refresh your dashboards or datasets in response to specific events, such as the completion of an ETL pipeline or a database trigger. This is known as **event-driven refresh**, and it ensures that data is refreshed only when necessary, reducing unnecessary API calls.

Event-Driven Refresh Using Database Triggers

Database triggers can detect changes in the underlying data and send a signal to Superset to invalidate the cache and refresh the dataset or dashboard.

Example: PostgreSQL Trigger

In PostgreSQL, you can set up a trigger that makes an HTTP request to Superset's API to refresh a dataset whenever a specific table is updated.

```
CREATE OR REPLACE FUNCTION refresh_superset_data()
RETURNS TRIGGER AS $$
BEGIN
   PERFORM pg_notify('superset_refresh', 'refresh dataset');
   RETURN NEW;
END;
$$ LANGUAGE plpgsql;

CREATE TRIGGER data_update_trigger
AFTER INSERT OR UPDATE ON your_table
FOR EACH ROW EXECUTE FUNCTION refresh_superset_data();
```

Further, event **`pg_notify`** can be monitored, and an API call towards Superset could be triggered through running a script or a service, which listens to such triggers.

ETL Completion Signals for Refresh

The refresh can now start in Superset once the ETL process is done. Most of the time, this refresh is issued directly from ETL tools to ensure that new information exists–Apache Airflow, Talend, and dbt.

Using External Tools for Data Refresh Automation

However, for more complex workflows, external orchestration tools such as Apache Airflow may be used to automatically refresh, and this function is often incorporated into an overall ETL workflow.

Automated Refresh of Data through Airflow: Apache Airflow is a workflow orchestration tool that enables users to establish a DAG in automation for many tasks, data extraction, transformation, loading (ETL), and dashboards refreshing. Superset's API, being integrated with Airflow, allows automatic refreshing of data after the completion of some predefined tasks.

Example: Airflow DAG to Refresh Superset Dataset

```
from airflow import DAG
from airflow.operators.python_operator import PythonOperator
from datetime import datetime
import requests
```

```
# Define the DAG
dag = DAG('superset_refresh', description='Superset dataset refresh',
          schedule_interval='@hourly', start_date=datetime(2023, 1, 1),
catchup=False)

# Python function to refresh Superset dataset
def refresh_superset():
    api_url = "http://your-superset-url/api/v1/dataset/<dataset_id>/
refresh"
    headers = {
        "Authorization": "Bearer YOUR_API_TOKEN"
    }
    response = requests.post(api_url, headers=headers)
    if response.status_code == 200:
        print("Dataset refresh successful")
    else:
        print(f"Failed to refresh: {response.content}")

# Airflow task to refresh dataset
refresh_task = PythonOperator(task_id='refresh_superset_dataset',
python_callable=refresh_superset, dag=dag)

# Set task dependencies (optional)
refresh_task
```

In this example, the Airflow DAG refreshes the Superset dataset every hour. You can also tie such a task to other ETL tasks to make sure that Superset refreshes only after new data has been loaded into the data warehouse.

Alternative Workflow Orchestration Tools: Besides Airflow, there are other tools such as Talend, dbt, and Luigi that allow refreshes to be started for Superset. Traditionally, these tools run ETL jobs, and after a successful run, they can send an API call to Superset to flush the cache on datasets or dashboards.

One would integrate an API invocation at the end of an ETL process within the Talend environment using the tRESTClient component to start the refresh. After running dbt run to update your data models, you can script an API call to Superset's refresh endpoint as a final step in your deployment pipeline.

Integrating with ETL Tools

The two principal ways to prepare data for the analytics and visualization tools of Apache Superset are called ETL (Extract, Transform, Load) and ELT (Extract, Load, Transform). The two processes are essentially the same—the art of taking data from numerous sources into a centralized repository, such as a data warehouse–but they differ in the order of their operations and how the data is processed.

Defining ETL and ELT in Data Engineering

The three steps of ETL are extract, transform, and load.

Data is extracted from more sources, such as databases, APIs, and CSV files. The data is cleansed, enriched, and transformed into a format to fit in with standardized schema forms; for instance, the sales data from different regions are merged together into one structure.

The processed data is then uploaded to a predetermined system, usually a data warehouse or database, from which it can be used for analysis and visualization.

In the ETL methodology, transformation of data is occurring before the data is loaded into the data warehouse. Therefore, by this approach, only sanitized and processed data is maintained.

ELT is actually the more recent approach that has the order of operations reversed:

From there, data is solicited from different `sources. Data` is fed directly into the designated system, typically a scalable cloud-based data warehouse, for example, Google BigQuery or Snowflake.

Transformation occurs in the data warehouse wherein raw data is cleaned and structured using SQL or a comparable query language.

It leverages the full computing power of cloud data warehouses, which can process a large amount of raw data and transform it in real-time. This usually means reduced time to load data.

- **ETL versus ELT: Key Differences in Transformation Timing:** In ETL, transformation occurs before loading, whereas in ELT, transformation occurs after a process of loading.
- **Storage Requirements:** Because ETL only loads clean data into it, storage is usually less. But ELT loads all raw data, and the storage requirements are higher, but it is flexible and can perform late transformations.
- **Performance:** Since the online data warehouse can easily process direct raw data through its distributed processing, ELT is often preferred in a cloud-based environment.

The Role of ETL Tools in Preparing Data for Superset Dashboards

The bottom line is that whether using ETL or ELT, the core objective is to have data in a structured and clean format, ready for analytics and visualization. ETL tools automate the tasks of extraction and transformation into an actionable format and subsequently load it into the warehouse. Doing so ensures that Superset receives trustworthy, clean, and up-to-date data to build dashboards on.

The number of ways ETL is crucial in the data preparation process for Superset:

- **Data Integration:** They combine data from multiple sources (for example, databases, APIs, and third-party services) into a single source of truth.
- **Data Cleansing:** The ETL tool will handle missing values, outliers, and inconsistent formats to ensure that only high-quality data is available for analysis.
- **Data Transformation**: The datasets are prepared through restructuring, aggregation, and enrichment by ETL tools for visualization in Superset.
- **Data Loading**: Once transformed, these tools load the cleaned data into a warehouse (Redshift, BigQuery, and so on) so that Superset can connect to and visualize.

Overview of Popular ETL Tools and Superset Integration

There are many ETL and ELT tools. All of them have their strengths in a given use case, scalability, and integration capabilities. A few of the popular ETL tools and their compatibility with a Superset-integrated data pipeline are summarized as follows:

- **Apache Airflow**

  Overview: Apache Airflow is an open-source, programmatically controllable, free platform to author, write, schedule, and monitor workflows. This is targeted at orchestrating complex data pipelines and managing ETL tasks.

  Superset Integration: Airflow can automatically trigger the refreshing of Superset dashboards after the completion of ETL jobs by calling the REST API of Superset.

- **Talend**

  Overview: Talend is a powerful ETL data-integration platform with open-source as well as enterprise versions for data integration, transformation, and governance. Talend can provide many connectors for various data sources.

  Superset Integration Talend will be used for the automation of data extraction, transformation, and loading. It calls the API of Superset after the completion of ETL jobs, refreshing all the dashboards.

- **Apache NiFi**

  Overview: Apache NiFi software is used to automate data flow between two systems; it provides real-time streaming ETL capabilities and high customization in the management of data flow from on-premise to cloud systems.

  Using APIs, it can integrate with Superset and be used for real-time ingestion of data; hence, it is useful when dashboards require near-real-time data.

- **Data Build Tool (dbt)**

  Overview: dbt is an ELT tool, specifically intended to build a data transformation within a data warehouse. It assists teams with modeling and transforming raw data in SQL.

  Transformations in dbt can be set up to make a call to the Superset API when refreshing dashboards so that the most recent data are rendered.

  Superset sits at the end of the data pipeline. Here, visualization and the BI layer is constructed on top of a data warehouse. While ETL toolset focuses more on the data preparation steps, Superset uses prepared data to come up with interactive dashboards and reports. Here is how Superset comes into the overall ecosystem:

Data Sources Accrued from Many Sources: Such as databases, APIs, CSVs, and so on. ETL/ELT transforms, cleans, and loads data into a data warehouse.

Superset: It pulls data from the warehouse to build dashboards, visualizations, and reports.

Setting Up Apache Airflow to Orchestrate Superset Data Pipelines

Apache Airflow is a popular choice for managing ETL workflows, and it integrates seamlessly with Superset via its API. Here is how to configure Airflow to manage ETL workflows for Superset.

Configuring Airflow for ETL and Superset

Install Airflow: Use **`pip`** to install Apache Airflow:

```
pip install apache-airflow
```

Install Additional Operators: Install the necessary operators for your data sources, for example, for PostgreSQL, MySQL, or AWS services.

```
pip install apache-airflow-providers-postgres
pip install apache-airflow-providers-amazon
```

Set Up DAGs for Orchestration: Airflow orchestrates workflows using **Directed Acyclic Graphs (DAGs)**. These are Python scripts defining tasks and their dependencies.

Example: DAG for ETL and Superset Dashboard Refresh

This example shows how to orchestrate an ETL process that extracts data from PostgreSQL, loads it into a data warehouse, and then triggers a Superset dashboard refresh.

```
from airflow import DAG
from airflow.operators.python_operator import PythonOperator
from airflow.providers.postgres.operators.postgres import PostgresOpera-
tor
from airflow.providers.http.operators.http import SimpleHttpOperator
from datetime import datetime

# Define the DAG
dag = DAG('etl_superset_refresh', start_date=datetime(2023, 1, 1),
schedule_interval='@hourly')

# Task to extract data from PostgreSQL
extract_task = PostgresOperator(
    task_id='extract_data',
    postgres_conn_id='postgres_default',
    sql='SELECT * FROM source_table',
    dag=dag
)

# Task to load data into the warehouse (dummy example)
def load_to_warehouse():
    # Load transformed data into your warehouse (Snowflake, Redshift, and
so on)
    pass

load_task = PythonOperator(
    task_id='load_to_warehouse',
    python_callable=load_to_warehouse,
    dag=dag
)

# Task to trigger Superset dashboard refresh
refresh_superset_task = SimpleHttpOperator(
    task_id='refresh_superset_dashboard',
    http_conn_id='superset_api',
    endpoint='/api/v1/dashboard/1/refresh',
    headers={"Authorization": "Bearer YOUR_API_TOKEN"},
    method='POST',
```

```
    dag=dag
)

# Set task dependencies
extract_task >> load_task >> refresh_superset_task
```

In this DAG:

- Data is extracted from PostgreSQL, loaded into a data warehouse, and then Superset is triggered to refresh its dashboards.

Talend Integration with Superset

Talend is a powerful ETL tool that provides a graphical interface for creating data flows. It offers pre-built components for connecting to databases, APIs, and cloud storage, making it an excellent choice for preparing data for Superset.

Overview of Talend's Role in Data Transformation

Talend's graphical interface allows you to design complex ETL workflows, including:

- **Extracting**: Talend can pull data from various sources (databases, files, cloud and services).
- **Transforming**: Data can be cleaned, aggregated, and enriched using Talend's data transformation tools.
- **Loading**: Talend loads the transformed data into the data warehouse for analysis.

Automating Superset Dashboard Refreshes with Talend

After Talend completes an ETL job, you can use the `tRESTClient` component to trigger a Superset dashboard refresh.

Steps to Automate Dashboard Refresh in Talend

1. **Design ETL Job**: Use Talend's GUI to design your ETL pipeline.
2. **Add `tRESTClient`**: Add the `tRESTClient` component to make an API call to the Superset API after the ETL process is complete.
3. **Configure `tRESTClient`**: Set up the API call in `tRESTClient` to refresh the dashboard:
    - **URL**: `http://superset-url/api/v1/dashboard/<dashboard_id>/refresh`
    - **Method**: POST
    - **Authorization Header**: Use the Superset API token for authentication.

4. **Deploy and Automate**: Deploy the Talend job to automate the ETL process and trigger the Superset refresh after data is loaded.

ETL (Extract, Transform, Load) and ELT (Extract, Load, Transform) processes are essential to prepare data for visualization tools such as Apache Superset. By integrating Superset with popular ETL tools such as Apache Airflow and Talend, organizations can automate data workflows, ensuring that dashboards always display fresh, actionable insights. Whether handling batch ETL jobs or real-time data pipelines, Superset fits seamlessly into the broader data pipeline ecosystem, offering flexibility, scalability, and real-time data visualization.

Building Real-Time Dashboards

In the contemporary digital context, agile and competitively responsive organizations must have real-time analytics for their mere survival. Unlike old-school analytics, real-time analytics allows the organizations to acquire instant insight on the basis of the flow of incoming data, and it supports immediate decisions on the basis of incoming trends and changing challenges or events.

- **Real-Time Dashboards Matter:** Real-time dashboards offer an always-updated view of the critical metrics. Whether one is interested in the analysis of consumer behavior, monitoring financial markets, or tracking the IoT devices, these dashboards provide real-time access to the most critical information needed for decisions involving prompt responses. They remove the delay typically associated with batch processing and hence allow stakeholders to even take action immediately. This is particularly true for fraud detection or performance analysis.
- **Common Uses of Real-Time Dashboards:** Real-time dashboards are widely applied in various industries and reflect their application to many key areas:
  - **Customer Behavior Monitoring**: E-commerce sites can monitor user behavior and track what people browse. Therefore, it is not difficult for marketers to get real-time abandonment rates and change their promotions or strategies accordingly.
  - **Financial Market Monitoring**: In case of financial market monitoring, there is real-time information on every minute stock price, currency value, and trading volume that will guide the trader.
  - **IoT Device Monitoring**: IoT-based dashboards monitor in real-time machine metrics, environmental conditions, and asset statuses that lead to timely maintenance, efficient operations, and stable systems.

Creating and Configuring Auto-Refreshing Dashboards

Setting up real-time dashboards requires configuring auto-refresh intervals so that data is updated at regular intervals, usually every few seconds to a minute, depending on the use case.

Steps to Create an Auto-Refreshing Dashboard:

1. **Create a New Dashboard**: Begin by creating a new dashboard in Superset or modifying an existing one.
2. **Add Charts and Filters**: Add the charts you want to display and apply filters, if necessary. Filters allow users to drill down into specific datasets or timeframes.
3. **Configure Refresh Intervals**: In Superset, set the dashboard to auto-refresh. A common interval is every 30 seconds, but for more time-sensitive dashboards, it could be set as low as 5-10 seconds.
4. **Test for Latency and Performance**: Ensure that the refresh rate does not overload your database or cause latency issues in Superset.

For example, if an e-commerce manager sets a 30-second refresh cycle on customer behavior data, he or she can watch and see changes in user interactions almost in real-time. If product views are growing, marketing can respond almost in time by altering recommendations or running flash promotions.

Real-Time Query Optimization Techniques

Efficiently managing real-time data is critical for performance. Here are some optimization techniques to keep your queries responsive and your dashboard fast.

Best Practices for Efficient Queries

- **Use Windowing Functions**: Rather than pulling in all data each time, use windowing functions to limit the data to a specific time range, such as the last 5 minutes.
- **Apply Time-Based Filters**: Filters such as “last 1 hour” or “last 24 hours” can restrict data to recent records, reducing the amount of data processed per query.
- **Optimize Indexes and Partitioning**: Index the fields that are frequently queried or filtered. Partitioning tables by time can also help by isolating recent data from historical data.
- **Limit Columns and Granularity**: Select only the necessary columns and avoid

querying at unnecessarily granular levels if broader data views can still meet requirements.

With mighty tools such as Apache Superset, Apache Druid, Kafka, or Kinesis on hand, businesses will be in a position to build such ever-updating dashboards actionable in customer engagement, financial analysis, and even IoT monitoring. Real-time dashboards have dramatically altered the face of data-driven operations with their features such as auto-refresh, query optimization, and efficient streaming data integration. This has allowed organizations to react effectively to key events and refine strategies towards better results.

Monitoring Data Pipelines

Pipeline monitoring is highly relevant to any data-related environment, primarily because it impacts the quality, reliability, and timeliness of the information produced in such an environment. In a pipeline feeding into analytics and decision-making tools, failure in one pipeline may mean poorly reported facts, opportunities missed, or even operational risks. This sections covers the key aspects of pipeline monitoring by discussing techniques for monitoring ETL using Apache Airflow and visualization tools such as Superset.

Significance of Pipeline Surveillance to Data Integrity

Data pipelines collect or gather raw data from several sources, transforming and loading them into data warehouses to facilitate analytics. It is necessary to monitor pipeline performance to ensure that pipelines do what is expected, providing quality information to downstream applications.

Monitoring is one component of ETL health. ETL operations are complex, involving data from many sources–some of high quality–in some formats, and accessible with varying degrees of ease. Continuous monitoring enables us to detect

- **Early Failures:** It can monitor network outages, changes in corrupted data in the schema, or resource overloads leading to pipeline failure. This enables teams to correct the problems before users get affected.
- **Assurance of Data Freshness:** Old or stale data reveals the wrong insights. Latency monitoring helps ensure data freshness and availability on time.
- **Quality Assurance and Consistency** Monitoring Quality issues, such as null values, duplicates, or data anomalies, may be caught when bringing in incorrect analytics.

Impact on Analytics by Pipeline Failure

This has downstream consequences, for instance, a pipeline failure.

- **Inaccurate Analytics**: Incorrect or inconsistent information may distort reporting and make insights invalid, therefore perhaps leading to expensive decisions.

- **Operational Disruptions**: Latency in the process of data processing will delay the responsiveness of various applications such as fraud detection, supply chain management, financial trading, and so on.
- **Very High Operation Maintenance Cost**: Repair and re-execution of defective pipes require a lot of time and money. Proactive surveillance decreases reactive maintenance and thus, low operation cost.

Monitoring ETL Pipelines with Apache Airflow

Apache Airflow is a powerful tool to orchestrate workflows, such that users can build, schedule, and monitor ETL pipelines. These monitoring capabilities, including native visualization and alerting functionalities, support complex data flow management.

Manage ETL Jobs Through Airflow's Monitoring Tools

Airflow gives a mixture of monitoring tools that allows data engineers to monitor the status of ETL jobs:

- Airflow supports representations for workflows as DAGs—each task with its dependencies—showing the entire sequence of those tasks. It provides a very good visualization of which set of stages is probably a bottleneck or a failure.
- **Gantt Charts**: Gantt charts in Airflow graph the run times of every task in a DAG. They provide insight into which tasks might be slowing down a pipeline, impacting its overall efficiency.
- **Task Time Monitoring**: Airflow captures the time taken by tasks, which facilitate the baselining process by identifying tasks that are running longer than predicted. This may indicate problems in data volume or processing inefficiency.
- **Task Logs**: All the task's logs with details of error messages and diagnostics that could be useful for debugging.

Visualization of pipeline performance and failure in Superset Availability of Airflow data will enhance integration with Superset and offer richer visualization options for pipeline performance.

- **Export Airflow Metrics**: Configure Airflow to log metrics, such as task success/failure rates, task run times, and DAG execution times, to a relational database that can be queried by Superset.
- **Connecting Superset**: This connects Superset to the database of Airflow logs. This integration helps in visualizing the ETL metrics and makes it much easier to analyze performance.

Implement Alerts and Notifications

Pipeline monitoring basically means building alerts that notify data engineers in case of a problem with the pipeline. In relation to issues concerning data quality, alerting is easy to set up with Apache Superset using SQL-based alerting.

Configuration of SQL-Driven Alerts in Superset

- **Define Alert Conditions:** Write queries based on SQL in Superset to identify conditions that require attention, such as task failures above a percentage threshold.
- **Notifications:** Use Superset's alerting feature that can send emails or a Slack notification when certain conditions are met. With such integrations, pipeline problems could be identified right away, hence a quick solution for the process.

Integration with Messaging Platforms

- **Slack Integration**: Pipeline health alerts should be integrated into Slack channels. That way, any member can stay updated on pipeline health. That would actually help both the DevOps and data engineering teams.
- **Email Notifications:** Enable Superset to send email notifications for major events such as an ETL process failure or a delay in the ingestion of data. This pushes the critical problems to reach the right people as early as possible.

Testing and Debugging Non-Working Pipelines

Proper logging could be the only way to quickly locate possible failures in an ETL pipeline. It offers detailed context on what went wrong and how not to let it happen again.

Adding Log Data to Superset Dashboards

Airflow maintains a log entry for any task, and the record can further be exported to a logging platform or relational database.

- **`VIEW LOGS IN SUPERSET`**: Create Superset charts to view logs associated with a failed task by either DAG or error type.
- **Interactive Filtering**: Filters based on error messages, task designations, or timestamps might make it possible to filter log entries relevant to specific issues.

Optimal Implemented Solution Monitoring Failed ETL Procedures

It should be set up so that Airflow documents comprehensive error messages containing schema, transformation, and source information related to the failure.

- **Retries**: Configure jobs to have Airflow manage retry policies and to ensure that transients such as net-timeout do not "**`deadlock`**" your pipeline. Introduce post-failure verification procedures. After failure, introduce data integrity checks so that the data remains valid and accurate.

Maintain data integrity and ETL operations continuously with oversight on data pipelines. Tech stacks, such as Apache Airflow and Superset, ensure a framework for detailed monitoring that includes dashboards, alerts, and logging working in unison. Thus, with these pipeline anomaly fixes happening instantly, functionality does not pause but continues, ensuring high-quality data availability for analytics and decision-making.

Conclusion

High benefits are yielded through the integration of Apache Superset in data pipelines. It improves the decision-making process significantly. Superset enables organizations to have real-time visibility into deep processes that include data. It allows them to monitor, analyze, and respond to fluctuations effectively in their data environments. As Superset can connect to numerous databases and data warehouses, it offers refreshing and flexible dashboards that are constantly dynamic in nature, providing instant snapshots of key pipeline metrics, such as latency, error rates, and throughput.

This integration further arms data teams with the much-needed tools to handle data quality and the state of pipelines. Superset offers instant alerts with respect to pipeline breakdowns or misalignments in the data so that issues are addressed in time and ensure data reliability. The high degree of visualization capabilities in Superset makes the complex patterns of data vivid, therefore enabling stakeholders at every level to have a better understanding of pipeline efficiency and make decisions in the right and informed manner. It breeds a culture of data, encourages constant optimization, and ensures strategic decisions across an organization by integrating them into data pipelines.

The next chapter will guide readers through basic EDA using Apache Superset, exploring data visually with histograms and scatter plots to identify trends and anomalies. They will learn to refine insights through filters, drill-downs, and customizations, followed by hypothesis testing to validate assumptions. By the end, readers will be able to design EDA dashboards, create reports, and effectively present their findings.

CHAPTER 9
Exploratory Data Analysis and Hypothesis Testing

Introduction

Indeed, organizations of all kinds in the data world collect more information than ever before in history. Yet, raw data alone cannot be translated into actionable knowledge. The secret to using data depends on how the data is mined and understood—a process that begins with Exploratory Data Analysis (EDA). EDA forms the bedrock of any data science or analytics project because it exposes underlying patterns and anomalies in the relationships within the dataset and hence guides decision-makers toward informed action.

EDA forms the basis of most analytics, modeling, and decision-making activities. In that regard, it should point out trends or patterns, seasonality, or long-term changes that affect business strategies. EDA can also be helpful in identifying outliers or anomalies. These could represent low data quality or something worth investigating in more detail. The chapter concludes with the generation of hypotheses and preparing data for advanced modeling, in turn ensuring that it will be in a suitable form for complex analyses. Finally, it encourages an intuitive understanding of the "personality" of the data in relation to real-world assumptions and predictions.

Structure

In this chapter, we will cover the following topics:

- Introduction to Exploratory Data Analysis (EDA)
- Connecting and Preparing Data for EDA
- Exploring Data with Basic Charts (Histograms, Scatter Plots, and More)
- Identifying Trends, Outliers, and Patterns

- Using Filters and Drill-Downs for Deeper Insights
- Generating Insights and Sharing Reports
- Creating an EDA Dashboard
- Introduction to Hypothesis Testing in Data Analysis
- Conducting Hypothesis Tests in Apache Superset

Introduction to Exploratory Data Analysis (EDA)

EDA is an essential step in the data analysis process that demonstrates a firsthand understanding of the structure of a dataset, with instances of trends and anomalies. EDA is designed to enable data scientists and analysts to examine and explore their data prior to modeling or hypothesis testing so as to discover insights that are not immediately apparent when raw data is observed. This section captures the purpose of EDA, its general benefits, and how Apache Superset is part of the toolset to achieve efficient and insightful data exploration.

Purpose of EDA

EDA is crucial in any project that is data-driven, as it allows analysts to understand the details of the data they work with. Goals of EDA:

- It then has a tendency to detect patterns and relationships underlying some variables that might be hidden, which guides further analysis.
- **Identification of Data Quality Issues:** EDA might reveal inconsistencies, missing values, or outliers in the data using various visualizations and summary statistics that need to be addressed before modeling.
- **Analyze and Modeling Strategy:** Analyzes the distribution of data to be able to assume the right type of model or analysis technique to be used for the particular dataset.
- It refines questions and hypotheses; insights from EDA often generate or refine hypotheses to provide direction to the analysis process. Through the course of these steps, EDA acts as a discovery phase that helps analysts make smart decisions regarding preprocessing data, feature engineering, and the way toward an analytical approach.

EDA versus Traditional Analysis

EDA is also different from the traditionally conceived, confirmatory data analysis in terms of being exploratory and flexible. Here are some of those differences:

- **Exploratory versus Confirmatory:** EDA allows one to explore the data with flexibility and often without any kind of predefined hypotheses. The analyst uses charts, plots, and summary statistics to see what patterns emerge, and therefore, it is perfect for open-ended questions.

  EDA is hypothesis-driven and follows a more structured path as compared to the other. In EDA, one analyzes the data with respect to specific hypotheses or expectations that are to be confirmed or rejected. This is normally the step following EDA involving hypothesis testing, significance levels, and other statistical techniques to validate findings.

- **Iterative Process:** EDA is often an iterative process in which, as analysts find patterns or anomalies, they clean the data, transform variables, or establish new metrics to start interpreting the dataset.

  Traditional analysis is more formal and used mainly in deriving conclusions or making predictions with prior settings of assumptions.

- **Flexibility versus Formality:** This, instead, fosters a more flexible approach where analysts feel free to try several visualizations and analyses without strict statistical requirements. Confirmatory analysis, on the other hand, depends on specific methodologies, such as hypothesis testing and regression analysis, to produce statistically valid insights. This means that although there is a complementarity between EDA and confirmatory analysis, the two differ in their purposes. EDA is about exploration and discovery, laying the groundwork for confirmatory analysis and hypothesis testing.

Benefits of EDA

EDA offers several benefits that extend across the data lifecycle:

- **Improves Data Quality:** EDA is able to make quick errors or anomaly detection by inspecting data using graphical display and statistical summary that makes future datasets cleaner and more dependable. This activity, thereby, not only builds confidence in the analytical result but also in the decision-making and modeling activities themselves.

- **Detecting Outliers and Anomalies:** EDA makes it easier to spot unusual values, which might skew results if left unaddressed.

  In general, EDA will highlight missing or inconsistent data through summary statistics and possibly some visualizations that may need cleaning or imputation.

- **Helps in Feature Selection**: EDA will unfold features most relevant to a given analysis or model, concerning the exploration of correlations, distributions, and relationships between variables. All this may decrease the number of dimensions in data, provide better models, and reduce computational complexity.

- **Improves Understanding of Context of Data**: From EDA, analysts may gain an intuition about the context in which the dataset lives–for example, seasonality, possible causal relationships, or demographic patterns–and build upon that basis a more robust analysis and predictive models.
- **Hypothesis Formulation and Testing Guides Patterns in EDA**: It may be used to refine or even hypothesize the look that should then be confirmed or tested statistically through formal analysis. For example, if they find a trend in EDA, they can hypothesize something that can then be tested via formal analysis. All these advantages make EDA an essential part of the data analysis process, enhancing accuracy and efficiency and offering insightfulness in downstream analyses.

Role of Apache Superset in EDA

A cursory look would say that Apache Superset is the open-source Business Intelligence tool, capable of versatile interactive data visualization. In Superset, one can connect to their data sources, create dashboards, and build visualizations, making it ideal for EDA. Here is how Superset supports each phase of EDA:

- **Prep and Join Data:** Superset is highly pliable to support numerous data sources such as SQL databases, cloud-based warehouses, and CSV files, making it very practical for other architectures.

  Transformations can take place directly in Superset using SQL-based transformation, which does make data preparation via aggregations and filtering very easy.
- **Graph Developments**: The interface of Superset allows for the generation of different types of charts, such as bar charts, line graphs, scatter plots, and heatmaps. Therefore, these are the most important visuals in EDA when looking for trends, distributions, and relationships.

  The tool further supports the application of more complex visualizations, such as box plots and violin plots, for the purpose of analyzing the variability, outliers, and clusters of data.
- **Build Interactive Dashboards:** Superset enables analysts to combine a number of charts and views, giving a panoramic view of the data in dashboards.

  Dashboards can be designed with interactive filtering and drill-down capabilities so that users can interact dynamically with the data by filtering or zooming into certain areas for deeper insights.

- **Customizable Reporting and Sharing**: Superset enables exporting dashboards and reports. This makes it easy to share findings with team members or stakeholders. Reports can also be personalized in terms of how the data should be reported, summarized, and interpreted. It is also open-source, so it is a highly customizable and accessible tool for data teams of any size. Superset makes the EDA process much easier and faster by transforming data into actionable insights.

EDA is an essential phase in any data analysis project, as it allows analysts to delve into their data before they start drawing a basis for hypothesis testing or model building. EDA with Apache Superset can, therefore, become very smooth and visually driven, thereby helping teams deeply understand the trends, patterns, and relationships in the data. Everything laid down by EDA puts analysts in a better standing to design meaningful hypotheses, optimize data quality, and make data-driven decisions.

Connecting and Preparing Data for EDA

Data preparation plays an important role in working with the Pre-Exploratory Data Analysis process in the workflow of data analysis. The process includes connecting to appropriate data sources, cleaning up and transforming data, and preparing virtual datasets before analyzing the data. Apache Superset is an open-source BI tool that has the proficiency to connect with multiple data sources and prepare data for analysis using SQL-based transformations. This section digs deeper into the preparation steps so that users can easily transit to the EDA stage with quality and well-prepared data.

Overview of Data Sources

Apache Superset supports a wide variety of data sources, allowing users to connect to both structured and semi-structured data from numerous database platforms. This flexibility makes it suitable for diverse data environments, from small-scale setups to large enterprise data warehouses.

- **Relational Databases:**
    - **Supported Databases**: Superset can connect to popular relational databases, including **MySQL**, **PostgreSQL**, **SQLite**, and **MariaDB**.
    - **Use Case**: Relational databases are ideal for structured data with defined relationships, allowing Superset users to perform SQL queries and join tables for comprehensive data exploration.
- **Data Warehouses:**
    - **Supported Warehouses**: Superset integrates with cloud-based data warehouses such as **Amazon Redshift**, **Google BigQuery**, **Snowflake**, and **Microsoft Azure SQL Data Warehouse**.

- **Use Case**: For large-scale analytics, data warehouses are well-suited due to their ability to handle massive datasets and provide high performance for complex queries. They are ideal for enterprises managing extensive historical data or conducting business intelligence across multiple departments.

- **File-Based Sources:**
  - **CSV and Excel Files**: Superset can import flat files (for example, CSVs) for smaller or ad-hoc datasets that may not be stored in a database.
  - **Use Case**: Flat files are helpful for smaller, one-time analyses, or when pulling data from web sources, surveys, or other external systems that may not directly connect to a database.
- **NoSQL Databases:**
  - **Supported NoSQL Databases**: Superset has support for **MongoDB**, **Elasticsearch**, and **Druid**, which are commonly used for semi-structured or unstructured data.
  - **Use Case**: NoSQL databases are useful for data that lacks a strict schema, such as logs, text data, or large JSON datasets. Superset can connect to these databases, though complex transformations may still require pre-processing.
- **Data Lake Integrations:**
  - **Apache Hive** and **Presto** allow Superset to pull data directly from data lakes.
  - **Use Case**: Data lakes store vast amounts of raw data and are optimized for unstructured or varied formats, providing a cost-effective storage solution for big data analysis. By connecting Superset to data lakes, users can run SQL queries across massive data repositories, making it possible to perform EDA on raw or lightly processed data.

Data Cleaning and Transformation

Data cleaning is an essential process to ensure EDA has clean, unambiguous, error-free data. Cleaning and transformation make sure nothing such as missing values or outliers skews the results of analysis. It is not that Apache Superset has such advanced data-cleaning tools, but ideally, data should be pre-processed in a database or a data pipeline before being connected to Superset.

Handling Missing Values:

- **Identifying Missing Data**: It is essential to identify any columns or rows with missing data to avoid skewing analysis.

- **Methods for Handling Missing Values**:
    - **Imputation**: Replace missing values with the mean, median, or mode, depending on the variable type.
    - **Deletion**: Remove rows or columns with a high percentage of missing values, especially if they are not critical to analysis.
    - **Placeholder Values**: In some cases, filling missing data with placeholder values (for example, "*Unknown*" for categorical data) can help maintain dataset integrity.
- **Execution**: Ideally, handle missing values within your data warehouse or through ETL (Extract, Transform, Load) processes before importing into Superset. Alternatively, users can write SQL expressions within Superset's virtual datasets to apply basic handling for missing data.

Handling Outliers:

- **Identifying Outliers**: Use statistical methods (such as standard deviation or interquartile range) to spot outliers, which are unusually high or low values that may distort the results.
- **Methods for Handling Outliers**:
    - **Capping**: Set outlier values to a maximum or minimum threshold if the values are implausible but could impact analysis (for example, capping salary data to an upper threshold).
    - **Transformation**: Apply transformations (for example, log transformations) to normalize data with extreme outliers.
    - **Exclusion**: For extreme cases, exclude outliers from the dataset if they are not relevant to the analysis (for example, excluding abnormal sales spikes).
- **Execution**: Outlier handling can be performed in Superset by creating SQL-based virtual datasets to filter or cap values dynamically during analysis.

Standardization and Normalization:

- **Standardization**: Standardizing data to have a mean of 0 and a standard deviation of 1 helps when comparing data with varying scales, such as age and income. This can be particularly useful in visualization, as it ensures a more consistent representation.
- **Normalization**: Rescaling data to a range (for example, 0 to 1) can be useful for ratio-based comparisons or specific types of charts.
- **Execution**: Standardization and normalization are best done within a database or data pipeline. Superset allows basic transformations using SQL expressions if more flexibility is needed on a case-by-case basis.

Data Type Consistency:

- Ensuring consistency in data types (for example, integers, dates, and strings) prevents issues in analysis or visualization. Superset will automatically detect data types upon import, but analysts should verify them to ensure data is interpreted correctly.

Creating Virtual Datasets in Superset

Superset allows users to transform, filter, and customize data right within the platform using its virtual dataset. Once virtual datasets are defined, after the first usage of SQL expressions, it will enable highly sophisticated versions of the data and, thereby, better EDA than the original source.

- **Setting Up Virtual Datasets**: Superset offers a SQL Lab interface through which one can create virtual datasets where one would be able to write a custom SQL query that defines one's dataset.

  Now, with virtual datasets, customized filters, aggregations, and joins can easily be applied to combine a couple of tables or extract special subsets of data. For instance, a sales and operations planning analyst may create a dataset that only has sales data from the last year grouped by product category.

  - **Using SQL Expressions for Transformation**: Calculated fields can be assigned using SQL functions. Thus, for example, the "`Sales_Per_Product`" calculated field can be assigned with just a simple division of total sales by the products sold.
  - **Filtering Data**: SQL "`WHERE`" clauses can be used to filter a dataset by criteria, for example, records that would indicate sales greater than some amount.
  - **Date Transformation**: The SQL function can be used to date format or group data by specific time periods, which helps when working with a time-based analysis.

- **Optimizing for Performance**: Users can also create summary tables with virtual datasets. Summary tables enable user data to be pre-aggregated, which helps improve query performance. For example, a virtual dataset may have the monthly sales aggregated. This means when Superset is generating a visualization, Superset does not have to take time querying raw transactional data every time.

  Indexing fields commonly used in filtering or joins can sometimes help performance but largely applies only in big data.

- **Using Virtual Datasets for Drill-Downs and Explorations**: Virtual datasets in Superset provide multiple tiers of filtering, aggregation, and calculated fields, so they support deeper drill-down and exploration on dashboards. For example, users can set up a virtual dataset based on joined customer demographics and purchase data that provides a single context for exploring the purchases by age or by geographic region.

It would allow analysts to focus on a set of questions or insights that can be derived from the data, thus streamlining their analysis and improving the responsiveness of Superset. Virtual datasets can also be a very natural foundation for creating visualizations and interactive dashboards, thus leading to a very customized and insightful EDA experience.

Connecting and setting up data for EDA in Apache Superset requires understanding the origin of the data sources and then performing necessary data cleaning tasks and creating virtual datasets for refined analysis. This cleaning of data gives proper accuracy in the visualizations produced by Superset. Moreover, virtual datasets allow filtering, transforming, and drilling down into the data without affecting the source. It is here that analysts can then proceed accordingly and confidently to either the visualization or the exploratory phases of EDA, with clean and relevant data.

Exploring Data with Basic Charts in Apache Superset

EDA, it seems, acts around the whole visualization process–taking raw data and bringing insights into different types of visuals that are readable and analytical. Apache Superset provides a rich variety of visualization options, from very basic to sophisticated, to enable the user to explore data trends, distributions, relationships, and patterns using interactive charts and dashboards. In this section, we will go over the available chart types in Superset, show how to create common charts for EDA, and provide guidance on choosing the right chart type for various data analysis goals.

Overview of Available Charts and Visualization Tools in Superset

Apache Superset provides a rich selection of visualization tools, divided into **basic** and **advanced** categories:

- **Basic Chart Types:**
  - **Bar Charts**: Used to compare categorical data or summarize numerical data by category.
  - **Line Charts**: Ideal for visualizing data trends over time, where data points are connected to show continuous change.

- **Area Charts**: Similar to line charts but with filled areas, area charts emphasize volume or magnitude over time.
- **Scatter Plots**: Used to observe the relationship between two numerical variables, helpful for identifying correlations and clusters.
- **Histograms**: These are essential for viewing the distribution of a single variable, showing the frequency of data points within different ranges.

- **Advanced Chart Types**:
  - **Box Plots**: Box plots display the spread and distribution of data, highlighting quartiles and outliers.
  - **Violin Plots**: Similar to box plots, violin plots provide additional information about data density, showing the distribution shape along with data spread.
  - **Heatmaps**: A heatmap visualizes data density across two variables using color, often used to show correlation or intensity in a grid format.
  - **Pie and Donut Charts**: Used to show proportional data or composition within a single category, often limited to fewer data points to avoid clutter.
  - **Geospatial Maps**: Superset offers geospatial visualizations for location-based data, allowing users to plot data points or heatmaps on geographic maps.
  - **Bubble Charts**: Similar to scatter plots but with an additional dimension represented by bubble size, often used for data with three variables.
- **Other Interactive Features**:
  - **Filters**: Interactive filters let users customize data views and explore subsets within visualizations, enhancing analysis flexibility.
  - **Drill-Downs**: Superset supports drill-down options, where users can click on a data point to explore further details or related metrics.

With these chart types, Superset empowers analysts to perform a wide range of EDA tasks, from simple comparisons to complex multidimensional analyses.

Creating Basic Charts for EDA

Using Superset's charting capabilities, we will go over a few essential chart types that are fundamental to EDA.

Histograms: Understanding Data Distribution

Histograms are used to examine the distribution of a single variable. This chart divides the data into bins (intervals) and counts the frequency of data points within each bin, helping analysts identify data distribution patterns, skewness, and modality.

1. **Creating a Histogram in Superset**:
    a. In the chart creation interface, select "**`Histogram`**" as the chart type.
    b. Choose the variable you want to analyze (for example, "**`Sales`**" or "**`Age`**").
    c. Define the number of bins to control the granularity of the distribution (for example, 10 or 20 bins).
2. **Insights from Histograms**:
    a. **Skewness**: Whether the data leans towards higher or lower values (right-skewed or left-skewed).
    b. **Modality**: The number of peaks in the histogram (unimodal, bimodal, and so on).
    c. **Outliers**: Unusually high or low values will appear as isolated bars at the ends of the histogram.

Scatter Plots: Exploring Relationships Between Variables

Scatter plots help visualize the relationship between two numerical variables, often used to examine correlations and clustering.

1. **Creating a Scatter Plot in Superset**:
    a. Choose "**`Scatter Plot`**" as the chart type.
    b. Select the X-axis and Y-axis variables you wish to explore (for example, "**`Ad Spend`**" on the X-axis and "**`Revenue`**" on the Y-axis).
    c. Adjust point size and color if there is a third variable you did like to represent, such as the number of customers.
2. **Insights from Scatter Plots**:
    a. **Correlation**: A clear upward or downward trend indicates positive or negative correlation, respectively.
    b. **Clusters**: Groups of points can reveal natural segments within the data.
    c. **Outliers**: Isolated points far from the main distribution can indicate outliers or anomalies.

Line and Area Charts: Analyzing Trends Over Time

Line and area charts are particularly useful for examining time series data, where the focus is on trends over a continuous time period.

1. **Creating a Line Chart in Superset**:
   - Select "`Line Chart`" as the chart type.
   - Choose a date/time variable for the X-axis and a numerical variable for the Y-axis (for example, "`Date`" on the X-axis and "`Monthly Revenue`" on the Y-axis).
   - Customize line color, thickness, and add markers for clarity.
2. **Creating an Area Chart in Superset**:
   - Select "`Area Chart`" and follow similar steps to those for line charts.
   - The area beneath the line will be filled, emphasizing volume over time.
3. **Insights from Line and Area Charts**:
   - **Trend Detection**: Identify long-term increases or decreases in values.
   - **Seasonality**: Look for recurring peaks and valleys that indicate seasonal patterns.
   - **Volatility**: Sharp spikes or dips in the line reveal high volatility in the data.

Box Plots and Violin Plots: Identifying Data Spread, Variance, and Outliers

Box plots and violin plots are helpful for understanding the spread of data, variance, and the presence of outliers. These charts display the median, quartiles, and outliers, providing a visual summary of data distribution.

1. **Creating a Box Plot in Superset**:
   a. Choose "`Box Plot`" as the chart type.
   b. Select the categorical variable for grouping (for example, "`Region`") and the numerical variable to analyze (for example, "`Sales Amount`").
   c. Configure whiskers to control how far the plot extends to capture outliers.
2. **Creating a Violin Plot in Superset**:
   a. Choose "`Violin Plot`" for a view that includes data density along with spread.
   b. Like box plots, assign a categorical and a numerical variable, and adjust settings to control smoothing for a clearer shape.
3. **Insights from Box and Violin Plots**:
   a. **Outliers**: Extreme values appear as points outside the whiskers in box plots or as bumps on the edges of violin plots.

b. **Data Spread and Variance**: The length of the box or width of the violin indicates variability; a wider spread means higher variance.

c. **Comparing Groups**: Multiple box or violin plots can show differences in spread or central tendency between categories (for example, comparing sales across regions).

Choosing the Right Chart Type

Selecting the right chart type is crucial for effectively communicating insights. Here are some tips to help you choose based on your data type and analysis goals:

- **Data Distribution**: Use **histograms** for single-variable distributions and **box or violin plots** when comparing distributions across groups.
- **Trend Analysis**: For time series or trend analysis, use **line** or **area charts** to reveal patterns and seasonal effects.
- **Relationships and Correlation**: To explore relationships between two numerical variables, use a **scatter plot**. Add bubble size or color to represent additional variables if needed.
- **Comparative Analysis**: For comparing categorical data, **bar charts** are ideal. When comparing continuous data across categories, **box or violin plots** can show differences in spread, median, and outliers.
- **Geospatial Analysis**: For data with a geographic component, **map visualizations** (such as points or heatmaps) can highlight location-based patterns.
- **Composition Analysis**: **Pie** or **donut charts** are best for showing proportions within a single category, though they work well only for datasets with few categories.

From there, users can select the best chart for their data type and the objectives of analysis to maximize clarity and effectiveness in their visualizations. The lengthy list of charts that Superset provides guarantees analysts are set up for any EDA scenario they will need to quickly generate actionable insights and communicate those conclusions quickly and effectively.

Identifying Trends, Outliers, and Patterns

In general, there are trends, outliers, and patterns. Exploratory Data Analysis is a technique that can help the analyst find the underlying structure in data, gain knowledge of how the data evolves with time, and inform decisions, all of which can be done easily using the visualization tools of Apache Superset: line and area charts, box plots, scatter plots, and so on.

Identifying Trends

Trends are long-period movements in the data over time. It means trends can basically indicate a general uptrend, a downtrend, or even stable values. In certain situations, trends can also include seasonal patterns–the periodic changes that occur at established, anticipated intervals, such as the cyclical monthly peaks in sales or yearly revenue fluctuations.

Using Line Charts to Detect Trends:

- **Long-Term Trends**: Line charts are ideal for visualizing trends over extended periods, such as years or quarters. A clear upward or downward movement in the line indicates a trend.
- **Trend Smoothing**: In cases where data is volatile, adding a moving average to the line chart can help smooth out fluctuations and make the underlying trend more apparent.

Using Area Charts for Trends and Magnitude:

- **Area Emphasis**: Area charts are particularly useful for displaying cumulative values over time (for example, total sales), emphasizing the magnitude of change.
- **Stacked Area Charts**: These are useful when analyzing multiple trends simultaneously, as each layer's size reveals the contribution of different categories over time.

Detecting Seasonality:

- Recurring peaks or valleys on line or area charts indicate seasonal patterns. For example, a line chart of monthly sales data may show higher sales every December, suggesting a seasonal trend around the holidays.
- **Example**: A retail business might see an annual spike in sales around Black Friday and Christmas. By examining these seasonal trends, the company can better forecast demand and manage inventory.

Detecting Outliers

Outliers are data points that are significantly removed from the rest of the data set. They may depict errors, unusual events, or even occurrences that require closer observation. If left uncontrolled, outliers can distort analysis and, worse, lead to false conclusions.

Using Box Plots to Spot Outliers:

- **Box Plot Structure**: A box plot displays the median, quartiles, and outliers of a dataset. Data points that fall outside the "whiskers" (typically 1.5 times the interquartile range) are considered outliers.

- **Interpreting Outliers**: Points outside the whiskers indicate data that deviates from typical values. For example, a box plot of customer purchase amounts may reveal that a few customers have unusually high purchase totals.

Using Scatter Plots for Outlier Detection:

- **Scatter Plot Dynamics**: Scatter plots help identify relationships between two variables, making it easy to spot data points that fall far from the main distribution.
- **Isolated Points**: Outliers in scatter plots are often represented as isolated points away from clusters. These may signify data entry errors, unusual events, or legitimate, unique cases.

Role of Outliers in Analysis:

- Outliers may represent valuable insights or critical events (such as a one-time surge in web traffic) that should not be disregarded.
- **Example**: In a financial dataset, outliers could be fraudulent transactions. Identifying these transactions helps in detecting unusual behavior and improving security.

Recognizing Patterns

Patterns in data reveal relationships and associations among variables, helping to identify correlations, clusters, or groupings.

- **Finding Correlations:**
  - **Scatter Plots for Correlation**: Scatter plots are effective for spotting correlations between two variables. A positive or negative slope in the scatter plot points indicates correlation strength and direction.
  - **Example**: In a marketing dataset, a positive correlation between "`Ad Spend`" and "`Sales`" may indicate that higher ad spending leads to increased sales.
- **Identifying Groupings with Heatmaps and Clustered Scatter Plots**:
  - **Heatmaps**: Heatmaps can be used to detect data density, helping identify regions where data points are highly concentrated. These patterns can reveal relationships or high-activity areas in the data.
  - **Clustered Scatter Plots**: Scatter plots can show natural clusters of data points. For example, grouping customers by purchase amount and frequency may reveal distinct segments, such as high-value or infrequent buyers.

- **Recurring Patterns:**
    - **Visual Analysis for Patterns**: Visualizing recurring patterns–such as seasonal patterns in time series or repeated sequences–helps predict future behavior.
    - **Example**: An analysis of website traffic data might reveal recurring spikes on Mondays, indicating that users are more active at the beginning of the workweek.

Using Filters and Drill-Downs for Deeper Insights

The drill-downs and filters will prove useful to translate a high-level view into a more specific view in the exploration of the data to understand finer details. The functionalities built into Superset enable analysts and end-users to access the data on much more granular levels, going down into subsets to compare segments or explore details that otherwise get lost in visualization at the higher levels. This describes the configuration and use of filters and drill-downs in Superset, aiming to help you find deeper insights from your data.

Setting Up Filters in Superset

Superset makes it easy to apply various types of filters to visualizations. Here is a step-by-step guide to setting up filters to refine your data view:

1. **Access the Chart Builder**: Start by creating or editing a chart in Superset. Go to the `Chart Builder` and choose the desired chart type (for example, line chart and bar chart).
2. **Select Filter Options**: In the chart configuration panel, locate the "`Filters`" section. Here, you can add multiple filters based on different criteria.
3. **Apply Different Types of Filters**:
    - **Time-Based Filters**:
        a. Use time-based filters to focus on specific periods (for example, year, quarter, and month).
        b. Select the "`Time Range`" option to filter data for a particular date range, such as "`Last 30 days`" or "`Previous year`."
    - **Category Filters:**
        a. Apply category filters to focus on specific attributes, such as "`Region`," "`Product Category`," or "`Customer Segment`."

b. Add filters by selecting a column and specifying criteria (for example, "`Region = North America`" or "`Product Category = Electronics`").

- **Numeric Filters:**

a. For numeric data, set conditions such as "`greater than`," "`less than`," or "`equals`." For instance, filtering "`Sales > 1000`" isolates data where sales exceed a certain amount.

4. **Testing and Viewing Results**: After applying filters, review the chart to see the refined data view. Adjust or add multiple filters, if needed, to drill further into specific insights.

Filters can be saved with the chart or dashboard, making it easy for users to view data with the same criteria applied each time they access the visualization.

Drill-Down Capabilities

It creates a drill-down effect, allowing the users to "`drill`" from high-level view to more specific points from within a visualization. Thus, it ensures that data is layered for the users to click its constituent element to unveil finer details from it.

Setting Up Drill-Downs in Superset:

1. **Enable Drill-Down for Relevant Charts**: Select charts that support drill-downs (for example, bar charts or pie charts with category groups).
2. **Define Hierarchies**: Set up hierarchies in your data (for example, `Year` > `Quarter` > `Month` for time-based analysis or `Region` > `Country` > `City` for geographic analysis).
3. **Using Drill-Down Interactively**:
   - Once drill-down is enabled, users can click a category or data point in the chart. This action reveals a deeper view, such as breaking down "`Region`" into "`Country`" or viewing a specific year's sales by quarter.
4. **Multiple Drill-Down Levels**: In Superset, it is possible to add multiple layers to drilldown further, allowing users to go as deep as necessary into the data.

For example, in a sales dashboard, clicking a bar representing total sales for a region could drill down into specific countries within that region, then down further into cities, revealing precise sales performance across different geographic levels.

Apache Superset's amazing tools in filtering and drill-downs are to be used for the refinement of views of data, comparison of segments, and getting drilled down for more insight. The integration of such features allows analysts to do very detailed comparative analyses as well as provide user-centric dashboards that give stakeholders interactivity in working with data. Such interactivity helps improve the quality of insights derived and fosters engagement so as to make informed decisions.

Generating Insights and Sharing Reports

Actionable insights will be the final and most important step in any data analysis process. The visualization and reporting capabilities of Apache Superset make it easier to break complex data into meaningful insights, summarize the findings, and share them with the stakeholders. This is the section describing how one can get insights from visualizations, summarizing insights made, exporting and sharing reports, and collaborating with other team members.

Creating Insights from Visuals

Visualizations are powerful tools, but turning them into actionable insights requires interpretation and context. To extract valuable insights, analysts should focus on patterns, trends, relationships, and anomalies presented by the visuals.

Steps for Translating Visuals into Actionable Insights:

1. **Identify Key Patterns and Trends**: Look for long-term trends, recurring seasonal patterns, or any noticeable shifts in the data. For example, if a line chart shows a steady increase in sales over a few quarters, this trend might indicate positive growth momentum.

2. **Examine Anomalies and Outliers**: Highlight outliers or unusual spikes/drops in the data, as these may indicate significant events, errors, or unique cases. For example, a sudden spike in website traffic might coincide with a marketing campaign.

3. **Evaluate Relationships and Correlations**: Assess correlations in scatter plots or grouped patterns in heatmaps to determine if variables are related. For instance, a scatter plot showing a strong positive correlation between customer satisfaction and repeat purchases suggests that improving satisfaction could boost customer retention.

4. **Provide Context**: Add context by correlating findings with external factors, historical data, or known business activities (for example, a seasonal sales increase around holidays).

5. **Develop Recommendations**: Convert observations into recommendations. For example, if data shows that product sales peak during certain months, the insight might be to increase stock or run targeted promotions during those months.

By consistently following these steps, analysts can ensure that each visualization tells a clear story, making it easier for stakeholders to understand and act on the insights.

Summarizing Findings

Summarizing findings effectively allows stakeholders to quickly grasp the essence of an analysis. Superset's dashboard and reporting capabilities make it possible to compile visualizations and insights into a cohesive report.

Best Practices for Summarizing Insights in Superset:

- **Highlight Key Takeaways**: Start each report section with a brief summary of the most important insights. Use bullet points or headers to keep this section concise.
- **Use Annotations and Labels**: Add annotations, titles, and labels to visualizations in Superset to guide readers. For example, use captions to highlight an upward trend or to note a particular outlier.
- **Organize Findings by Themes**: Group insights based on related themes or metrics, such as "Sales Performance," "Customer Retention," or "Marketing Impact." This organization makes it easier for readers to focus on specific areas of interest.
- **Provide Context and Background**: Give background information for significant findings. For example, if reporting a dip in sales, include potential reasons, such as seasonality or market factors.
- **Include Actionable Recommendations**: Conclude the report with recommendations that stem from the analysis, connecting the findings with possible business actions.

Following these best practices will ensure that reports are clear, focused, and valuable to decision-makers.

Exporting and Sharing Reports

Apache Superset provides various methods for exporting visualizations and dashboards to facilitate reporting and presentation. By sharing insights in formats that stakeholders can easily access and understand, analysts can broaden the reach and impact of their findings.

Methods for Exporting Reports in Superset:

1. **Exporting as PDF**: Superset allows users to export dashboards and reports as PDFs. This format is ideal for distributing reports via email or printing hard copies for meetings. To export as PDF:

a. Open the dashboard or chart.

b. Select the export option and choose "`Export as PDF`."

c. Save the PDF file to distribute as needed.

2. **Exporting Visualizations as Images**: Individual charts can be exported as images (for example, PNG or JPEG), making it easy to include specific visuals in presentations, documents, or emails.

   a. Right-click the visualization or select the export option to save it as an image.

3. **Exporting to CSV**: For stakeholders interested in the raw data behind the visualizations, Superset allows data exports to CSV files.

   a. Go to the chart or dataset and select "`Export to CSV`" to download the data.

4. **Embedding Dashboards and Charts**: Superset supports embedding dashboards and charts into other platforms (for example, intranet sites or presentations) by generating an iframe link or embedding code.

   a. This setup allows live data updates in embedded reports, providing real-time insights without manual updating.

These exporting options make it easy to customize reports to meet the needs of different stakeholders, whether they prefer PDFs, images, or direct data access.

Collaborative Sharing Options

Effective data collaboration often requires that team members work together on reports, access updated versions, and provide feedback. Superset offers various features that support collaborative work, version control, and access management.

Options for Collaborative Sharing in Superset:

- **Report Sharing and Access Control**: Superset allows for controlled sharing of dashboards and reports. User roles and permissions can be configured to define who can view, edit, or manage each report.

  a. Go to the dashboard or report settings to configure user access permissions.

  b. Define roles (for example, viewer, editor, or administrator) to ensure the right people have the appropriate level of access.

- **Versioning for Report Updates**:

  a. To maintain accuracy and consistency, create a versioning system for updates. Superset does not have built-in versioning, so teams may create a versioning policy for major report updates (for example, "**`Dashboard_v1`**," "**`Dashboard_v2`**") to track changes.

b. When updates are made, save a copy of the previous version for reference and communicate changes to relevant stakeholders.

- **Annotations and Comments**: Superset allows users to add annotations to charts and dashboards, enabling team members to highlight important findings, add context, or suggest edits directly on the visualization. While it does not support in-platform commenting, annotations act as a way to communicate context within the dashboard itself.
- **Integrating with Other Collaboration Tools**: Superset can be integrated with other project management or BI platforms, making it easier to share insights across tools. For instance, connecting Superset with a platform such as Slack or an internal messaging tool enables automated sharing of updated reports.
- **Scheduled Reports**: Use Superset's scheduling feature to automate report distribution. Schedule reports to be generated and shared at regular intervals, such as weekly or monthly, ensuring stakeholders always have the latest data.

Example of a Collaborative Workflow:

- A marketing team needs to review and update a dashboard on campaign performance. The team lead sets the access control so that analysts have editing permissions while executives have view-only access.
- The team saves an initial version of the report and labels it "**`Campaign_Performance_v1`**." As the team continues to update the report, new versions are saved with incremental labels (for example, "**`_v2`**," "**`_v3`**") to keep a record of changes.
- Annotations are added to highlight performance milestones, such as the launch date of a new campaign or a specific week's surge in conversions.
- The team schedules the dashboard to be shared with executives every Monday morning, keeping them informed of campaign performance.

By leveraging these collaborative options, teams can ensure that reports are accessible, up-to-date, and contextually enriched for all stakeholders.

Since effective sharing generates actionable insights that are crucial for the impact of data analysis, in addition to all these, through Apache Superset, analysts can derive meaningful insights from visualizations, create well-organized summaries, and use export and sharing options for easy report distribution. Collaboration features include access control, versioning, annotations, and scheduled sharing that support teamwork allowing various stakeholders to engage with the data and make informed, data-driven decisions.

Creating an EDA Dashboard in Apache Superset

It is ensured that the well-crafted dashboards provide users with ease to understand the key insights and interact with the data for making informed decisions. Good dashboards are visually characterized by hierarchies of charts, interactivity, and user-friendly interfaces. This part revolves around the principles of dashboard design, interaction, and charts, along with integrating them, adding interactivity to them, and reusable templates for the common needs in EDA.

Designing a Dashboard Layout

The layout of a dashboard plays a vital role in enhancing its readability and usability. A well-organized dashboard uses layout, color, and visualization hierarchy to guide users' attention and ensure that insights are easy to find and interpret.

1. **Visualization Hierarchy**:

    a. **Top-to-Bottom and Left-to-Right Structure**: Place the most important information at the top-left of the dashboard, as this is where users typically start viewing. Use this area for high-level KPIs or summary metrics.

    b. **Group Related Visuals Together**: Arrange charts that are related close to each other to help users connect related insights. For example, place monthly sales charts alongside quarterly sales charts for a cohesive view.

    c. **Progressive Detail**: Organize information so that the most general insights appear first, with details or breakdowns below or to the side. For instance, start with total revenue and then display revenue by region or product category.

2. **Color Scheme**:

    a. **Consistent Colors**: Use consistent colors across charts to represent the same variables or categories. If "`Revenue`" is green in one chart, it should be green in all charts to maintain consistency.

    b. **Highlighting Key Metrics**: Use bright or contrasting colors to highlight critical metrics or data points, such as goals achieved or outliers. Muted colors work well for less critical information.

    c. **Accessible Color Choices**: Use color schemes that are color-blind-friendly and avoid overusing red/green combinations, which can be challenging for users with color vision deficiencies.

3. **Spacing and Alignment**:

    a. **Balanced White Space**: Use white space effectively to prevent visual clutter and to make the dashboard easier to navigate.

    b. **Alignment and Symmetry**: Align charts and text boxes symmetrically to improve readability and to make the dashboard look polished and professional.

4. **Typography**:

    a. **Font Hierarchy**: Use larger fonts for titles, medium fonts for section headers, and smaller fonts for labels and captions to create a clear reading hierarchy.

    b. **Concise Labels**: Label sections and visuals concisely, avoiding long descriptions that can clutter the view.

These design principles make the dashboard easy to navigate and help users quickly locate and interpret essential data.

Integrating Charts and Visualizations

Bringing various EDA charts into a single dashboard in a cohesive way enables users to gain a holistic understanding of the data. In Superset, a dashboard can contain multiple charts, each with a specific purpose in the analysis workflow.

1. **Selecting Appropriate Charts**:

    a. Choose charts based on the type of data and insights they reveal. For instance, use line charts for trends, scatter plots for correlations, and histograms for data distributions.

    b. Limit the number of chart types to avoid a cluttered appearance. Aim for consistency across visuals by using similar styles and color schemes.

2. **Establishing Flow Between Visuals**:

    a. Arrange visuals logically to lead users through the analysis. For example, start with an overview chart (such as total revenue) and place more specific charts (such as revenue by product or region) below or beside it.

    b. Use tooltips and titles on each chart to provide context so that users understand each chart's purpose without needing extra explanation.

3. **Linking Charts to Show Relationships**: Use filters and drill-down options to connect related charts. For example, clicking a bar in a revenue chart can reveal a more detailed breakdown of that revenue by customer segment or product category in a linked chart.

By integrating visuals in this structured way, you create a comprehensive dashboard that tells a clear data story from high-level trends to detailed breakdowns.

Adding Interactivity

Interactivity transforms static dashboards into dynamic tools, allowing users to customize their views, focus on specific data subsets, and gain insights that are relevant to their needs. Superset supports several interactive features, such as filters, dropdowns, and drill-downs.

1. **Filters**:
   - **Global Filters**: Set up global filters that apply to multiple charts, allowing users to filter data across the entire dashboard. For example, a "`Year`" filter might update all charts to show only data from the selected year.
   - **Individual Chart Filters**: Enable specific filters on charts to let users refine data within a single visualization without affecting other visuals.
2. **Dropdowns and Selectors**:
   - Add dropdowns or selectors for categorical variables, such as "`Region`" or "`Product Category`." This setup allows users to toggle between different data segments, providing a flexible way to view detailed information.
   - **Example**: A dropdown selector for "`Region`" enables users to switch between different geographic areas, updating all relevant charts accordingly.
3. **Drill-Downs**:
   - Drill-downs allow users to click a chart element to view more granular data. For instance, clicking a bar in a sales chart could show monthly sales within that quarter, offering additional context without cluttering the primary chart.
   - Set up drill-downs by defining hierarchies in the data, such as "`Year` > `Quarter` > `Month`" or "`Country` > `State` > `City`."
4. **Dynamic Tooltips and Annotations**:
   - Use tooltips to display additional details when users hover over data points, helping them interpret values without overwhelming the dashboard visually.
   - Annotations or notes can be added to key charts, providing contextual information or highlighting insights that may be relevant to decision-making.

These interactive elements empower users to explore data in ways that suit their specific questions, making dashboards more valuable and engaging.

Best Practices for User-Friendly Dashboards

Creating a user-friendly dashboard requires attention to accessibility, responsive design, and clarity.

1. **Accessibility**:
   - **Color Contrast**: Ensure text, labels, and visuals have enough color contrast for readability.
   - **Color-Blind-Friendly Palettes**: Use color schemes that are accessible to users with color vision deficiencies, such as blue-orange color schemes instead of red-green.
2. **Responsive Design**:
   - Design dashboards that adapt well to different screen sizes. Superset supports responsive design, so test the dashboard on both desktop and mobile views.
   - Avoid overly complex layouts or too many visuals in one view, as these may become difficult to read on smaller screens.
3. **Concise Labeling and Tooltips**:
   - Keep titles, labels, and descriptions concise to avoid cluttering the dashboard.
   - Use tooltips to add context and reduce on-screen text. Tooltips can show detailed information without overwhelming users with text in the main layout.
4. **User Testing and Iteration**:
   - Test the dashboard with a sample of end-users to gather feedback on usability. Users may suggest improvements or identify issues that were not initially obvious.
   - Iterate on the design based on feedback, making adjustments to improve clarity, interactivity, and overall user experience.

These best practices help ensure that dashboards are intuitive, easy to navigate, and accessible to all users.

Dashboard Templates and Reusability

Creating reusable templates for dashboards can save time and ensure consistency in reporting, especially for recurring analyses. Templates allow analysts to replicate and customize dashboards for different datasets or projects without starting from scratch.

1. **Designing a Base Template**:
    a. Identify recurring components, such as common charts (for example, revenue trends and customer segmentation) and layouts.
    b. Create a generic dashboard with placeholders for specific data sources and filters, setting up the layout, color scheme, and filter options as needed.
2. **Customizing for Different Use Cases**:
    a. Templates can be adapted for different datasets by changing filters, data sources, or metrics. For example, a sales dashboard template could be reused by changing the filters to focus on different regions or products.
    b. Save templates with clear, descriptive names to indicate the base format, such as "`Monthly Performance Dashboard Template`" or "`Customer Segmentation Template`."
3. **Cloning Dashboards**:
    a. Superset allows dashboards to be cloned, which is ideal for creating a new version of a dashboard based on an existing template. Analysts can duplicate a dashboard and then modify data sources, visualizations, and filters without affecting the original template.
4. **Maintaining Template Consistency**:
    a. Regularly review and update templates to reflect best practices, new data sources, or improved visualizations.
    b. Standardize design elements such as color schemes, font styles, and layout structures across templates to create a consistent look and feel.

Using reusable templates streamlines the dashboard creation process, promotes consistency in reporting, and reduces the time spent on building dashboards for routine analysis.

Introduction to Hypothesis Testing in Data Analysis

Hypothesis testing is a statistical procedure that is used to determine whether sufficient evidence exists in a sample of data to reject an assumption or hypothesis. Analysts do not make decisions based on assumptions, speculations, or anecdotes but based on the rigorous testing of hypotheses. Hypothesis testing is a very basic tool applied in business and analytics to explain trends, relations, or impacts and hence optimize strategies and improve data.

Purpose of Hypothesis Testing

The primary purpose of hypothesis testing is to validate or refute assumptions about a dataset. It provides a structured framework for decision-making, helping to ensure that conclusions are based on evidence rather than chance. Here is how hypothesis testing serves this purpose:

- **Validating Assumptions**: Hypothesis testing confirms whether observed patterns in a sample are statistically significant and likely to be seen in the broader population.
- **Reducing Risk in Decision-Making**: By determining if an assumption holds under statistical scrutiny, hypothesis testing reduces the risk of acting on flawed conclusions.
- **Guiding Business Strategies**: Hypothesis testing allows businesses to test theories such as "*increasing marketing spend will lead to higher sales*" or "*changes in product design will improve customer satisfaction*," making it a fundamental tool in optimizing and refining strategies.

For example, a company may want to know if a new training program has improved employee productivity. Hypothesis testing can be used to analyze productivity data before and after the program to determine if there is a significant improvement.

Types of Hypotheses

In hypothesis testing, two primary hypotheses are formulated: the **null hypothesis (H_0)** and the **alternative hypothesis (H_1)**.

1. **Null Hypothesis (H_0)**:
   - The null hypothesis represents the default or baseline assumption. It posits that there is **no effect, difference, or relationship** between the variables under study.
   - **Example**: In testing the effectiveness of a new ad campaign, the null hypothesis might state, "*The new ad campaign has no impact on sales*," implying that any observed difference in sales is due to chance.
2. **Alternative Hypothesis (H_1)**:
   - The alternative hypothesis represents the opposing view to the null hypothesis. It suggests that there **is an effect, difference, or relationship** between the variables.
   - **Example**: In the ad campaign case, the alternative hypothesis might state, "The new ad campaign increases sales," suggesting that observed differences are due to the campaign and not random variation.

During hypothesis testing, data is used to determine if there is sufficient evidence to reject the null hypothesis in favor of the alternative hypothesis. However, if there is insufficient evidence, the null hypothesis remains accepted as the status quo.

Formulating Hypotheses in Business Contexts

Hypotheses can be formulated to address various business questions, helping analysts to explore relationships between variables or assess performance changes. Here are some examples:

1. **Testing Relationships Between Variables**:
    - **Example**: "Is *there a relationship between customer satisfaction and repeat purchases?*"
    - **Null Hypothesis (H_0)**: "*Customer satisfaction is not associated with repeat purchases.*"
    - **Alternative Hypothesis (H_1)**: "*Higher customer satisfaction leads to an increase in repeat purchases.*"
    - **Use Case**: If the null hypothesis is rejected, this could inform the company's strategy to invest more in customer satisfaction initiatives.
2. **Assessing Performance Changes**:
    - **Example**: "*Has the new product design reduced the return rate?*"
    - **Null Hypothesis (H_0)**: "*The new product design has no effect on the return rate.*"
    - **Alternative Hypothesis (H_1)**: "*The new product design has reduced the return rate.*"
    - **Use Case**: A significant reduction in returns can validate the effectiveness of the design changes, supporting continued investment in the product.
3. **Impact Analysis of Marketing Campaigns**:
    - **Example**: "*Did the email marketing campaign increase user engagement?*"
    - **Null Hypothesis (H_0)**: "*The email marketing campaign has no effect on user engagement.*"
    - **Alternative Hypothesis (H_1)**: "*The email marketing campaign increases user engagement.*"
    - **Use Case**: Proving this hypothesis can justify further investment in email marketing as an effective engagement tool.

Formulating hypotheses this way allows businesses to systematically test the impact of changes, strategies, or external factors on key performance metrics.

Basic Statistical Concepts

Several core statistical concepts play a vital role in hypothesis testing, helping to interpret and assess the results of the test.

- **Confidence Intervals and Significance Levels**:
    - **Confidence Interval**: A confidence interval is a range of values, typically around a sample statistic, that is likely to contain the population parameter. A 95% confidence interval means that if the study were repeated multiple times, 95% of the calculated intervals would contain the true population parameter.
    - **Significance Level (α)**: The significance level, often denoted as α (alpha), is the threshold for determining whether an observed result is statistically significant. Commonly set at 0.05 (5%), it indicates that if the null hypothesis were true, there would be only a 5% chance of obtaining a result as extreme as the one observed.
    - **P-Value**: The p-value is the probability of observing the test results given that the null hypothesis is true. If the p-value is lower than the significance level (for example, $p < 0.05$), it suggests strong evidence against the null hypothesis, supporting rejection of $\mathbf{H_0}$.
- **Interpreting Results**:
    - If $\mathbf{p < 0.05}$: The result is statistically significant, and we reject the null hypothesis.
    - If $\mathbf{p \geq 0.05}$: There is insufficient evidence to reject the null hypothesis, and it remains accepted.
- **Example**: In testing a marketing campaign's impact on sales, if the p-value is 0.03 and α is set at 0.05, the results are statistically significant, indicating that the campaign likely had an effect on sales.

Errors in Hypothesis Testing

In hypothesis testing, two types of errors can occur, which have implications for decision-making:

- **Type I Error (False Positive)**: A Type I error occurs when the null hypothesis is falsely rejected, meaning we conclude an effect exists when it actually does not. This is equivalent to a "*false positive.*"
    - **Example**: Concluding that a new marketing campaign increased sales when it actually did not.
    - **Impact**: Type I errors can lead to wasted resources, as a company might invest in strategies that are ineffective.

- **Type II Error (False Negative)**: A Type II error occurs when the null hypothesis is falsely accepted, meaning we fail to detect a true effect. This is equivalent to a *"false negative."*
    - **Example**: Concluding that a new customer loyalty program had no effect on retention when it actually did increase retention.
    - **Impact**: Type II errors can result in missed opportunities, as a business might overlook effective strategies.

Understanding these errors is crucial, as they affect the reliability of conclusions drawn from hypothesis testing.

Balancing Type I and Type II Errors:

- The significance level (α) controls the probability of a Type I error, while the sample size and statistical power influence the likelihood of a Type II error.
- In some contexts, reducing Type I errors may be more critical (for example, in drug testing, where false positives have serious consequences), while in others, minimizing Type II errors might be prioritized (for example, when trying to detect potentially impactful marketing strategies).

It is a methodical process to decide whether data supports or rejects a given assumption. Using the creation of null and alternative hypotheses, along with significance levels, confidence intervals, and knowledge of types of errors, analysts make data-driven decisions. It is a rigorous testing method that verifies assumptions while also fine-tunes strategy and mitigates risk in decision-making for business.

Conducting Hypothesis Tests in Apache Superset

In Apache Superset, analysts can quickly leverage SQL integrations and several statistical functions to set up and run common hypothesis tests. This section describes what the basic steps are to set up data for testing, outlines the statistical functions in Superset, describes what common tests, such as t-tests, Chi-square tests, and ANOVA, are, and provides guidance on the best way to interpret results.

Setting Up Data for Hypothesis Testing

The first step in hypothesis testing is preparing the data. For accurate and reliable results, you need to set up control and test groups and ensure data quality.

- **Defining Control and Test Groups**:
    - **Control Group**: The control group represents the "`status quo`" or baseline condition. It is not exposed to any changes, treatments, or interventions. This group helps provide a point of comparison.

- **Test Group**: The test group is the segment of data that receives the treatment or change you want to measure. Any differences observed between the control and test groups can be attributed to this change.
- **Example**: Suppose a company wants to test the impact of a new marketing strategy on sales. The control group would be the sales data from a period without the new strategy, while the test group would be sales data from the period with the strategy applied.

- **Random Sampling and Ensuring Similarity**:
  - If possible, use random sampling to assign data points to control and test groups. This ensures that the groups are similar and that any observed differences are likely due to the intervention and not pre-existing differences.
- **Handling Confounding Variables**:
  - Confounding variables can skew results if they affect the dependent and independent variables. For example, if testing a new sales promotion, seasonality might be a confounding variable. Try to control these by selecting similar time periods or accounting for them in the analysis.

By setting up clear control and test groups, analysts can ensure a valid and reliable hypothesis test.

Overview of Statistical Functions in Superset

Apache Superset offers SQL-based functionalities that allow users to perform certain statistical analyses. While Superset does not have built-in statistical tests, you can integrate SQL expressions to calculate key metrics such as averages, variances, and counts, enabling hypothesis testing workflows. Here is how Superset's capabilities can support these tests:

- **SQL Integrations for Statistical Calculations**: Use SQL queries in Superset's SQL Lab to calculate means, variances, counts, and other basic statistics required for hypothesis testing.

  Examples:
  - **Average (Mean)**: `SELECT AVG(column_name) FROM table_name WHERE condition;`
  - **Variance**: `SELECT VARIANCE(column_name) FROM table_name WHERE condition;`
  - **Count**: `SELECT COUNT(column_name) FROM table_name WHERE condition;`
- **Custom Queries for Hypothesis Tests**:
  - Superset enables custom SQL queries, making it possible to conduct basic

hypothesis testing by calculating metrics for control and test groups and comparing results.

  - For advanced tests, you may need to run calculations externally (for example, in Python or R) and import the results back into Superset for visualization.

- **Connecting to SQL Databases for Extended Functions**:
  - When using a SQL database with built-in statistical functions (for example, PostgreSQL), you can perform t-tests or ANOVA directly within the database. Then, Superset's SQL Lab allows you to visualize the output.

While Superset provides foundational support, more advanced hypothesis tests often require external statistical software or SQL databases with comprehensive statistical functions.

Common Hypothesis Tests

Multiple hypothesis tests are commonly used to explore different types of relationships and differences in data. Here is an overview of three frequently used tests: t-tests, Chi-square tests, and ANOVA.

- **t-Tests (One-Sample and Two-Sample t-Tests):**
  - **Purpose**: A t-test assesses whether the mean of one or two groups differs significantly from a hypothesized value or from each other.
  - **One-Sample t-Test**: Compares the mean of a single group to a known or hypothesized population mean.

    Example: Testing if the average monthly sales for the current year significantly differ from last year's average.
  - **Two-Sample (Independent) t-Test**: Compares the means of two independent groups to see if there is a statistically significant difference.

    Example: Testing if the average revenue of customers exposed to a new ad campaign differs from those who were not exposed.
  - **SQL Implementation**: Calculate the mean, variance, and sample size for both groups using SQL, then perform the test externally (for example, in Python). Import and visualize results in Superset.
- **Chi-Square Test for Association**:
  - **Purpose**: A Chi-square test examines the association between two categorical variables.
  - **Usage**: It tests whether observed frequencies of categorical outcomes differ from expected frequencies.
  - **Example**: A retailer might use a Chi-square test to check if the customer

age group is associated with product preference. This test would reveal if certain age groups are more likely to purchase specific product types.

- **SQL Implementation**: Use SQL to generate frequency tables for each category combination. The Chi-square test can then be calculated externally using a tool, such as Python or Excel, and visualized in Superset if desired.

- **Analysis of Variance (ANOVA)**:
  - **Purpose**: ANOVA tests for statistically significant differences among the means of three or more groups.
  - **Usage**: ANOVA is commonly used when comparing the performance or behavior of different segments within a dataset.
  - **Example**: A company might use ANOVA to test if the average customer satisfaction scores vary across regions (for example, North, South, East, and West).
  - **Types of ANOVA**:
    - **One-Way ANOVA**: Compares the means of multiple groups based on one independent variable (for example, region).
    - **Two-Way ANOVA**: Compares the means of multiple groups based on two independent variables (for example, region and customer segment).
  - **SQL Implementation**: Use SQL to calculate the means and variances of each group. Perform the ANOVA test externally and then import and visualize results in Superset.

These hypothesis tests are essential tools for exploring relationships, differences, and dependencies in data, and they can guide strategic business decisions.

Interpreting Test Results

After performing a hypothesis test, interpreting the results correctly is critical. This involves analyzing p-values and confidence intervals and drawing conclusions based on the data.

1. **Understanding the p-Value**:
   - **Definition**: The p-value represents the probability of observing a test statistic at least as extreme as the one computed, assuming the null hypothesis is true.
   - **Interpreting p-Values**:
     - **$p < \alpha$ (for example, 0.05)**: The result is statistically significant, meaning there is enough evidence to reject the null hypothesis.

    - **p ≥ α**: There is insufficient evidence to reject the null hypothesis, suggesting the observed difference might be due to a random chance.
  - **Example**: If testing a new customer service process yields a p-value of 0.03 with a significance level of 0.05, the result is statistically significant, indicating that the new process likely had an impact.

2. **Confidence Intervals**:
   - **Definition**: A confidence interval provides a range of values likely to contain the true population parameter.
   - **Interpreting Confidence Intervals**:
     - If a 95% confidence interval for the difference between two means does not include zero, this suggests a significant difference at the 5% significance level.
     - **Example**: A 95% confidence interval for the mean difference in customer satisfaction between two products might be (1.2, 2.5), suggesting a significant positive difference in satisfaction.

3. **Drawing Conclusions**:
   - Based on the p-value and confidence interval, conclude whether there is strong enough evidence to reject the null hypothesis.
   - **Example**: After testing for differences in average sales between two regions, a p-value of 0.01 and a confidence interval that does not include zero would indicate a statistically significant difference, suggesting that one region performs better than the other.

4. **Documenting and Communicating Results**:
   - Clearly communicate findings in terms of business impact. Instead of reporting a "*p-value of 0.04*," interpret the results to convey that the tested factor (for example, marketing campaign) had a statistically significant positive effect.
   - Summarize findings in a dashboard or report in Superset for ease of sharing with stakeholders.

Interpreting test results accurately ensures that business decisions are based on reliable insights, reducing the risk of making changes based on random variation or incorrect assumptions.

The analyst confirms assumptions, identifies the significant difference through hypothesis testing in Superset, and derives a thrust for business decisions. It sets control and test groups and then calculates different tests through SQL, such as t-tests, Chi-square tests, and ANOVA, and interprets the meaning of p-values and confidence intervals in the derivation of meaningful results. Superset offers very few statistical functions, but owing to SQL-based calculations and working with external tools for complex testing, powerful data-driven insights are achievable.

Conclusion

EDA and hypothesis testing are essential parts of every data professional's toolkit. They allow you to take raw, unrefined data and transform it into useful insights for your analysis. In this chapter, we walked through the process of EDA using the powerful, open-source BI platform, Apache Superset, which has been designed to facilitate easy and intuitive data exploration.

We covered how to combine multiple datasets, clean and pre-process data, and then apply a range of visualizations to tease out trends, patterns, and outliers. At every step of the EDA process, you learned how to understand the distinctive story that your data had to tell–from big-picture, broad trends to smaller details. Finally, with filters, drill-downs, and all the dashboarding features of Superset, you are now ready to do a deeper and more interactive exploration that will unearth hidden insights and communicate them effectively.

We also covered hypothesis testing, a middle ground between EDA and more formalistic statistical analysis. Testing relationships more confidently will help one not only validate assumptions but also choose between any two choices. Learning how to set up, test, and interpret hypotheses has given you the skills you need to make your analysis more rigorous and provide the bases for sound decision-making.

In the next chapter, we will take the reader through the deployment of Apache Superset in a production environment, built to scale for large-scale, high-performance applications. This includes ways to scale Superset for extensive teams, multi-tenant environments, and lots more using either Kubernetes or Docker Swarm. Readers will learn best practices for reliability and uptime that enable the development of robust, production-ready Superset deployments tailored to an organization's needs

CHAPTER 10
Scaling and Deploying Superset in Production

Introduction

Apache Superset is a powerful, open-source business intelligence and data visualization platform. However, moving from development to production environments requires strategic planning and scaling to ensure high availability, performance, and reliability, especially for larger teams or multi-tenant applications. This chapter will guide you through essential strategies to deploy Apache Superset in a robust, production-ready setup.

Structure

In this chapter, we will discuss the following topics:

- Production Deployment Strategies
- Scaling Superset for Large Teams
- Managing Multi-Tenant Environments
- Deploying Superset on Kubernetes or Docker Swarm
- Ensuring Reliability and Uptime

Production Deployment Strategies

When deploying Apache Superset in a production setting, considerations regarding architecture must be made concerning stability, security, and scalability. Each component contributes to helping Superset perform optimally and securely. Following is a detailed account on each component, with code snippets where applicable, illustrating how to build a robust production deployment of Superset.

Environment Configuration

Ensure Superset manages its secrets and settings securely and never stores sensitive data in the environment–database credentials, and so on–to maintain a consistent and safe configuration. With projects based on Docker, values should ideally remain inside a **.env** file, which will be referred to in the Docker Compose configuration. Following is an example of environment configuration for Superset:

```
SUPERSET_SECRET_KEY=my_secure_secret_key
DATABASE_URL=postgresql+psycopg2://user:password@db_host:5432/superset
REDIS_URL=redis://redis:6379/0
```

In Docker Compose, these variables can be accessed directly. More complex configurations use secrets managers such as AWS Secrets Manager, HashiCorp Vault, or Kubernetes Secrets for greater security and flexibility, especially for the rotation of credentials without restarting services. This is a small snippet of **docker-compose.yml** loading in the values of **.env**:

```
version: '3.7'
services:
  superset:
    image: apache/superset:latest
    env_file: .env
    environment:
      - SUPERSET_SECRET_KEY=${SUPERSET_SECRET_KEY}
      - DATABASE_URL=${DATABASE_URL}
      - REDIS_URL=${REDIS_URL}
```

Database Management

Apache Superset stores its internal metadata–such as user settings, dashboards, and permissions–in a dedicated "metadata database." By default, this metadata database can be SQLite, but for a production setup, you can configure an external database such as PostgreSQL, MySQL, or MariaDB.

Your **analytics data** (the data you query and visualize) can reside in one or more external data sources or data warehouses (for example, BigQuery, Snowflake, and Redshift). Superset connects with these warehouses to run queries and generate dashboards, while the metadata database tracks and manages your Superset configuration itself.

Caching with Redis

This will involve caching to improve performance, especially on complex visualizations or a large number of concurrent users. Popular caching systems for Superset are Redis or Memcached. For example, Redis would allow you to store cached query results, which would alleviate load on the database and make the dashboard load faster. In your superset configuration file, superset_config.py, you can use a few simple settings to set Redis as the cache backend:

```
from cachelib.redis import RedisCache
CACHE_CONFIG = {
    'CACHE_TYPE': 'redis',
    'CACHE_DEFAULT_TIMEOUT': 300,
    'CACHE_KEY_PREFIX': 'superset_',
    'CACHE_REDIS_URL': 'redis://localhost:6379/0'
}
```

This type of caching will enable the most frequently accessed dashboards to open much faster. This happens because their data does need not be fetched again from the database on every request.

Reverse Proxy and SSL with NGINX

The first priority of the production is security, and an important step includes the fact that all traffic must go over HTTPS to the Superset. Because NGINX acts as a reverse proxy, traffic may be made secure via SSL while, at the same time, balancing load on multiple instances of Superset if needed. Here is an example NGINX configuration with Let's Encrypt:

```
server {
    listen 80;
    server_name your_superset_domain.com;

    location / {
        return 301 https://$host$request_uri;
    }
}

server {
    listen 443 ssl;
    server_name your_superset_domain.com;

    ssl_certificate /etc/letsencrypt/live/your_superset_domain.com/full-
chain.pem;
    ssl_certificate_key /etc/letsencrypt/live/your_superset_domain.com/
privkey.pem;

    location / {
        proxy_pass http://superset:8088;
        proxy_set_header Host $host;
        proxy_set_header X-Real-IP $remote_addr;
```

```
        proxy_set_header X-Forwarded-For $proxy_add_x_forwarded_for;
        proxy_set_header X-Forwarded-Proto $scheme;
    }
}
```

This setup ensures NGINX forwards any incoming HTTP request to HTTPS, all while making the gateway an SSL-secure front end to the Superset application. Because Let's Encrypt has certificates that automatically renew by default, there are constant SSL covers.

Configure Load Balancer

High-traffic deployments also need to ensure that the incoming requests are spread out to several instances of Superset through a load balancer to ensure scalability. It prevents getting a bottleneck, and the load will be appropriately spread out. In AWS Cloud, for example, ELB is a pretty straightforward choice that offers auto-scaling. On-prem or self-hosted installations may use NGINX as a load balancer. To use NGINX as a load balancer, point lots of Superset instances behind an NGINX instance, such as:

```
http {
    upstream superset_cluster {
        server superset1:8088;
        server superset2:8088;
        server superset3:8088;
    }

    server {
        listen 443 ssl;
        server_name your_superset_domain.com;

        ssl_certificate /etc/letsencrypt/live/your_superset_domain.com/
fullchain.pem;
        ssl_certificate_key /etc/letsencrypt/live/your_superset_domain.
com/privkey.pem;

        location / {
            proxy_pass http://superset_cluster;
            proxy_set_header Host $host;
            proxy_set_header X-Real-IP $remote_addr;
            proxy_set_header X-Forwarded-For $proxy_add_x_forwarded_for;
            proxy_set_header X-Forwarded-Proto $scheme;
        }
    }
}
```

This will spread incoming requests over three instances of Superset: `superset1`, `superset2`, and `superset3`. Using this approach, you can scale Superset horizontally as traffic spikes behind NGINX in response to adding a load balancer.

All these strategies put together–environmentally variable secure configuration, metadata database, caching, reverse proxying over SSL, and load balancing–will result in a Superset production deployment that is scalable, high-traffic tolerant, and resilient against production loads. Each layer is added to the last one, so Superset is a production-ready deployment that is both secure and efficient, built to handle enterprise-level workloads.

Scaling Superset for Large Teams

This would be one of the areas in scaling Superset for big teams and even high-visualization demand while keeping it fast. The use case dictates scaling both vertically and horizontally, where, with a rise in usage, both approaches help manage complex queries on data and concurrent users without slowing down or going offline. Now let us outline this approach and the tools for a smooth scale-up in Superset in production.

Vertical Scaling

The first type of scaling allocated to individual components of Superset is vertical scaling or resource boosting. The most vital resources are, given that Superset deals with enormous datasets and complex visualizations, memory and CPU. By default, **NGINX is used as a proxy** for Apache Superset. However, **Superset itself** can be **installed either on-premises or in a cloud environment** such as AWS or GCP. For example, if your visualization workload requires more computing power or memory, you could:

- **On AWS**: Scale up by using larger Amazon EC2 instances. A common deployment flow might be **Route53 (DNS) → Elastic Load Balancer (ELB) → EC2 instances** running Superset, with NGINX acting as a proxy or load balancer in front of the Superset application.
- **On GCP**: Provision more powerful virtual machines on Google Compute Engine (GCE) and configure a similar load-balancing setup with NGINX.

In each scenario, the idea is that **Superset can be deployed where you have infrastructure**–whether that is on your own servers (on-premises) or in the cloud–while NGINX ensures that requests are routed appropriately and securely. By choosing higher-end instances or VMs, you can ensure that Superset has the necessary resources to handle **memory-intensive** or **graphics-intensive** visualization tasks.

Metadata, including Superset's internal configurations, user data, and dashboard definitions, can be scaled vertically like any traditional database (for example,

PostgreSQL or MySQL). By **upgrading to a larger, more powerful instance**, you reduce the likelihood of the metadata database becoming a bottleneck during under peak usage.

If you are **deploying Superset in a cloud environment**, you can also offload database management by **using services such as Amazon RDS or GCP Cloud SQL**. These managed database services streamline administration tasks (for example, backups, patches) and often provide **built-in connection pooling** features (such as the Amazon RDS Proxy), ensuring optimal resource usage when multiple users issue simultaneous requests.

Database connection pooling–whether configured manually on-premises or through a managed service–optimizes how Superset handles concurrent reads and writes, balancing load and minimizing latency for all users.

Horizontal Scaling

This does, however, require horizontal scaling for the high concurrency. All you do is distribute the workload across the cluster by having multiple instances of Superset. Therefore, more users can access it simultaneously. A containerized setup in Docker would work best. With Docker, you can spin up and down multiple instances of Superset rapidly. Therefore, each container runs the isolated instance of Superset, which can then be orchestrated collectively through a platform such as Kubernetes. In the instance of deployment in Kubernetes, it would look something like the following:

```
apiVersion: apps/v1
kind: Deployment
metadata:
  name: superset-deployment
spec:
  replicas: 3
  selector:
    matchLabels:
      app: superset
  template:
    metadata:
      labels:
        app: superset
    spec:
      containers:
      - name: superset
        image: apache/superset:latest
        ports:
        - containerPort: 8088
        resources:
```

```
        requests:
          memory: "2Gi"
          cpu: "1000m"
        limits:
          memory: "4Gi"
          cpu: "2000m"
```

It is going to the configure setting, **replicas: 3**, deploy three instances of Superset, and each of these will be managed by the Kubernetes to ensure redundancy and load distribution. They will run separately in containers, allowing multiple instances of Superset to operate simultaneously. With a load balancer, the workload is evenly distributed, preventing any single instance from becoming overloaded, which enhances overall performance.

Task Queue Management with Celery

It needs background processing to process those asynchronous jobs, including query execution and scheduling refreshes into the dashboard. For this, there needs to be a task queue using Celery. Celery helps make the tasks run in different worker processes—this would be handy in letting Superset have several background jobs without getting in the user's experience on the front end. In this case, it makes use of Redis or RabbitMQ as a message broker to coordinate with Superset and the Celery workers. To install Celery with Redis, add the following to your **superset_config.py** file:

```
from celery import Celery
import os

class CeleryConfig:
    broker_url = 'redis://redis:6379/0'
    result_backend = 'redis://redis:6379/1'
    task_annotations = {'*': {'rate_limit': '10/s'}}
    worker_concurrency = 4  # Adjust based on your CPU availability

app = Celery('tasks')
app.config_from_object(CeleryConfig)
```

In doing so, Celery connects to Redis and tasks are distributed across four worker processes. Since you are adding more workers depending on how much traffic your application experiences, scalability in this setup ensures that background tasks do not interfere with any user-facing features.

User Sessions and Caching Using Redis

The scaling of user sessions and caching of the most accessed data are important to make sure that the users have a smooth time across the various instances of Superset.

Redis can be used for managing distributed sessions, whereby when routed to other Superset instances, the session of the user is not disconnected. Redis works well as a cache where one does not have to rerun complex queries since it caches the frequently requested data. Configuring Redis for both session and query caching needs to be done in **superset_config.py**.

```
from cachelib.redis import RedisCache

# Set up caching
CACHE_CONFIG = {
    'CACHE_TYPE': 'redis',
    'CACHE_DEFAULT_TIMEOUT': 300,
    'CACHE_KEY_PREFIX': 'superset_',
    'CACHE_REDIS_URL': 'redis://redis:6379/0'
}

# Configure session management
SESSION_TYPE = 'redis'
SESSION_REDIS = RedisCache.from_url('redis://redis:6379/1')
```

In this arrangement:

1. **CACHE_CONFIG**: Redis cache and recently accessed data are stored in Redis, and cache entries expire after 300 seconds. As a result, frequently accessed visualizations and dashboards load quickly without constantly querying the database.

2. **SESSION_TYPE** and **SESSION_REDIS**: This will enable Redis as the session store, so the user session persists across different instances, ensuring smooth user interactions with Superset.

Scaling Apache Superset for a large team that relies on data visualization requires a strategic and planned combination of vertical and horizontal scaling, appropriate task management, and effective use of caching. These strategies enable Superset to handle a large number of users by assigning additional resources to different components, utilizing multiple instances with load balancing, leveraging Celery for background task management, and using Redis for caching and session management. This approach ensures high availability, strong performance, and readiness to handle heavy loads on scalable infrastructure.

Managing Multi-Tenant Environments

The reason managing multi-tenant environments in Apache Superset is very important for an organization is that it must be able to offer data visualization and analytics capabilities to different user groups with varied data sets and permissions. In a multi-tenant architecture, you must separate user access to data, custom visualizations, and manage secure authentication across diverse tenants. Here are some strategies to set up an effective multi-tenant environment in Superset: database isolation, role-based access control (RBAC), custom authentication, and dedicated workspaces.

Isolated Databases

A multi-tenant environment benefits from database isolation, where each tenant has a dedicated database or schema. Superset supports multiple database connections, allowing administrators to configure specific data sources for each tenant. This, in turn, enhances security and ensures proper data management, as users from one tenant cannot access data belonging to another.

Distinguish separate databases in Superset: Use the UI and configure a connection for each tenant in Superset's connections. Each tenant requires a dedicated schema or instance, which must be added in the configuration files. Following this approach, when defining a database setup configuration for SQLAlchemy-based Superset, you can specify it in a superset_config.py file, as follows:

```
SQLALCHEMY_BINDS = {
    'tenant1': 'postgresql+psycopg2://user:password@db_host1/tenant1_db',
    'tenant2': 'postgresql+psycopg2://user:password@db_host2/tenant2_db',
}
```

This configuration allows Superset to forward tenant-specific queries to particular databases. Moreover, tenant users will only be able to access their respective databases based on manual configurations or programmatic rules set according to their tenant roles.

Role-Based Access Control (RBAC)

Superset's RBAC system is a feature that offers permissions and access levels for different types of user roles. Critical in maintaining the multi-tenancy setup as safe and manageable, it allows you to create roles such as data-set or dashboard limits and limits on the usage of SQL Lab features within a multi-tenancy environment. For example, you may have **`Tenant1_Viewer`** and **`Tenant1_Admin`** roles. The data sources, charts, and dashboards of Tenant 1 are only accessed by these roles.

The administrator can apply role-based customization for various role kinds using Superset's permissions architecture. Using the "**`Security`**" menu or the "**`Roles List`**" in the user interface, he can specify roles in Superset. For instance, the administrator can turn off permissions like **`can_write_on_sqllab`** and **`can_access_sqllab`** to stop viewers from accessing SQL Lab. Access to datasets can also be limited; for example, some roles may only be able to view the datasets that correspond to their tenant. This guarantees that every user can only access the information and functionalities pertinent to their position within the application.

```
# Example role permissions for Tenant1 Viewer in `superset_config.py`
ROLE_PERMISSIONS = {
    'Tenant1_Viewer': [
        'can_view_on_Dashboard',  # View dashboards
        'can_read_on_Datasource', # Read access to Tenant1 data sources
        'can_view_on_Chart',      # View charts only for Tenant1
    ],
}
```

Superset's multiple-tenant setup prevents an unauthorized user from accessing some data using flexible resource isolation through role-based access controls.

Custom Authentication OAuth LDAP SSO

Any multi-tenant setup has inherent authentication. User access with OAuth, LDAP, or SSO IDPs makes this extremely easy. Custom authentication integration for user management centralizes user management via a Superset setup that reduces admin overhead and eases the process of onboarding users for multiple tenants. Superset natively supports multiple authentication mechanisms, which can be configured in **superset_config.py**. For example, to enable SSO, select an OAuth-based provider. Configure OAuth authentication through the config file: client credentials and endpoints.

```
from authlib.integrations.flask_client import OAuth

AUTH_TYPE = AUTH_OAUTH
OAUTH_PROVIDERS = [{
    'name': 'google',
    'icon': 'fa-google',
    'token_key': 'access_token',
    'remote_app': {
        'consumer_key': 'your_google_client_id',
        'consumer_secret': 'your_google_client_secret',
        'base_url': 'https://www.googleapis.com/oauth2/v2/',
        'request_token_url': None,
        'access_token_url': 'https://accounts.google.com/o/oauth2/token',
        'authorize_url': 'https://accounts.google.com/o/oauth2/auth',
        'request_token_params': {
            'scope': 'email profile'
        }
    }
}]
```

Google OAuth is also accepted, one of the alternative login options. The functionality will forward people directly at the set-up time via Google, where, with Google's verification, this sends people back to Superset with a secure established session.

User management goes across the IDP level; therefore, this is advantageous as people come on-board and then leave; it is convenient.

Otherwise, LDAP can be integrated for organizations that already apply directory services for authentication. Since LDAP is configured, it validates users against the organization's LDAP server, and for large enterprises with an already existing directory infrastructure, this has been ideal.

Dedicated Spaces

You can use the workspaces within Superset to manage data resources for each tenant to further organize and isolate tenant data and visualizations. Workspaces are a mechanism to logically partition data and visualizations so that tenants can only see the resources relevant to them. Superset does not have built-in workspaces, but you can simulate workspace-like environments by using RBAC in conjunction with naming conventions and access controls. For instance, the dashboards, charts, and datasets would be named with tenant-specific prefixes, for example, **`Tenant1_Sales_Dashboard`** and **`Tenant2_Marketing_Dashboard`**. Such a configuration would apply while implementing access control to the effect that all users view or update only its tenant prefix-containing items such that the number of those from Tenant 1 with access to the resources created for Tenant 2 is lowered.

This is an example of how to apply permissions to simulate workspaces:

```
# Assign permissions to each role
ROLE_PERMISSIONS = {
    'Tenant1_Admin': [
        'can_write_on_Tenant1_Sales_Dashboard',
        'can_write_on_Tenant1_Charts',
        'can_read_on_Tenant1_Datasets',
    ],
    'Tenant2_Admin': [
        'can_write_on_Tenant2_Marketing_Dashboard',
        'can_write_on_Tenant2_Charts',
        'can_read_on_Tenant2_Datasets',
    ],
}
```

This way, tenants can work in their dedicated "**`spaces`**" without data or visualizations mixing, keeping the environment organized and tenant-specific.

This would allow the isolation of a database, role-based access control, custom authentication, and resource organization to be configured in a dedicated workspace within a multi-tenant environment in Apache Superset. All these aspects enable the formation of a safe, manageable platform for servicing diverse user groups with unique data access and visualization. The approach permits teams to use Superset effectively but with clear demarcations between the tenant's data and their visualizations.

Deploying Superset on Kubernetes and Docker Swarm

Even Kubernetes and Docker Swarm, as container orchestration platforms, make it easy to deploy, scale, and manage Apache Superset in a production environment. Following is a detailed walkthrough on setting up Superset on both Kubernetes and Docker Swarm, including configuration recommendations for each.

Deploy to Kubernetes

Kubernetes is an excellent containerized application orchestrator with plenty of alternatives to install and run Superset on a production-ready environment.

Namespace and Deployment Configuration

When deploying Superset in Kubernetes, you will define a Deployment resource to manage the Superset pods. A deployment configuration includes specifications for CPU, memory, and storage resources. Additionally, Kubernetes Namespaces can separate tenant-specific resources, which is useful in multi-tenant environments to organize and secure resources by user group or project. The example Kubernetes **`superset-deployment.yaml`** is as follows:

```
apiVersion: apps/v1
kind: Deployment
metadata:
  name: superset
  namespace: superset-namespace
spec:
  replicas: 3
  selector:
    matchLabels:
      app: superset
  template:
    metadata:
      labels:
        app: superset
    spec:
      containers:
      - name: superset
        image: apache/superset:latest
        ports:
```

```
        - containerPort: 8088
        resources:
          requests:
            memory: "2Gi"
            cpu: "1000m"
          limits:
            memory: "4Gi"
            cpu: "2000m"
```

In this configuration:

1. **Namespace**: A namespace, such as superset-namespace separates Superset resources from other deployments and provides logical isolation within your cluster.
2. **Resource Limits**: By setting CPU and memory requests and limits in the configuration, **you ensure** a baseline allocation of resources for each pod while also preventing resource overuse. **This optimizes** performance and stability.

Persistent Storage

Persistent storage is required for Superset's metadata database, as user configurations and dashboards need to persist over time. In Kubernetes, Persistent Volume Claims (PVCs) allow data to be retained even when pods are removed or rescheduled. Create an example Persistent Volume and Persistent Volume Claim:

```
apiVersion: v1
kind: PersistentVolumeClaim
metadata:
  name: superset-pvc
  namespace: superset-namespace
spec:
  accessModes:
    - ReadWriteOnce
  resources:
    requests:
      storage: 10Gi
```

This will ensure that Superset's database holds some dependable storage, crucial for the integrity of the data, and makes the operation scale.

Horizontal Pod Autoscaler

HPA Auto-Scaling uses an HPA to scale with variable loads of traffic. It automatically scales Superset pods based on metrics such as CPU usage and memory usage, thereby modifying your deployment based on the dynamic increase in the load of traffic.

```
Example HPA configuration:
apiVersion: autoscaling/v2
kind: HorizontalPodAutoscaler
metadata:
  name: superset-hpa
  namespace: superset-namespace
spec:
  scaleTargetRef:
    apiVersion: apps/v1
    kind: Deployment
    name: superset
  minReplicas: 2
  maxReplicas: 10
  metrics:
  - type: Resource
    resource:
      name: cpu
      target:
        type: Utilization
        averageUtilization: 70
```

The HPA will set the number of replicas to scale up Superset pods from 2 to 10 based on CPU usage, creating pods when the CPU usage exceeds 70%.

Helm Charts for Simplified Deployment

Helm is the package manager for Kubernetes. Superset comes with an official Helm chart that makes it easy to deploy. It allows easy dependency management and scaling and upgrading configurations.

```
Installation of Superset using Helm:
helm repo add superset https://apache.github.io/superset
helm install superset superset/superset --namespace superset-namespace
```

It has made deployment and management easy with teams managing large-scale, complex deployments for Superset on Kubernetes.

Deployment to Docker Swarm

Conversely, Docker Swarm is usually less complex than Kubernetes and provides key functionality for getting Superset up and running in an environment where Kubernetes itself is too heavyweight to be applied.

Service Stacks with Docker Compose

The services defined in the docker-compose files can be managed by Docker Swarm. For example, a simple stack for Superset could consist of the Superset application,

Redis for caching and sessions, Celery for managing tasks, and a metadata database such as PostgreSQL. An example **docker-compose.yml** for Docker Swarm:

```
version: '3.7'
services:
  superset:
    image: apache/superset:latest
    deploy:
      replicas: 3
      resources:
        limits:
          cpus: '1.0'
          memory: 2G
    environment:
      - SUPERSET_SECRET_KEY=mysecretkey
      - REDIS_HOST=redis
      - DATABASE_URL=postgresql://user:password@db:5432/superset
    networks:
      - superset-net

  db:
    image: postgres:13
    environment:
      POSTGRES_DB: superset
      POSTGRES_USER: user
      POSTGRES_PASSWORD: password
    volumes:
      - superset-db-data:/var/lib/postgresql/data
    networks:
      - superset-net

  redis:
    image: redis:6
    networks:
      - superset-net

networks:
  superset-net:

volumes:
  superset-db-data:
```

In this **docker-compose.yml**, Docker Swarm will manage replicas of the Superset service, Redis, and PostgreSQL—all in one defined network. Using Docker Swarm, it can deploy this stack with a single command on any host running Docker:

```
docker stack deploy -c docker-compose.yml superset_stack
```

Scaling Services

With Docker Swarm, it is pretty easy to scale your services by simply modifying the replicas value in your **docker-compose.yml** file. You can see in the previous example that replicas: 3 ensures three instances of Superset are running. This is easily changed to scale the application up or down based on demand:

```
docker service scale superset_stack_superset=5
```

This command will scale the Superset service up to five replicas. Docker Swarm will automatically distribute the load between them, resulting in smooth scaling of the service.

For deploying, scaling, and managing Apache Superset in a production setting, Kubernetes and Docker Swarm are both excellent choices. Kubernetes is ideally suited for big and intricate deployments because it offers sophisticated capabilities like namespaces, persistent storage, and auto-scaling using Horizontal Pod Autoscalers. Conversely, Docker Swarm is more suited for smaller-scale or less complex environments due to its easier orchestration, scaling through replicas, and straightforward secrets management. You may create and manage a scalable, highly available Superset environment that is customized to your team's requirements by being aware of each platform's features and options.

Ensuring Reliability and Uptime

High availability and reliability in the Apache Superset production environment are of utmost importance, with downtime at the minimum. Users never experience a time when they lack Apache Superset. Tactics such as backups, high availability of databases, monitoring, health checks, and deployments with zero downtime are explained as follows:

Backup Strategy

A good backup plan should ensure safety against data loss and speed up recovery in the occurrence of any unexpected failure. The critical pieces that should be backed up on Superset are metadata, which stores configurations, dashboard information, user roles, and any data warehouse on which Superset is dependent to query data.

Managed cloud database services, such as AWS RDS, GCP Cloud SQL, or Azure SQL, will make the metadata DB backup management easier. Services do support automatic backup, snapshots, and even point-in-time recovery.

AWS RDS also provides auto-backup features that could be designed to keep daily snapshots and hold backups for an assigned period. GCP Cloud SQL offers daily automatic backups and can also retain them. Such features are also included in Azure SQL Database.

In addition, the strategy for manually backing up before any major update or schema can be considered. This can be done with the use of tools such as **`pg_dump`** for PostgreSQL and mysqldump for MySQL. Metadata are exported in SQL files that are placed within a secure cloud storage bucket or in a backup repository.

High Availability of Metadata Database

In multi-Availability Zone (AZ) deployment, the metadata database needs to be used for achieving high availability. Managed database services usually allow for deployment in multiple AZs and replicate the database across various availability zones to provide automatic failover in case of an outage within one of the zones.

For example:

AWS RDS will automatically replicate your database from the main instance to a secondary instance residing in another availability zone based on the multi-AZ deployment.

GCP Cloud SQL, as well as Azure SQL, share the configuration, so on failure, a standby instance can take over without any sort of manual intervention.

This redundancy ensures that the metadata database is always available even if one of the data centers or availability zones fails.

Monitoring and Logging

Tools to use for proactive management of issues and optimization of performance would include Prometheus, Grafana, and the ELK Stack–a combination of Elasticsearch, Logstash, and Kibana. Each of these brings essential capabilities for real-time visibility into your Superset environment.

Prometheus is an open-source monitoring system that provides tracking of time-series data. With Prometheus, CPU usage, memory consumption, and query latency can be tracked. The user can also set alert rules and let them execute automatically in case of threshold excess.

Grafana: In case of visualization, one should use Prometheus with Grafana. By using Grafana dashboards, you would be able to track response time, query loads and errors easily. The Grafana alerting system alerts teams every time certain thresholds are attained so you can intervene quickly.

The ELK Stack offers logging capabilities for Apache Superset. Log information is stored in Elasticsearch, ingested and processed through Logstash, and visualized in Kibana with dashboards. Setting up the ELK Stack further allows for the analysis of logs to identify errors or user activity and performance issues with the application, which may be resolved faster and possibly with data-driven optimizations.

In Kubernetes, logging and monitoring can be integrated using Helm charts or custom configurations. In Docker environments, lightweight log shipping solutions such as Fluentd or Beats can route logs to ELK or Prometheus.

Health Checks and Auto-Restarts

With Kubernetes or Docker Swarm, liveness and readiness probes can be set easily so that Superset deployments can continue running with failed containers automatically restarting.

Kubernetes Liveness and Readiness Probes

The state of the containers in Superset is monitored by Kubernetes liveness and readiness probes that can remediate as needed. The liveness probe would identify non-responsive instances, which are then restarted. However, the readiness probe will determine whether an application is ready to accept traffic before sending it to the application. An example of liveness and readiness probes applied in a Superset deployment is as follows:

```
livenessProbe:
  httpGet:
    path: /health
    port: 8088
  initialDelaySeconds: 30
  periodSeconds: 15

readinessProbe:
  httpGet:
    path: /health
    port: 8088
  initialDelaySeconds: 10
  periodSeconds: 5
```

It checks the **/health** endpoint on Superset every 15 seconds for liveness and every 5 seconds for readiness. If the **/health** endpoint becomes unresponsive, the container is restarted, minimizing downtime.

Docker Swarm Restart Policy

You can set up a restart policy on Docker Swarm for Superset containers to define the conditions under which Docker should attempt to restart a failed container.

```
restart_policy:
  condition: on-failure
  delay: 10s
  max_attempts: 3
```

With this setup, Docker Swarm will automatically try to restart the Superset service in case it fails. It will retry three times with a delay of 10 seconds between each attempt.

Zero-Downtime Deployments

Zero-downtime deployments ensure that users are not affected by updates or maintenance. Kubernetes supports rolling updates, which incrementally replace Superset instances while keeping some existing pods available as new pods come online.

An example of rolling update strategy in Kubernetes is as follows:

```
strategy:
  type: RollingUpdate
  rollingUpdate:
    maxUnavailable: 1
    maxSurge: 1
```

In this environment:

`maxUnavailable: 1`

It ensures that at any time, only one pod is unavailable. With **`maxSurge: 1`**, a second pod is created during the update, maintaining availability. The number of unavailable and newly scaled pods is controlled by rolling updates, ensuring a smooth transition before fully exposing the updated deployment to users accessing the database.

This can be made possible in Docker Swarm through the setting of a policy in the **`docker-compose.yml`**.

```
update_config:
  parallelism: 1
  delay: 10s
```

Here, Docker Swarm will apply changes to one container at a time with minimal disruption, leaving 10 seconds between all changes, with parallelism set to 1.

Apache Superset can run in a stable, highly available environment thanks to a thorough backup plan, a highly available metadata database, full monitoring with appropriate health checks, zero-downtime deployment, and other best practices. When combined, these safeguards prevent downtime for your Superset deployments and allow for proactive, effective management, both of which are essential for meeting production's business-critical intelligence requirements.

Conclusion

This chapter provided the readers with a comprehensive guide to get Apache Superset up and running in a production environment. It began by discussing how to deploy it in production, using approaches that emphasized on scalability and high availability. The topic taught audiences how to configure Superset for large teams and multi-tenancy environments to enable successful collaboration across user populations.

Further exploration of the implementation of Superset on modern orchestration platforms, such as Kubernetes or Docker Swarm, emphasized the procedures necessary for effective resource management and containerization. It also addressed strategies related to reliability and uptime, providing readers with tools required to maintain a resilient, high-performing Superset configuration in a production environment.

The next chapter will focus on using Apache Superset for business reporting and data-driven decision-making. It will cover report automation, KPI visualization, and best practices for sharing insights effectively.

CHAPTER 11
Superset for Business Reporting

Introduction

Apache Superset is now a very solid business intelligence tool for teams that require open-source, customizable, and feature-rich solutions for reporting and visualization. Superset has an extremely friendly user interface and good compatibility with data sources. It offers very rich visualization options. Therefore, whenever the company wants to transform raw data into actionable insights, it uses Superset. This chapter discusses the general characteristics of Apache Superset as a BI tool and unique benefits it can provide towards business reporting.

Overview of Apache Superset Reporting

Apache Superset is a free, open-source business intelligence (BI) system that allows users to build and share rich visualizations and dashboards. Because of its technical and non-technical construction, Superset can meet the needs of organizations that vary in degrees of data literacy among group members. It has evolved from its early development at Airbnb into one of the Apache Software Foundation BI solutions that attracted organizations from all over the world. It ranges from simple data visualization up to more complex interactive dashboards. This supports several different data sources including SQL databases, cloud-based storage systems, even big data platforms, making it flexible enough to accommodate almost any organizational need. With its interactive SQL editor, users can query data directly through the platform, create calculated metrics, and build up visualizations to reveal information in real time. Furthermore, its integrated features for report scheduling and alerts make it a complete tool for both routine and real-time business reporting.

Structure

In this chapter, the following topics will be covered:

- Building Reports for Business Users

- Automating Report Generation
- Visualizing Key Performance Indicators (KPIs)
- Sharing Dashboards and Reports
- Best Practices for Business Reporting

Building Reports for Business Users

Superset is unique in the BI space, offering several compelling advantages for business reporting. Here are some of the core advantages:

- **Cost and Open Source**: Superset is free to use and customizable, thereby reducing the costs associated with BI and reporting software; proprietary BI tools, such as Tableau or Power BI. Superset is an open-source approach preferred for organizations that want to avoid licensing fees but still need access to quality reporting tools.
- **Customizability**: As Superset is open-source, it is highly customizable, allowing organizations to use it for their specific reporting needs. Developers can add or modify functionality, integrate it with custom data pipelines, and even contribute to improving the tool.

  It also supports many visualizations ranging from simple bar charts to very complex geospatial maps. All this variety helps in building dashboards based on the specific kinds of information required for any given business need.
- **Interactive Data Exploration**: Superset's SQL Lab enables the analyst and data engineer to directly write SQL queries in the platform, create temporary tables, and start exploring data before creating any visualization. This is probably the most useful feature of business reporting when fast data exploration and validation are needed.
- **Scalable and Secure:** Superset is engineered to meet the scale up requirements of big data volume for tens and hundreds of users at the organization. It holds all the best security facilities including role-based access controls, and even supports certain integrations with LDAP and OAuth protocols, preventing delicate information from coming into illiterates' hands.

  Driven by its active community of developers and users, Superset is constantly evolving. It is more advanced in data visualization and BI trends because its updates or features are regularly added. This means the organizations that use it benefit from a long-term solution to their needs.

Key Features of Reporting and Visualization

With such diversified functionalities, Superset really helps in business reporting. Some of the core features that would be worthy of note for business users include:

- **Diverse Visualization Types:** Superset includes many visualization options, which can accommodate different business reporting needs. Common visual types include:
    - **Line and Area Charts:** Ideal for monitoring trends over time, such as sales, web traffic, performance metrics on operations, and more. Use bar and pie charts to compare by value across categories, such as product performances or market segmentations.
    - **KPI Indicators**: Single-value indicators ensure interested parties focus on the really important values, such as revenue, churn rates, or scores for customer satisfaction.
    - **Scatter and Bubble Charts**: These charts are excellent for showing relationships between variables, such as sales versus marketing expenditure.
    - **Heatmaps and Maps**: This allows for geolocation or categorical breakdown. It makes them helpful for multi-location businesses or operating demographics.
- **Dashboard Creation and Customization:** Superset allows for structuring a set of visualizations into coherent dashboards with filters, drill-downs, and layouts customized toward the needs of the end-user. Interactive dashboards enable the business user to filter through data, zoom into specified time frames, and then make data-driven decisions in real time.
- **SQL Lab and Data Exploration**: SQL Lab allows users to query, explore, and validate data before creating visualizations. This provides analysts with the tools to manipulate raw data and prepare it for reporting. It also supports temporary tables and query caching, which can save time and improve report performance
- **Report Scheduling and Alerts:** Superset has also enabled rich scheduling features to automatically create and send reports. There is a feature in this application that allows scheduling dashboards or any number of charts to be delivered as email or alerts. This helps stakeholders to stay up to date with the change of KPI or other significant metrics. Users receive important insights in real time which makes support for proactive decision-making easier.
- **Role-Based Access Control:** In Superset, role-based access control allows reports and dashboards to be accessed by the right people. For the firm working with sensitive information, this will thus allow strict regimes of data governance policies to ensure and secure compliance in full. Superset offers APIs for integration with other business tools and for automating the workflows of data. It is useful for integrating the Superset visualizations within the external applications and pulling the data from other platforms or to meet more complex reporting requirements.

Apache Superset is a power reporting tool for businesses purely because of flexibility, its cost-effectiveness, and wide-ranging capabilities in visualizing. Superset would allow companies to transform raw data into meaningful insights informing business decisions at all levels: its combination of automated reporting, the ease of real-time exploration, and easy-to-avail visualization options. A well-rounded platform ensures not just scalability but security within which the platform will take up the organization's next leaps, thus ensuring no possibility of future obsolescence.

Building Business Reports with Apache Superset

Among the most important steps in developing extensive business reports in Apache Superset is creating connections to relevant sources of data, proper data organization, selection of visual presentations suitable for the intended purposes, development of user-friendly dashboards, and the availability of interactive features that make reports both informative and accessible to business users.

Creating Effective Data Sources

To begin creating effective reports, it is essential to connect data sources that meet the specific reporting needs of the business.

1. **Connecting to Data Sources**: Superset supports a wide range of databases (for example, PostgreSQL, MySQL, SQLite, Google BigQuery, and more). To connect a data source:
    a. Go to the "`Data`" tab in Superset and select "`Databases`."
    b. Click "`+ Database`" to configure a new connection, entering details such as database URI, username, password, and any necessary connection parameters.
    c. Test the connection to ensure data is accessible.
2. **Organizing Data for Reporting**: Once connected, it is important to organize and prepare data with reporting needs in mind:
    a. **Data Quality Checks**: Ensure data integrity by checking for duplicates, inconsistencies, and missing values.
    b. **Defining Tables and Views**: Use predefined tables or views that aggregate, filter, or format data specifically for reporting. For example, a "`Sales Summary`" view may aggregate sales data by region, product, or quarter.
    c. **Standardizing Metrics**: Create standardized metrics (for example,

revenue, churn rate, customer lifetime value) to maintain consistency across reports.

3. **Data Security and Governance**: Set up role-based access controls for sensitive data to ensure only authorized users can access specific datasets or columns.

Using SQL Lab to Prepare Data for Reports

The SQL Lab is a powerful tool in Superset for data preparation, allowing analysts to write SQL queries to filter, join, and aggregate data before creating visualizations.

1. **Querying Data in SQL Lab**:

   a. Navigate to SQL Lab from the Superset menu and select "`SQL Editor`."

   b. Choose a connected database and write SQL queries to filter and structure the data. For example, a query may join customers and order tables to calculate average order value by customer segment.

   c. Run the query to preview results and ensure accuracy.

2. **Creating Temporary Tables**: Superset allows the creation of temporary tables in SQL Lab, which is useful for simplifying complex joins or aggregations. These tables can then be saved as virtual datasets, making it easier to create visualizations without re-running heavy queries.

3. **Saving Queries for Reuse**: Save queries to streamline workflows, especially for recurring reports. Saved queries can be accessed and modified for future needs, maintaining consistency across multiple reports.

Creating Visualizations

Superset offers a wide range of chart types to visualize data effectively. Choosing the right type of visualization is essential to communicate insights clearly.

- **Chart Types and When to Use Them**:
  - **Bar Chart**: Great for comparing categories (for example, sales by region, product popularity). Use it for side-by-side comparisons across dimensions.
  - **Line Chart**: Ideal for tracking trends over time, such as monthly revenue or customer acquisition. Line charts excel at showing change over time and identifying patterns.
  - **Scatter Plot**: Useful for visualizing relationships between variables, such as marketing spend versus sales. It is often used for trend analysis and correlation studies.

- **Heatmap**: A color-coded grid that displays the intensity of metrics across two dimensions, such as customer satisfaction scores by region and month.
- **Pie and Donut Charts**: Useful for showing proportions within a whole, such as market share by product. However, they are best used with fewer categories for clarity.
- **KPI Metric Card**: Useful for displaying single values, such as total revenue or customer count. These are typically highlighted at the top of dashboards to provide a quick snapshot.
- **Map Visualizations**: Useful for geospatial data, showing metrics by location. They are effective for businesses with location-based insights, including retail chains or logistics.

- **Building Visualizations in Superset**:
  a. Go to "`Charts`" and select "`+ Chart`."
  b. Choose the desired chart type and connect it to a data source.
  c. Configure the visualization by selecting metrics, dimensions, and any necessary aggregations or filters.
  d. Customize visual elements, such as colors, labels, and legends, to enhance readability.
- **Design Tips**: Keep visualizations clean and avoid overcrowding with too many dimensions. Use color intentionally to highlight key data points or trends.

Composing Dashboards for Business Users

After creating visualizations, combine them into dashboards that present a comprehensive view of the data for business users.

- **Organizing Dashboards:**
  - **Thematic Grouping**: Arrange visualizations by themes or business areas (for example, revenue, customer behavior, operational metrics) to make data easier to navigate.
  - **Hierarchical Layout**: Place key metrics and KPIs at the top for quick access, followed by supporting visualizations. This layout guides users through high-level insights to detailed analysis.
  - **Using White Space**: White space between visualizations improves readability, preventing dashboards from looking cluttered.
- **Aesthetic Appeal**:
  - **Consistent Color Schemes**: Use a consistent color palette across the dashboard to enhance visual coherence.

- **Font Consistency**: Keep fonts standardized to maintain professionalism and clarity.
- **Aligning Elements**: Align charts, headers, and text boxes for a cleaner, more professional look. Superset's grid-based layout can assist with alignment.

- **Using Text Boxes for Context**: Add text boxes or headers to describe sections, provide context, or explain metrics. This helps users understand the data more easily.

Customizing Filters and Interactivity

Adding filters and interactive elements makes dashboards more flexible, allowing business users to explore data dynamically.

1. **Adding Filters**:

   a. **Global Filters**: These allow users to filter all visualizations on a dashboard based on selected criteria, such as time range or region. To add a global filter:

      i. Select "`Edit Dashboard`" and add a filter widget.

      ii. Choose the data field(s) to filter by, and configure any default settings.

      iii. Apply the filter to relevant charts to sync data based on user selections.

   b. **Chart-Specific Filters**: For cases where only certain visualizations need filtering, apply filters directly within individual charts.

2. **Adding Drill-Downs**:

   a. **Hierarchical Drill-Downs**: Organize data so that clicking a high-level metric (like total revenue) can lead users to more detailed views (such as revenue by product or region).

   b. **Linking Charts for Contextual Exploration**: For instance, clicking a bar representing a region could trigger a new dashboard tab with more specific information about that region.

3. **Using Interactive Features**:

   a. **Tooltip Customization**: Tooltips provide additional context when hovering over data points. Customize tooltips to show additional metrics, trends, or calculated fields.

   b. **Cross-Filtering Between Visualizations**: Enable cross-filters to create connections between charts. For example, selecting a region in one chart may update metrics in other related charts to reflect only that region's data.

4. **User Guidance and Instructions**: Add brief tooltips or instructions on dashboards to guide users on how to use filters, drill-downs, and other interactive elements effectively.

Following the procedures within Superset, the user will be able to build very efficient and agile business reports. Proper integration of the data sources, preparation in SQL Lab, generation of suitable visualizations, and creation of interactive dashboards allows for intuitive and proper extraction of insights at the right pace. This empowers teams to make informed decisions, track performance metrics, and discern trends from raw data to make it actionable business intelligence.

Automating Report Generation in Superset

Business reporting is central to automation as it makes information timely and relevant without depending on constant manual intervention. Apache Superset is highly enabled by functionalities such as scheduling reports, creating alerts, and integration with other systems; this makes it easy to keep stakeholders informed continually. This section details how one can create schedules and alerts and manage notifications and also interface with external systems as well as best practices while trying to automate reports in a very efficient way.

Setting Up Schedules and Alerts

Apache Superset includes features for scheduling reports and setting up alerts, which allows stakeholders to receive timely updates on key metrics and insights.

1. **Scheduling Reports**:

    a. To set up a report schedule, go to the "**`Alerts & Reports`**" section in Superset.

    b. Choose "**`+ Report`**" and select the dashboard or specific chart you want to schedule.

    c. Configure the schedule details:

        i. **Frequency**: Set how often you want the report to be delivered (for example, daily, weekly, or monthly).

        ii. **Time of Day**: Choose an optimal time for delivery based on stakeholder needs or data update schedules.

iii. **Delivery Method**: Options include sending reports via email or Slack (if integrated).

d. **Customizing Report Content**: Add specific metrics, descriptions, or highlights in the email body to give recipients a clear understanding of the report's focus.

2. **Setting Up Alerts**:

   a. Go to "`Alerts & Reports`" and select "`+ Alert`."

   b. Choose the metric or KPI to monitor and configure an alert condition. For instance, set an alert to trigger if website traffic drops below a certain threshold or if monthly revenue exceeds a target.

   c. Define the frequency and delivery method for the alert.

   d. **Thresholds and Conditional Alerts**: Alerts can be set based on conditions such as "`greater than`," "`less than`," or custom SQL expressions, making it easy to monitor metrics against predefined targets.

Integrating with External Systems

In many cases, business reports need to be accessible across various systems used by different departments. Apache Superset supports integration with external systems, which allows for streamlined report delivery across platforms.

- **Integration with Slack**:
  - Superset offers native support for Slack notifications, allowing scheduled reports or alerts to be sent directly to specified Slack channels.
  - To set up a Slack integration, configure your workspace's webhook URL in Superset's settings under "`Slack API Integration`". This enables automated notifications to team channels, enhancing accessibility.
- **Using Webhooks and APIs**:
  - Superset's API allows it to interact with other platforms, enabling custom integrations with third-party systems such as Microsoft Teams, Jira, or custom web applications.
  - **Creating API-Based Integrations**:

    a. Use the Superset API to retrieve data or visualization images from reports.

    b. Program the API to trigger at specific times or based on external conditions, allowing reports to be sent to users on demand or on a schedule.

   c. Set up webhooks for specific events, such as notifying team members when an alert is triggered or a KPI threshold is reached.

- **Exporting and Embedding Reports**:
    - Superset allows reports to be exported as images, PDFs, or CSV files, which can then be imported into other BI tools or report aggregation platforms.
    - Use the **`embed option`** to display Superset visualizations within external dashboards, websites, or intranet portals. This is especially useful for embedding real-time data into widely accessible locations for broader organizational visibility.

Managing Automated Notifications and Alerts

For automation to be truly effective, notifications and alerts need to be managed carefully. Setting up customized notifications for KPIs and conditions can prevent over-alerting while ensuring that important updates are not missed.

- **Customizing Notification Settings**:
    - When creating alerts, set conditions carefully to avoid triggering unnecessary notifications.
    - For KPI-based reports, consider sending daily summaries rather than immediate notifications. For example, use conditions such as "**`day-over-day`**" or "**`week-over-week`**" percentage changes to highlight significant shifts only.
- **Setting Alert Prioritization**:
    - **Critical Alerts**: For high-impact metrics (for example, revenue drop, user churn increase), set alerts that send instant notifications via email or Slack. Designate a specific team channel for critical alerts to centralize urgent issues.
    - **Routine Summaries**: For routine KPIs, set up weekly or monthly summaries rather than instant alerts. This helps to prevent notification overload while still providing regular insights.
- **Frequency Management**:
    - Balance alert frequency based on metric importance and frequency of change. For instance, customer satisfaction metrics might warrant monthly alerts, while operational KPIs (like error rates) might be monitored daily.
    - Limit notification volume to prevent alert fatigue. This involves setting only essential alerts and choosing to batch less critical metrics into periodic summary reports.

Best Practices for Report Automation

To maximize the value of report automation, it is essential to follow best practices in scheduling frequency, performance optimization, and alert management.

- **Optimizing Report and Query Performance**:
  - Scheduled reports should be optimized for performance to minimize load times and server impact. Cache results whenever possible to reduce query load, especially for reports that aggregate large datasets.
  - Use Superset's built-in `cache settings` to store report data temporarily, which can improve load times for frequently viewed reports and reduce strain on the database.
- **Avoiding Alert Fatigue**:
  - To reduce the risk of alert fatigue, segment alerts by priority and ensure that only actionable alerts are delivered. For example, critical business metrics such as revenue shifts or server downtimes can be prioritized for instant alerts, while others can be included in a weekly summary.
  - Regularly review alert conditions to ensure they are still relevant. Metrics that no longer require frequent monitoring should be adjusted or removed to keep alerts meaningful.
  - Encourage users to opt-in for specific reports and alerts relevant to their role to ensure that recipients only receive information directly applicable to their responsibilities.
- **Determining Ideal Frequency for Reports and Alerts**:
  - Base reporting frequency on data update rates and the speed of decision-making cycles. For fast-changing metrics (for example, daily active users, conversion rates), daily or weekly reports are more relevant, while slower metrics (for example, customer lifetime value) may be updated monthly.
  - Ensure alert frequency aligns with the reporting objectives. For example, operational teams may require hourly alerts for system uptime, while financial reports for C-level executives might only need weekly or monthly summaries.
- **User-Centric Automation Design**:
  - Design automated reports and alerts with the end user in mind. Segment reporting by department (for example, finance, marketing) to deliver specific insights tailored to different functional needs.
  - Provide dashboards with quick access to the most frequently requested metrics and establish clear labeling so users can quickly interpret information without extensive context-switching.

- Collect feedback from stakeholders to refine the automation setup over time, ensuring reports remain relevant and actionable.

Apache Superset gives teams real-time, relevant insights automatically. The capability to schedule and alert, plus third-party integration, lets stakeholders know about critical data without manually checking. Best practices around performance optimization, priority-based alerts, and user-centric design ensure the effect of automated reports increases value to decision-making rather than contributing to alert fatigue.

Visualizing Key Performance Indicators (KPIs)

KPIs are the most important metrics of the health, progress, and success of an organization in a particular area. Proper definition and expression of KPIs in Superset make data-driven decisions so that organizations remain on track with strategic goals. This section introduces the concept of KPIs in a business context, defines how to define them in Superset, best practices for visualizations, and design best practices for effective communication.

Understanding KPIs in the Business Context

KPIs are measurable values that indicate how well an organization is achieving key business objectives. Unlike general metrics, KPIs are strategically selected to align with company goals, making them central to tracking progress and guiding decision-making.

- **Significance of KPIs**:
  - **Performance Tracking**: KPIs enable teams to monitor performance in real time, such as monitoring monthly sales, profit margins, or customer acquisition rates.
  - **Goal Alignment**: KPIs link everyday activities to broader business goals, ensuring alignment from executives down to individual teams.
  - **Decision Support**: By focusing on meaningful metrics, KPIs help identify growth opportunities, reveal problem areas, and inform strategic decisions.
- **Choosing Relevant KPIs**:
  - KPIs should be **specific, measurable, attainable, relevant**, and **time-bound (SMART)**.
  - Each KPI should be directly linked to a specific business objective. For example, a digital marketing KPI might be "*Customer Acquisition Cost* (CAC)" if the goal is to optimize spending efficiency.
  - Avoid overcrowding dashboards with too many KPIs. Focus on the most

impactful metrics, such as revenue, customer satisfaction, or churn rate, depending on the audience and purpose of the report.

Defining KPIs in Superset

Superset allows users to define KPIs within charts or dashboards using calculated columns, expressions, and metrics, which help tailor data to specific reporting needs.

- **Creating Calculated Columns and Metrics**:
    - **Calculated Columns**: Go to "`Datasets`" and select a dataset. Under the "`Columns`" tab, add a new calculated column where you can define custom KPIs. For instance, create a calculated column for `profit margin` by dividing profit by revenue.
    - **Metrics**: In the dataset editor, go to the "`Metrics`" tab to define custom metrics (aggregations like `SUM`, `AVG`, `COUNT`) that represent KPIs, such as total revenue or average order value.
    - **SQL Expressions**: Use SQL expressions for more complex KPI definitions, such as customer lifetime value or average deal size. These expressions allow flexibility in combining or transforming data for custom KPIs.
- **Configuring KPI Widgets**:
    - Superset offers KPI widgets, which allow you to visualize single-value metrics, such as total sales or average customer satisfaction. Set up these widgets by selecting "`Single Value`" or "`Big Number`" charts, which are ideal for displaying KPIs prominently on dashboards.

Designing KPI Visualizations

To make KPIs actionable, they need to be visualized in a way that is easy to understand at a glance. Different chart types cater to different reporting needs, depending on the nature of the KPI.

- **Best Chart Types for KPI Visualization**:
    - **KPI Tiles (Big Number)**: Single-value displays such as "`Big Number`" are great for highlighting key metrics, such as revenue or churn rate, that stakeholders need to track continuously. These tiles are prominent and often located at the top of a dashboard.
    - **Trend Lines**: Use line charts to show KPI changes over time, such as sales growth, customer acquisition trends, or website traffic patterns. Trend lines are effective for spotting seasonality, growth, or decline in metrics.
    - **Bar Charts**: For KPIs that compare categories (for example, revenue by region or product), bar charts provide a clear comparison and are easy to interpret.

  - **Donut or Pie Charts**: Best for displaying the proportion of a KPI among categories. For example, a pie chart might show the percentage contribution of each product line to total revenue.
  - **Gauge or Progress Bars**: Use these for goal-oriented KPIs, such as progress toward a sales target. Gauges provide a visual representation of how close you are to achieving a specific threshold.
- **Using Superset's KPI Widgets**:
  - Create a "`Big Number`" chart or other KPI-specific visualization to add single-value KPIs directly to your dashboards.
  - Customize the font size, colors, and labels to ensure the KPI tile stands out and is easily interpretable. Include subtext or context (for example, "`compared to last month`") to make the KPI more meaningful.

Using Color and Layout for KPI Communication

Visual design plays a significant role in enhancing KPI dashboards by making data easy to interpret and emphasizing important metrics. Effective use of color, layout, and thresholds helps users focus on critical information.

- **Color Coding**:
  - **Highlight Key Data Points**: Use distinct colors to draw attention to important KPIs. For example, use green for positive performance (revenue growth) and red for areas that need improvement (increased churn).
  - **Threshold-Based Colors**: Set colors to indicate when a KPI reaches a certain threshold. For example, set a color range for a KPI tile that changes from green to yellow to red as a metric approaches a critical level.
  - **Consistent Palette**: Use a consistent color palette throughout the dashboard. This maintains visual harmony and avoids cognitive overload.
- **Thresholds and Conditional Formatting**:
  - Set up conditional formatting to emphasize when KPIs fall below or exceed certain thresholds. For instance, a profit margin KPI can turn red when it drops below a 10% threshold.
  - Thresholds should be aligned with business goals and strategic priorities, such as monthly revenue targets or customer satisfaction benchmarks, to give users clear visual cues on performance status.
- **Layout and Positioning**:
  - **Hierarchy of Information**: Position the most critical KPIs at the top of the dashboard, making them the first thing users see. Less critical or supporting data can be displayed below.

   - **Grouping Related KPIs**: Group similar KPIs together (for example, financial KPIs in one section, operational KPIs in another). This helps users quickly navigate the dashboard and understand relationships between metrics.
   - **White Space and Alignment**: Leave adequate white space between elements to avoid a cluttered appearance. Proper alignment and spacing improve readability and user focus.

- Text and Labels for Clarity:
   - Include explanatory text or tooltips with KPI visualizations to provide context, such as the formula or time period used. For example, a KPI showing "`Customer Satisfaction`" could have a tooltip describing the survey period and scoring method.
   - Add concise, descriptive labels to each KPI tile. Labels such as "`Monthly Revenue`" or "`Average Customer Lifetime Value`" clarify what the metric represents and guide users through the data.

Plan carefully the inclusion of KPIs into Superset dashboards; from the right metrics or defining them in Superset to choosing the right kind of visualizations. Apply thoughtful design principles by leveraging the power of KPI tiles, trend lines, bar charts, and threshold-based color coding to help users develop intuitive, action-oriented dashboards that really drive good decision-making.

Sharing Dashboards and Reports with Stakeholders

Apache Superset offers more than a dozen tools that help make the usage of data visualizations and insights effective, which can be used for sharing dashboards and reports. Links and embed codes are enabled, and real-time data refresh configurations are important to configure access controls. This section briefly talks about Superset's role-based access control, report sharing options, real-time data configurations, and ways of exporting and making data available for offline use.

Understanding User Roles and Access Control

Superset includes robust role-based access control (RBAC), enabling administrators to manage permissions and protect data by assigning roles to different user groups. This functionality ensures that users have access to only the data and dashboards they need while maintaining the security of sensitive information.

- **Superset User Roles**:

   a. **`Admin`**: The highest level of access, with permissions to manage users, configure databases, and edit all content.

b. **`Gamma`**: A role designed for data consumers who primarily need access to explore and view dashboards but cannot create or edit charts or datasets.

c. **`Alpha`**: This role has access to most features, including creating and editing dashboards and reports, but does not have access to administrative settings.

d. **`Public`**: This role allows limited access to public resources. Typically, users with this role can only view specific public dashboards or charts.

- **Assigning and Managing Roles**:

  a. Go to the "**`Security`**" tab and select "**`List Roles`**".

  b. Create new roles or edit existing ones to customize permissions based on business needs. For instance, finance team members may need access to specific financial dashboards but not to HR data.

  c. **Granular Permissions**: Superset allows administrators to assign permissions to specific datasets, dashboards, or charts, creating a customized experience for each role.

- **Data Security**: Role-based permissions in Superset help maintain data security by limiting access to sensitive information. For instance, roles can be set up so that only certain users can view personal data, financial metrics, or confidential reports.

Setting Up Report Sharing

Superset provides multiple options for sharing dashboards and reports, including direct links, embed codes, and exporting as PDFs or images for flexibility in distribution.

- **Sharing via Direct Links**:

  a. After building a dashboard, you can generate a **shareable link** for users within the Superset environment. To share a link:

     i. Open the dashboard and click the share icon to copy the URL.

     ii. Share the link with stakeholders who have appropriate permissions within Superset. Note that only users with the necessary permissions will be able to access the content.

- **Embedding Dashboards in External Applications**:

  a. Superset supports embedding dashboards or individual charts in other applications, including intranets or business portals.

     i. Enable the "**`Public`**" role for viewing-only access to dashboards that are widely shared or embed charts with iframe codes (for embedded HTML).

ii. **Embed Options**: Go to the desired chart or dashboard, select "`Embed Code`" from the share options, and paste it into the HTML of the destination site.

iii. Ensure embedded content remains secure by configuring access control to limit visibility based on the viewer's role.

- **Sharing Reports as PDFs**:

  a. Users can `export dashboards as PDFs` to facilitate sharing outside of Superset or for official documentation purposes.

  i. Go to the "`Share`" options and select "`Download as PDF`" to generate a PDF version of the current view.

  ii. These PDFs can then be distributed to stakeholders who may not have Superset access but need regular insights in a portable format.

Real-Time Data and Refresh Options

Real-time data access is essential for keeping reports accurate and actionable. Superset supports data refresh options that ensure dashboards and charts display the latest information.

- **Automatic Data Refresh**:
  - Superset allows users to configure automatic data refreshes at intervals to keep dashboards up to date without manual intervention.

    i. Go to the `dashboard` settings, select the refresh interval option, and choose a refresh frequency that matches the data update cycle (for example, every minute, hourly, or daily).

    ii. Frequent refreshes are recommended for operational dashboards where data changes rapidly, such as monitoring website traffic or real-time sales.

- **Configuring Cache Settings**:
  - Caching can improve performance by reducing the need to query the database each time a dashboard loads. To configure caching:

    i. Go to `Settings > Caching` and adjust cache durations based on data sensitivity and the frequency with which it changes.

    ii. For data that rarely changes, longer cache durations can reduce load on the database, whereas frequently updated data may require shorter cache intervals.

- **Query-Based Updates**: Superset also supports setting up SQL queries that dynamically pull real-time data for dashboards. For instance, a live data feed from an analytics system can update every time the dashboard is accessed, ensuring real-time reporting.

Exporting Reports for Offline Use

Superset allows users to export data and dashboards in several formats for offline access, which is useful for sharing with users who may not have Superset access or for archiving purposes.

- **Exporting as CSV**:
  - For data analysis outside of Superset, charts and datasets can be exported as CSV files.
    1. Open the desired chart, select "`Export Data`," and choose CSV format. The CSV can then be downloaded, allowing users to analyze or share the data in spreadsheets or other BI tools.
- **Exporting Images**:
  - Visualizations can be saved as images, making it easy to include in presentations or reports.
    1. Select "`Download as PNG`" for the chart or visualization. This feature is useful for static reports, such as monthly updates or snapshots for presentations.
- **Exporting Dashboards as PDFs**:
  - Dashboards can be exported as PDFs for offline sharing with stakeholders who need a complete view of all KPIs and metrics.
    1. Go to the "`Share`" options on the dashboard page and select "`Download as PDF`." The entire dashboard, including all charts and KPIs, is rendered as a PDF that can be saved or printed.
- **Scheduled Report Delivery**:
  - Superset supports scheduled report deliveries, such as automated emails with PDF or CSV attachments.
    1. Set up scheduled reports in `Alerts & Reports` by selecting the dashboard, setting a schedule, and choosing the desired file format (PDF or CSV). This enables automated report distribution for recipients who require offline access or regular updates.

The processes for figuring the appropriate roles and the corresponding access controls and distribution mechanisms are quite tedious in case of distribution of dashboards and reports in Superset. In this way, Superset facilitates the distribution of insights to organizations via building secure, role-centric access, combined with near-real-time data availability as well as offline reporting capabilities. Properly configured, these tools enable stakeholders in access analysis as well as response on time while taking informed decisions on the data.

Best Practices for Business Reporting in Superset

In Superset, big influential business reports need to be aesthetically pleasing, exact, prompt, secure, and user friendly. Any report has to be prepared with an eye for aesthetic detail such that the details it conveys reach the right persons. In addition, stakeholder input, including that of compliance, ensures that improvement will always continue. This section illustrates the best practices on how continuing improvement of business reports in Superset effectiveness are ensured.

Data Quality and Accuracy

Clean and accurate data is the foundation of reliable reporting. Without data quality, reports can lead to incorrect insights, poor decision-making, and a lack of stakeholder trust.

- **The Importance of Data Validation and Consistency**:
  - Inconsistent data can result from errors in data entry, differences in format, or incomplete data sources. Accurate reporting depends on systematic validation to maintain data integrity.
  - Data quality checks should be automated wherever possible, especially when dealing with multiple data sources or complex datasets.
- **Tips for Ensuring Data Quality**:
  - **Data Cleansing**: Use SQL Lab or other data preparation tools to clean datasets by removing duplicates, standardizing formats (example, date formats), and filling missing values before creating visualizations.
  - **Regular Audits**: Schedule periodic data quality audits, which include checks for data duplication, anomalies, and outliers. For example, ensure that monthly revenue numbers do not show extreme deviations unless expected.
  - **Data Governance Policies**: Implement data governance policies to define and maintain data standards. This can include creating a single source of truth for key metrics and ensuring alignment across departments.

Designing for Your Audience

Reports are most impactful when they are tailored to meet the specific needs and preferences of different business users or departments. Understanding the audience allows you to prioritize relevant metrics, choose appropriate visualizations, and design a dashboard that enhances data accessibility.

- **Tailoring Reports for Specific Departments**:
  - **Finance**: Finance reports often focus on metrics such as revenue, profit margin, cash flow, and ROI. These users may require line charts for historical trends, bar charts for comparisons, and KPI tiles to highlight high-level financial metrics.
  - **Marketing**: Marketing teams are likely to focus on engagement metrics, customer acquisition costs, conversion rates, and ROI. Visualizations such as funnel charts, time series charts, and customer segmentation heatmaps can provide valuable insights.
  - **Operations**: Operational reports may focus on metrics such as production efficiency, error rates, and uptime. Using gauges, trend lines, and scatter plots can help operations teams identify bottlenecks and track performance over time.
- **Effective Presentation for Non-Technical Users**:
  - Avoid data overload by focusing on essential KPIs and providing context for each metric with clear labels and tooltips.
  - Use interactive filters to give users control over the data they see, allowing them to explore subsets of information relevant to their role.

Ensuring Report Performance

Optimized performance is essential for dashboards to be both effective and accessible, especially when dealing with large datasets or complex calculations. Slow load times can hinder user experience and reduce report value.

- **Optimizing Dashboard Load Times**:
  - **Query Optimization**: Refine SQL queries by indexing commonly queried columns, simplifying joins, and removing unnecessary aggregations. This reduces query execution time and improves dashboard responsiveness.
  - **Caching**: Use Superset's caching feature to store frequently accessed data. Cached reports load faster because they retrieve data from a temporary storage layer rather than querying the database each time.
  - **Limit Data Scope**: Restrict data to the necessary timeframe or dimensions to reduce load time. For instance, load only the past year's data rather than the entire dataset unless historical data is required.

- **Balancing Real-Time Data Needs**:
    - For real-time dashboards, set appropriate refresh intervals based on user needs and data volatility. For example, high-frequency metrics (for example, website traffic) might refresh every minute, while others (for example, monthly revenue) might only need daily updates.
    - Enable real-time data selectively to avoid unnecessary server load. Use scheduled refreshes for metrics that do not need constant updating.

Privacy, Security, and Compliance

Maintaining data privacy, security, and compliance with regulatory standards is critical, particularly when reports contain sensitive or personally identifiable information (PII).

- **Role-Based Access Control (RBAC)**:
    - Superset's role-based access control enables you to assign specific access permissions to different user roles. This minimizes unauthorized access and helps ensure that users only see data that is relevant to them.
    - Regularly review and update roles to ensure they align with current data governance policies and organizational needs.
- **Data Privacy Compliance**:
    - If handling PII, ensure that data is anonymized or redacted where necessary to comply with GDPR, CCPA, or other privacy laws.
    - Avoid embedding or exporting sensitive information in reports that may be shared externally. Ensure that dashboards and exports are restricted to authorized users.
- **Secure Sharing and Distribution**:
    - Use SSL/TLS encryption for Superset's network traffic to secure data transfers.
    - For highly sensitive data, avoid embedding dashboards in external systems or use additional security measures, such as multi-factor authentication (MFA) or VPN access, to add layers of security.

Continuous Improvement and Feedback

Regularly gathering feedback from stakeholders and refining reports can significantly enhance their value and relevance. As business needs evolve, ongoing improvements ensure that reports remain aligned with organizational goals and user expectations.

- **Gathering Feedback**:
    - Schedule regular check-ins with report users to gather their input. Ask

about the relevance of metrics, the usability of the dashboard, and any additional insights they need.

  - Use surveys or feedback forms to capture quantitative and qualitative insights about report effectiveness and user satisfaction.

- **Iterating on Reports**:
  - Based on feedback, update or add new metrics, visualizations, and filters that meet users' evolving needs. For instance, if the marketing team wants to track a new campaign KPI, integrate it into their dashboard.
  - Implement an agile approach to reporting, where you iterate on report features and designs based on user feedback and changing requirements.
- **Documentation and Training**:
  - Provide updated documentation for each report to help users understand the data, metrics, and any new features added. This includes definitions of key metrics and how to interpret visualizations.
  - Offer brief training sessions, especially for complex reports, to help users make the most of interactive filters, drill-downs, and other features.

Conclusion

This chapter focused on the capabilities of Apache Superset-a powerful tool for facilitating business reporting and strategic decision-making. It started with setting up data sources, creating visualizations, and automating the workflows to generate detailed interactive dashboards that meet stakeholder requirements. The SQL Lab is another key feature of Superset that allows preparing and refining datasets to meaningful, analysis-ready reports.

Readers assessed the different types of graphical representations in Superset in the context of specific business questions, including line charts, heatmaps, and KPI tiles. This chapter also covered automation of report generation, setting of alerts, and integration with third-party systems to supplement reporting workflows and ensure information is properly propagated.

The relevance of KPIs in business reports has been stressed by emphasizing to readers how they can be defined and visualized by applying best practices for clarity and actionability. Tools such as role-based access control, data security, and flexible options of report sharing have been included for improving stakeholder engagement. Maintaining data accuracy, user-centric design, and evolutionary report through stakeholder input are suggested as the best practices in the last chapter.

Using such concepts, it enables organizations to use Superset to improve their reporting processes, foster better decision-making and cultivate a data-driven culture.

The next chapter is focused on enabling end-users to self-service business intelligence using the help of Apache Superset. Readers will understand how to enable non-technical users to discover data for themselves, create their reports, and get insights independently without relying on technical teams. Key topics include creating user-friendly dashboards, teaching non-technical users, and best practices for user enablement, all of which will foster easier and more collaborative reporting across the organization.

CHAPTER 12
Self-Service BI with Superset

Introduction

The essence of data-driven decision-making in the modern context is about quick access, interpretation, and actioning of insights that come from data. Traditionally, data analysis and business intelligence have always been the preserve of technical teams, which often acts as a bottleneck to the speed at which an organization may respond to critical insights about the business from data. Thus, self-service BI is the reverse, transform approach which empowers non-technical users to access, explore, and interpret data on their own with a minimum dependency on data or IT teams.

Apache Superset is an open-source BI tool that has surfaced as a very potent platform for self-service BI. The user-friendly interface and rich data visualization options provided along with flexible architecture support diverse users from various roles and technical backgrounds in making independent reports, metrics, and insights. This, in turn, brings the power of data to the desks of business users and eliminates their dependency on technical teams to make decisions more agile while encouraging a data exploration culture within organizations.

This chapter explores how to harness Apache Superset to create a robust self-service BI environment. We will cover essential aspects of setting up Superset, from enabling data democratization to creating intuitive dashboards tailored for non-technical users. We will also discuss effective strategies for training users, empowering them with the skills and confidence needed to explore data independently, and share best practices that facilitate a smooth transition to self-service BI.

By and large, this chapter will endow companies with a strategic guide toward constructing an Apache Superset-driven, self-service BI culture, empowering users to make smarter decisions based on sound data insights.

Structure

In this chapter, we will cover the following topics:

- Enabling Self-Service BI
- Training Non-Technical Users
- Creating Easy-to-Use Dashboards
- Best Practices for User Empowerment

Enabling Self-Service BI

In today's fast-paced business environment, organizations require data to become more accessible. Self-service Business Intelligence empowers non-technical users to access and analyze data independently, enabling swift, well-informed decisions without constant reliance on IT or data teams. Apache Superset, a powerful open-source BI tool, supports self-service BI by providing easy data access and visual analytics capabilities for both technical and non-technical users.

This section explores the fundamental principles of self-service BI, what makes Apache Superset different, and how it aids in democratizing access to data across an organization. We will then explore some strategies on data connectivity and governance to ensure data is secure and accurate in self-service BI environments.

Definition and Core Principles of Self-Service BI

Self-service BI refers to the tools and practices that allow end-users, even non-technical users, to directly access and analyze data. This cuts off reliance on IT departments or specialized analysts, democratizing access to data and making decisions with data-driven evidence in organizations.

Core Principles of Self-Service BI

Self-service BI enables users to independently determine and visualize the data they deem relevant, regardless of their technical skills. Key technical skills include:

- **Usability**: For BI to be truly self-service, the tools must be highly usable. Easy-to-read interfaces, intuitive controls, and simplified data querying help even those with minimal technical knowledge to navigate and utilize the BI platforms.
- **Accessibility**: Data has to be accessible to any legitimate user in the self-service

BI environment. This accessibility is a prerequisite for effective browsing and analysis with BI tools, minimizing constraints on relevant datasets.

- **Governance**: Although the primary purpose is ease of access, self-service BI still needs to be governed so that accuracy, security, and consistency of data are ensured. Governance fosters trust in the data and encourages users to follow best practices.

Value Proposition of Self-Service BI in Modern Organizations

- **Speed:** Self-service BI provides faster access to insights, eliminating delays caused by waiting for technical team responses. Real-time reports, analyses, and data access enable timely decision-making, a crucial competitive advantage in dynamic industries.
- **Sovereignty:** The dependency on the IT and data teams is eradicated, thus creating agility and responsiveness within the team, as the users can directly and independently access and analyze their data.
- **Accessibility:** Self-service BI breaks down data silos between departments. Cross-functional teams can access the data they need, enabling everyone from marketing to finance to contribute to data-informed strategies.

Key Features of Apache Superset for Self-Service BI

Apache Superset is an open-source data exploration and visualization platform widely used for accessibility, powerful visualizations, and ease of use by non-technical users.

Superset has intuitive, organized dashboards of data visualization views and interactive querying through a SQL lab. The structure of the application is most useful in an environment for non-technical users who are able to view, visualize, or explore data without extensive preparation or training.

- **Explore View:** This is a feature that allows a user to create and edit visualizations without knowing any SQL. Users can drag/drop data fields, apply filters, and then choose from various chart types, such as bar, line, and scatter plots, to gain analytical insights from raw data.
- **SQL Lab:** SQL Lab can be availed for direct data querying, especially for power and technical users. In SQL Lab, one may execute SQL queries, combine datasets, preview results and then visualize or export that result. Users may further create their custom calculations and metrics.
- **Dashboard Functions**: Dashboards in Superset can be customized and rolled out across the organization. It enables users to track and monitor key metrics,

filter it by various types of filters, and even schedule reports to track the moving KPIs in the system.

Understanding Data Democratization

It involves the democratization of data at the core. Here, the idea is to ensure that access to data is available to everyone, not just a select group of technical specialists. Superset supports the process of democratization by offering intuitive tools that makes data exploration manageable and understandable for all users.

- **Data Availability**: Superset's user-friendly interface and visualization tools break the technical barriers, and hence users from all walks of life can access and interpret data. Non-technical users can independently navigate data, create dashboards, and explore datasets, which significantly reduces their dependency on data specialists or IT support.
- **Creating a Self-Service Data Environment in Superset**: Superset enables data democratization, allowing teams to build a centralized, self-service data environment. Users can easily access predefined data sources, templates, and dashboards, which makes it easy to explore data and generate insights without having advanced technical skills. Access controls and permissions can be configured to ensure users can only access relevant datasets, thus balancing accessibility with data security.

Data Sources and Connectivity

A self-service BI environment must let the connection to data sources be done without much complexity. That way, the users' focus will shift to more analysis rather than to the technical configuration. Since Superset supports a wide variety of data sources, it is a suitable option for diverse data environments.

- **Connecting to Multiple Data Sources**: The Superset connects different types of data storage, such as SQL databases (MySQL, PostgreSQL), a cloud data warehouse (BigQuery, Redshift), and a data lake. It can access data from all the sources, giving an organization a complete view of the data.
- **Simplify Data Connectivity to Minimize Technical Involvement**: Once the data sources are connected, users can begin querying and visualizing data directly in the interface of Superset without a care in the world for integration or ETL processes. Pre-configured data connections and metadata make it easy to access data for insights rather than connectivity.
- **Best Practices in Managing and Organizing Data Sources in Superset**: It will be easy to access with department or use case-specific data sources: sales, finance, and customer insights.

- Data Source Descriptions: All data sources will provide brief descriptions so that every dataset can be easily recognized.
- **Monitor performance:** Data connections must be monitored frequently for efficient data loading into the system, especially in cases where bulky datasets are used.

Data Governance in Self-Service BI

In the self-service BI environment, effective data governance is that which will balance accessibility and security. Through Apache Superset, strict governance policies can be created to maintain data integrity while allowing users to responsibly consume data.

Balance Freedom with Data Security and Accuracy

While data democratization is important, it is also important to control access to and modification of the data. Superset features role-based access control and therefore allows administrators to manage access rights so that only certain individuals can access sensitive information.

Role and Permission Configuration for Users in Superset

In Superset, administrators can assign specific roles as Admin, Alpha, and Gamma, which significantly varies in access levels.

- **Admin**: It has access to manage and configure the Superset environment, including data sources and permissions.
- **Alpha**: It can view and build visualizations and dashboards but lacks full administrative rights.
- **Gamma**: It can view dashboards and the data but cannot modify data sources or configurations.

These roles guarantee that users have only the necessary level of access for their job functions, ensuring secure, self-service access.

Ensuring Integrity in Data Based on Clear Policies and Quality Checks

- **Data Quality Checks**: Quality checks should run continually in self-service BI environments to ensure data quality; in fact, data quality issues can erode trust.
- **Define Data Usage Policies:** Include best practices for data exploration,

analysis, and sharing. Ensure that users verify a data source or methodology for consistent and reliable insights.

- **Audit Logs**: Superset tracks user activity, so the administrator will know how people use the application to spot anomalies and ensure compliance with data governance policies.

Self-service BI, made possible by Apache Superset, equips all types of users with accessible data insight and actionable data through independence, speed, and accessibility. The functionality behind Superset's enabling tools for data democratization along with its reduction of dependence on the technical teams makes every such organization balance the desired levels of freedom of the use of self-service BI without compromising on security or reliability in the data-driven environment.

Training Non-Technical Users

Effective training is crucial for empowering non-technical users to effectively leverage self-service BI tools such as Apache Superset. This approach, in turn, not only builds foundational skills but also creates confidence and independence, thereby allowing the users to discover data and create insights without constant technical support. Here are some of the key elements for designing a well-rounded training program to equip non-technical users with the essential skills needed to navigate Superset and encourage continuous learning.

Structuring an Introductory Training Program

Empowering the user in self-service BI capabilities requires structured training to help users gain confidence and independence. This section provides an all-encompassing approach in introducing non-technical users to Apache Superset starting with clear goals in training, such as navigation, exploration of datasets, and basic visualizations.

Users will acquire fundamental competencies such as dashboard navigation, filter application, and visualization interaction, presented in a structured manner to facilitate comprehension. Practical modules designed for hands-on experience offer targeted instructions, gradually elevating the level of difficulty to improve skill mastery.

In order to foster sustainable development, continuous resources such as tutorials, workshops, and feedback mechanisms are in place, empowering users to independently investigate data and generate reports with confidence. This strategy fosters an environment characterized by curiosity, collaboration, and decision-making informed by data throughout the organization.

1. **Setting Clear Training Goals**
    - Begin with defining specific, achievable goals for the introductory program, focusing on equipping users with:

- Basic navigation skills within the Superset interface.
- Familiarity with dashboards, filtering, and fundamental visualizations.
- Confidence in exploring and interacting with datasets.

- Outline the program's objectives, emphasizing ease of use, fostering curiosity, and building user independence.

2. **Breaking Down the Essentials**
   - **Dashboard Navigation**: Start with a brief introduction to the main components of the Superset interface, explaining how to:
     - Access and switch between dashboards.
     - Identify key sections such as Explore view, SQL Lab, and main dashboard view.
   - **Applying Filters**: Teach users how to apply filters to narrow down data, focusing on filtering types and how filters affect visualizations.
   - **Interacting with Visualizations**: Cover how to interpret different chart types, customize views, and use interactive features such as zooming or hovering for deeper insights.
3. **Building Hands-On Practice Modules**
   - Structure hands-on activities around common tasks, such as using filters or customizing a chart. These modules should focus on:
     - **Task-Specific Guides**: Use step-by-step guides for navigating charts, applying filters, or adding annotations.
     - **Incremental Complexity**: Gradually introduce more complex interactions, ensuring users build confidence as they progress.
4. **Offering Ongoing Training and Resources**
   - After completing introductory training, provide ongoing learning resources to support user growth:
     - **Tutorial videos and webinars** for specific use cases.
     - **Monthly workshops** that allow users to tackle real-life data challenges.
     - **Regular feedback loops** through surveys or check-ins to identify additional training needs.

Empowering Users with Core Skills

Facilitating user empowerment in core competencies related to Apache Superset requires arming them with the necessary knowledge and resources to navigate and utilize the platform effectively. As a data visualization and business intelligence tool,

Apache Superset enables users to explore and visualize datasets, build complex dashboards, and perform extensive analytical activities efficiently.

Empowerment starts with user onboarding in the Superset interface. They will be exposed to all skills necessary for working with important elements such as Explore view, SQL Lab, and dashboards. Such foundational understanding leads to user comfort with the platform and thereby enhances the users' ability to access and utilize the tool functionalities confidently.

1. **Navigating Superset's Interface**
    - Make users comfortable with the Superset layout by highlighting:
        - **Main Interface Components**: Show how to access the Explore view, SQL Lab, and dashboard.
        - **Using Breadcrumbs and Navigation Tabs**: Guide users on efficiently navigating between sections and revisiting recently accessed dashboards.
2. **Simplifying Essential Features**
    - **Filters and Sorting**: Teach users how to apply filters effectively to narrow down results and sort data based on their analysis goals.
    - **Grouping and Aggregating Data**: Help users understand the grouping and aggregation options available within Superset, demonstrating the importance of grouping in uncovering trends.
    - **Exporting Data**: Show users how to export data from Superset into spreadsheets or other formats they may need, supporting them in creating reports for different contexts.

Creating Interactive and Hands-On Training Materials

To maximize the value of Apache Superset for self-service BI, users require a solid grasp of key skills. This section aims to guide users in intuitively understanding the Superset interface, its main features, and their application to data analysis workloads.

Users will be empowered to master the core elements of the interface-comprising the Explore view, SQL Lab, and dashboards and also become masters of navigation tools such as breadcrumbs and tabs. The functionality of filtering, sorting, grouping, and aggregation would be optimized so that trends and insights can be extracted dependably. Export instructions will be in place so that users can get their findings communicated in formats suitable for reporting needs.

With these core competencies in hand, users can use Superset in self-servicing mode and add even more simplicity and convenience to the data exploration and reporting processes.

1. **Using Real-World Data Examples**
   - Tailor training materials to reflect data relevant to users' roles:
     - **Realistic Datasets**: Use datasets similar to those they will handle in their daily tasks (for example, sales data for sales teams, customer analytics for marketing).
     - **Role-Specific Exercises**: Customize training exercises around role-specific tasks, such as creating sales trends for the sales team or campaign performance for marketing.
2. **Incorporating Interactive Elements in Training**
   - **Quizzes and Knowledge Checks**: Embed quizzes at the end of each module to reinforce understanding and make learning engaging.
   - **Hands-On Labs**: Organize practical labs where users can try creating visualizations or reports based on guided exercises.
   - **Practice Dashboards**: Set up sample dashboards with mock data, allowing users to explore and modify visuals in a risk-free environment.
3. **Step-by-Step Guides for Creating Basic Visualizations and Charts**

   a. Provide easy-to-follow guides for users to create basic visualizations, starting with:
   - **Bar and line charts** for trend analysis.
   - **Pie charts** for categorical breakdowns.
   - **Tables** for detailed data inspection.

   b. Break down the chart creation process into manageable steps, emphasizing the value each chart type offers and its appropriate use.

Strategies for Building User Confidence

Empowering users goes beyond technical training, it requires instilling confidence and curiosity. This section describes ways to help users feel empowered and motivated as they navigate their data journey.

Clear, step-by step instructions on how to do common operations enable users to independently complete core tasks. A Sandbox environment encourages exploration by granting free access to all Superset features—sometimes "*getting it wrong*" is part of the learning process. Sharing impact stories and acknowledging user contributions creates an appreciative and encouraging community, making individuals feel valued and confident in their Superset accomplishments.

1. **Providing Comprehensive Step-by-Step Guides**

    a. Develop accessible guides for common tasks, helping users complete essential tasks on their own. Example guides include:

    - **How to filter data by date range**.
    - **How to create a simple bar chart with categorical breakdowns**.

    b. Include visuals with annotations for easy reference, focusing on key actions users will perform frequently.

2. **Encouraging Experimentation and Exploration**

    - Cultivate a culture that encourages users to explore data beyond set instructions. Highlight the following:
        - **Safe Spaces for Experimentation**: Create sandbox environments where users can try out different visualizations and filtering techniques without worrying about making mistakes.
        - **Experimentation as Learning**: Reinforce that trying different approaches leads to better insights and skill development.

3. **Celebrating Successes**

    - Share examples of how self-service BI has improved team or organizational outcomes, showcasing user success stories to inspire confidence.
    - Recognize and reward users who excel or creatively solve problems with Superset, helping foster a supportive environment.

Supporting Self-Sufficiency and Continuous Learning

Enabling success for users within self-service business intelligence environments such as Apache Superset requires not just initial training but also resources and support for continued growth. This section discusses ways to encourage continued learning and self-sufficiency among users.

It offers a comprehensive support system through FAQs, helpdesks, and peer-to-peer channels for instant support at all times. It develops peer learning, sharing of knowledge, and camaraderie by creating user communities and arranging collaborative sessions. Self-guided learning resources and rewarding users for their achievements help in developing motivation and engagement to use more complex features as desired.

These efforts allow a sustainable, data-centric culture, with users confident to leverage Superset for informed decision-making and fostering innovation and collaboration across teams.

1. **Setting Up a Support System**
   - **FAQ and Knowledge Base**: Compile frequently asked questions and guides for basic tasks. Update this resource based on user feedback and new Superset features.
   - **Helpdesk or Chat Support**: Set up a support channel where users can get quick help, either from a dedicated team or through a peer support model.
   - **Peer Support Channels**: Consider setting up internal forums or chat groups where users can discuss insights, ask questions, and share solutions. This helps foster a sense of community and collaborative problem-solving.
2. **Creating User Communities for Peer Learning**
   - Organize regular user meetings or "*lunch-and-learn*" sessions where users can present their dashboards, share tips, and discuss challenges. This helps in:
     - **Building Relationships**: Users can learn from each other's experiences and deepen their understanding of data analysis within their context.
     - **Sharing Best Practices**: Knowledge sharing within a user community helps propagate best practices and solutions.
3. **Encouraging Self-Guided Learning**
   - Provide resources for self-paced learning, such as tutorials, e-learning modules, or guides on more advanced Superset features (for example, custom SQL, advanced filtering).
   - Set up a reward system for users who complete self-guided training modules, fostering motivation and engagement.

An effective program for a non-technical user of Apache Superset requires structured guidance on balanced opportunities for independent exploration. Breaking down complicated ideas into manageable steps, practicing it through hands-on interaction, and maintaining avenues of continued support and learning allow an organization to develop user capability and confidence in using Superset for data-driven decision-making. This can foster a data-centric culture and encourages continuous engagement with self-service BI tools, encouraging experimentation and peer learning.

Creating Easy-to-Use Dashboards

Designing user-friendly dashboards is an essential requirement for any self-service BI initiative, especially if it is directed at non-technical users. A user-friendly dashboard empowers these users to engage with data, draw insights, and make informed decisions without deep technical skills. This section follows a structured approach in making accessible, intuitive dashboards in Apache Superset from planning and design principles, testing, and iterating based on feedback.

Planning the Dashboard: Needs Assessment

A successful dashboard will be built on understanding the purpose for which it is being used and aligning that with user needs. This section addresses how to conduct a comprehensive needs assessment to ensure the dashboard delivers relevant and actionable insights.

Organizations can define the boundaries and focus on planning the dashboard by identifying key stakeholders, understanding their needs, and prioritizing appropriate measures. This process includes gathering requirements for the types of graphics required, sources of information to include, and the level of interactivity expected. A good needs assessment ensures that a dashboard meets user needs and also acts as a tool for facilitating decisions and achieving objectives.

Requirements Prior to Design

Before designing a dashboard, understand the users' needs and objectives. Interviews or surveys with the stakeholders can reveal the following:

- **Core Metrics and KPIs:** Which of these metrics is crucial for users' day-to-day activities or strategic goals? For example, a sales team might focus on revenue, conversion rate, and customer acquisition, while a marketing team could track campaign performance or lead generation metrics.
- **Decision-Making Needs:** Identify the decisions users will make based on the data. For instance, if users need to monitor trends, historical line graphs or rolling averages would be appropriate.
- **Preferred Data Rate:** Determine the required data refresh rate, considering whether real-time data or monthly updates are sufficient.

Mapping Dashboard Structure for Non-Technical Users

It should thus be easy for even novices to navigate through; after all, the intuitive dashboards structuring is logical and user-centric. Key design principles include:

- **Layered Structure**: Places the most important KPI at the top (for example, Total Revenue, Customer retention Rate)., followed by supporting metrics (for example, Regional Sales Breakdown).
- **Grouping Similar Metrics:** Sort the metrics under relevant groups (for example, Sales Performance, Customer Metrics, and Operational Efficiency.

It means that users can navigate logically from high-level KPIs to more granular data. This reduces complexity, makes the experience simpler, and avoids overwhelming them with too much information.

Design Principles for Usable Dashboards

- **Simplicity**: Simplicity is crucial in dashboard design, especially for non-technical users. Consider these tips:
  - **Clear Visualizations:** Employ clear simple forms of visualizations that have high conveyance rates, such as bar chart or line graphs.
  - **Clean Design:** Avoid unnecessary gridlines, extraneous labeling, or too much color. It should be focused around key insights.
  - **Effective Labeling**: Use concise, descriptive labels and titles to clarify the meaning of each chart.
- **Accessibility:** Dashboards should be designed to be accessible to all users, including those with additional visual impairments:
  - **Color Schemes:** Use contrasting color combinations that are accessible to colorblind user. Avoid combinations such as red and green. Consider using a color blind-friendly palette or incorporating different shapes and patterns to distinguish data.
  - **Text Size and Readability:** The text, especially labels and legends, should be large enough to be read on any monitor size. Superset offers options for changing the fonts for accessibility.
- **Consistency:** Consistent design across dashboards allow users a sense of familiarity and reduces cognitive loads for non-technical individuals navigating the dashboards.
  - **Standard Templates and Styles**: It must carry the same templates and standards for designing, including standard color use, font, and bar charts layout throughout.
  - **Iconography and Naming**: Name standardized icon sets, vocabularies, and naming on the dashboard panels to minimize confusion.
  - **Consistent Placement of Interactive Elements:** Place interactive elements in the identical location across all dashboards: ideally at the left or top of a dashboard so that they are easily accessible.

Proper Selection and Use of Visualization

1. **Selecting Visualization Techniques**

   The right visualization type is vital to enabling non-technical users to interpret data fast and in proper detail.

- **Bar Charts and Line Graphs:** Provide excellent support for trend analysis and comparisons of value over time, and often intuitive designs, even to non-technical users.
- **KPI Cards:** Use the KPI cards for critical metrics, such as sales revenue or customer satisfaction scores, for an at-a-glance view.
- **Pie Charts and Donuts:** They are best suited for representing proportion within a whole; however, too many categories tend to cause confusion.

2. **Key Metrics and Insights**

   It draws attention to really important information, and insight becomes easy to interpret.

   - **Conditional Formatting:** Use color-coded or icons to indicate the status of a condition. For instance, Green for positive and Red for negative.
   - **Annotations and Callouts:** Annotations may be used in a table to highlight important data, trends and even outliers. For instance, you might annotate a sales drop due to an external event.
   - **Focus on Actionable Data:** Prioritize metrics relevant to decision making, and hide distracting or low-priority data by default, but bring it to attention if required.

Inclusion of Interaction within Dashboards

1. **Filters and Drop-Downs**

   Incorporate filters to allow users to customize their view without requiring technical skills:

   - **Date Filters:** Option for the user to view data by timeframes-crossing, for example, daily, monthly, or quarterly.
   - **Category-Based Filters:** Category-based filters such as region, department, or product line, so users could narrow down the most important data.
   - **Dropdown and Sliders:** These allow users to select individual observations or ranges for detailed analysis.

2. **Drill-Down Capability**

   Drill-downs let the user explore the data at different levels of detail, which is valuable for high-level overviews and deeper dives:

   - **Hierarchical Navigation:** Enables users to click from summary data down to revealing more detailed information, for example, from total revenue to revenue by region or product.

- **Data Granularity**: Allow users to switch between finer-grained data options such as displaying data for weeks instead of months.
- **Visual Cue Indicators:** Uses icons or arrows to show drill-down options, so the user intuitively knows where to click.

Testing Dashboards with End-Users

1. **Collecting Feedback from End-Users**

   Testing dashboards with end-users is crucial to ensure they meet real-world needs and are easy to use:

   - **Usability Testing**: Hold user sessions where the user completes common tasks on the dashboard. Observations of such interaction with the interface may uncover usability problems.
   - **Feedback Surveys:** Use surveys or forms to capture impressions and challenges, for instance problems in navigation through filters or suggestions for charts improvement.
   - **User Interviews**: Interview a sample of users about their dashboard usage, what they like, and what they do not understand.

2. **Iteration of Dashboards Based on User Feedback:**

   Utilizing an iterative design will ensure the dashboard continuously changes with user needs and technical advancements.

   - **Identify Pain Points:** Changes should be considered for what burdens users. Often this involves ambiguous names or too messy visualizations.
   - **Incremental changes:** Change gradually so the users are not shocked by sudden redesigns. Begin small changes in filters, visualizations, or layout based on feedback.
   - **Retest and Refine**: After the changes are implemented, retest the dashboard with end-users to ensure that the changes indeed address the issues that were identified. Repeat the testing and improvement process as needed to ensure usability.

Designing intuitive dashboards for the non-technical audience in Apache Superset requires careful planning, adherence to design principles, and a commitment to iterative improvement based on user feedback. Focus on user needs, keep it simple and accessible, empower users with interactive elements, and create dashboards that drive meaningful engagement and support data-driven decision-making at all organizational levels. It is best that the dashboards, following sufficient feedback and further refinement, should eventually enable users to search and interpret data on their own.

Best Practices for User Empowerment

Effective self-service BI would enable the users to make decisions based on data. It refers to an environment that would enable the users to confidently access, analyze, and act on data. Toward this end, organizations will have to focus on establishing a culture of data literacy, provide accessible templates with role-based permissions, and provide a system of continuous feedback and support in Apache Superset.

Some of the best practices for ensuring that self-service BI becomes a value-add, user-centric tool within any organization include the following:

Installing a Culture of Data-Driven Decision-Making

- **Data Literacy for Decision Making:** Provide data literacy education in workshops and other materials that enable users to learn the fundamental concepts of data, how to read visualizations, and derive insights. Describe how data influences decision-making and provide examples that are relevant to the user's role.

  Data-Driven Mindset: Explain how the data-driven approach is advantageous. Data-driven approaches will bring about improvements in efficiency, error minimization, and discovering new possibilities. For instance, data can be used for maximizing campaigns, whereas process efficiency can be improved by operations.

- **Encourage Curiosity and Experimentation**

  Safe Data Exploration: The user can experiment with everything about data in the "*sandbox*" environments that will not impact live reports. It fosters experimenting with varied filters, charts, and analyses, developing a culture of curiosity and comfort with data.

  Recognition and Rewards: Recognize and reward users to leverage data creatively. Thus, a dashboard designed by a non-technical person, which saves money, will be celebrated during the team meeting and also in the newsletter.

Quick Start with Templates and Examples

- **Templates ready for common metrics**
  - **Quick Win Templates:** These are dashboards and templates available that service common needs of the users. For example, sales performance, customer demographics, or operational efficiency. As a result, such insights may be available on demand by the user directly, reducing the cycle for getting insights.
  - **Templates for Common KPIs:** Preconfigured KPI cards and charts for

common metrics reduce the need for technical configuration. The users can only filter or change time periods to customize views.

- **Improving new user on-boarding speed**
    - **Clear Documentation:** Templates must be documented on how the user may use it for their needs. A sales template would contain instructions on how to add filters by region or product line.

    Give the user examples of use case or scenario where each one applies to give the user immediate access to which template aligns with the type of data that is needed.

Setting Up Role-Based Access and Permissions

Efficient access control in Apache Superset is necessary to provide users with the appropriate level of access to dashboards and datasets without jeopardizing data usability and security. A well-established access control policy enables organizations to control permissions based on roles of users so that users get access to only the data pertaining to their tasks. Role-based permissions enable customized access levels, avoiding accidental data exposure while enhancing productivity. Data minimization ensures that users get only the data required without complexity, enhancing usability.

- **A stated access control policy**
    - **Role-Based Permissions:** Apache Superset will allow the creation of specific roles (for example, Viewer, Explorer, Admin) that will determine which datasets and dashboards a user can access based on his needs. For instance, executives may require high-level KPIs, while department managers need more detailed data.
    - **Data Minimization:** Access data only when it is required for preventing clutter and swamping users with data not needed by them. Non-technical users should see only relevant metrics and reports of a role.
- **Permissions aligned with data needs and proficiency**

    Customize to accommodate different skill levels by granting access based on proficiency: Dashboard access with default filtering for beginners, SQL Lab for advanced users with flexible query capabilities.

Clear Permission Documentation: Provide resources that explain which features users can access based on their role. For example, a "`Viewer`" might be able to navigate dashboards and apply filters but not create new visualizations. This establishes a feedback and improvement loop.

- **Routine Feedbacks from Users**
    - **Feedback Mechanisms:** Introduce feedback surveys, comment sections,

or regular meetings for users to provide feedback about dashboards, templates, and training resources. This would help administrators know what needs are being experienced by users and what is paining them.

    - **Focus Groups and User Testing:** Sometimes focus groups are conducted for a small group of users, giving insight into the experience. This helps to bring up possible usability issues not appearing in survey feedback otherwise.

- **Response to Feedback: Adjustment of Self-Service Environment**
    - Dashboard iteration should improve and optimize based on the comments received through changes in the various types of charts, filters, or even rearrangement.
    - **User-Friendly Improvements**: Create more templates with new visualizations, and keep the dashboards simple. If a dashboard receives frequent requests about some customization variations, then make a pre-configured version that suits their needs.

Enabling On-Demand Assistance

- **Form a Support Team or Designate a Dedicated Resource**
    - **Designated Support Staff:** The support person or team is trained on Apache Superset to deal with questions and troubleshooting issues. This helps the non-technical users have assistance and not feel frustrated when navigating advanced functionality.
    - **Help Desk and Ticketing Systems:** Implement the use of a help desk or ticketing system by ensuring that users get good responses to problems or requests. A well-arranged support system is comforted to the user when they face an issue.
- **Suggest that Users Use the Help System for Advanced Features**
    - **Proactive Support for Complex Needs:** This encourages users to call the support team to help them create calculated metrics or configure a custom visualization. This makes them feel supported as they dive deeper into more advanced capabilities.
    - **Monthly Office Hours**: This encourages users to pop in during the monthly "*office hours*" to address a specific Superset function to ask questions and request assistance. Informal situations such as this one could resolve questions that don't warrant a formal support request.

Continuous Learning and Improvement for Employee-Orientation

- **An opportunity to learn advanced techniques**
  - **Workshops and Training Modules**: It can be conducted on various topics, for example, interpretation of data, Superset's SQL Lab, or customization of dashboards. Such constant learning will ultimately propel the users to up-grade their skills gradually.
  - **E-learning Resources**: An in-built library of e-materials, such as video lectures or tutorials, so that one could learn advanced techniques independent of time and schedule.
- **Non-Technical Users Hacking Data-Driven Projects**
  - **Promote Success Stories:** Public recognition of users who deliver significant value through Superset, such as insights that have guided the success of a project or cost-saving ideas. It inspires other users and espouses the value of data-driven decision making.
  - **Peer-Led Sessions:** Organize peer-led sessions where users can present their Superset projects or insights. The peer-led approach creates a learning community but also fosters a collaborative, data-centric culture.

The empowerment of using self-service BI tools should be strategically enabled in people, as this means inculcating a culture of data, resource-availability, proper permissioning and continuous improvement. Supporting templates, continuous learning, along with an adequate feedback cycle can give a culture and environment wherein each user gains the empowerment to look deeper into the data. These best practices lead to higher adoption and satisfaction among the users of self-service BI and drive more innovation and data-informed decision-making across the organization.

Conclusion

Organizations need to foster a data culture, simplify access, and build confidence in data exploration for non-technical users of self-service BI using Apache Superset. This involves promoting data literacy to foster curiosity and understanding of data's in informed decision- making.

Providing pre-built dashboards and templates gives users a head start, while clearly defined permissions within role-based access control ensure access to relevant data only. Establishing a feedback loop allows for continuous improvement based on user input, and readily available support resources, like a helpdesk or office hours, provide on-demand assistance.

Finally, nurturing continuous learning through workshops and celebrating data-driven successes creates a positive environment that encourages exploration and drives adoption of self-service BI, ultimately fostering a data-informed culture.

The last chapter focuses on what the future of data visualization and business intelligence looks like, examining how tools such as Apache Superset continue to help meet emerging demands.

It explores the transformative role of AI and machine learning in BI, focusing on next-generation analytics and predictive insights. Augmented analytics, which integrates AI with traditional BI workflows to enhance decision-making and automate insights, is also discussed. It further covers future trends and next-generation visualization use cases, indicating how advancements in design and interactivity are expanding the possibilities of BI tools.

CHAPTER 13

Emerging Trends and Innovations in Data Visualization

Introduction

Data has become the lifeblood of modern business, driving strategic decision-making and innovation across all sectors in today's digital landscape. The increasing abundance and complexity of data are transforming how it is visualized and interacted with. This chapter explores the current trends and technologies reshaping data visualization and Business Intelligence (BI), shifting the focus from simply seeing insights to truly experiencing them.

BI tools have evolved beyond static charts and graphs with the advent of AI-driven analytics, augmented analytics, and immersive visualization techniques. Tools such as Apache Superset are at the forefront of helping organizations leverage the power of artificial intelligence, machine learning, and advanced visualization to make data more accessible, insightful, and actionable. This chapter examines how these emerging trends break down barriers, democratize data, and empower businesses in previously unimaginable ways.

From integrating AI-enhanced visualizations and real-time analytics to virtual and augmented reality integrations, we will discuss how BI is becoming an interactive, intelligent, and inclusive domain. We will also consider the ethical implications of AI-driven analytics and explore how data visualization can be used to address sustainability and social impact challenges. This chapter equips you with insights into the innovations shaping the future of data visualization and BI, enabling you to stay ahead in this ever-changing, data-driven world. It inspires you to not only improve upon current data visualization practices but also, by embracing these emerging trends, to open new vistas in your business intelligence journey.

Structure

In this chapter, we will cover the following topics:

- AI-Driven Data Visualization
- Augmented Analytics and Natural Language Processing (NLP)
- Future of Augmented Analytics and NLP in BI
- Real-Time Data Visualization and Streaming Analytics
- Predictive and Prescriptive Analytics in Visualization
- Enhanced Data Storytelling and Narrative Visualization
- Immersive Visualizations: Virtual Reality (VR) and Augmented Reality (AR)
- Integration of BI with Collaborative Platforms
- Data Visualization in Edge Computing and IoT

AI-Driven Data Visualization

With the explosive growth of data, its increasing complexity and volume make it challenging to extract meaningful information. This is where AI-driven data visualization comes into play, it uses AI and ML algorithms to simplify, enhance, and automate the process of data visualization. This technology has revolutionized the way businesses interact with data - changing their ways of decision-making and offering a more profound understanding of complex datasets.

Data Visualization Shifting with Artificial Intelligence

The game-changing capabilities of AI-driven visualization tools comprise some, if not all, of the following:

- **Automated Choices for Charts:** There is much wastage of time in the process of choice, wherein one has to make a decision about the kind of chart or graph through which the data can be represented. AI algorithms can analyze the underlying data structure and can automatically recommend or select the most suitable visualization such that the insights are communicated at their best. This saves time while reducing the chances of misrepresentation due to incorrect chart choices.
- **Generate Insights:** AI-powered tools can identify patterns, correlations, and trends in data that human analysts might miss. They also highlight outliers and key findings, quickly drawing business attention to pinpoint opportunities or

hidden risks. This moves businesses beyond simply presenting data and assists in giving actionable insights.

- **Predictive Analytics:** It is possible to predict trends for the future through predictive analytics capabilities integrated with AI-driven visualization tools. Based on history data, they may forecast a rise and fall in sales, customers' behavior, or even a fluctuation in the market, thus bringing a competitive advantage for proactive decision-making.
- **Data Cleaning and Preparation:** Data visualization is only as good as the data it is based on. AI algorithmic functions can help in cleaning, structuring, and preparing datasets to be analyzed with minimal error or inaccuracy which will be carried over when visualized.

AI-Powered Visualization and Its Impact on Decision Making

The intervention of AI in data visualization indeed changes the process of decision-making in several ways.

- **Speed and Efficiency:** With AI, the pace at which one would take insights from data is accelerated because it reduces mundane work involved in preparing data, choosing charts, and then generating insights. Analysts and decision-makers spend less time on minding detail and can understand most of those insights.
- **Improved Accuracy:** The accuracy improves since all human bias and error are removed from the presentation and interpretation of data. Machine learning algorithms identify patterns and relationships that easily pass human analysts. These algorithms do make the interpretation more accurate and informed.
- **Accessibility for Non-Technical Users:** AI-driven data visualization democratizes access to data through the ability of non-technical users to read insights. Features such as automated insights and natural language descriptions allow all those in an organization to understand and subsequently act on data, thus fostering a data-driven culture.

Key Examples of AI-Driven Data Visualization Tools

Several major data visualization and BI platforms integrate AI-driven capabilities, including:

- **Superset's AI Enhancements:** Apache Superset, an open-source BI tool, is increasingly incorporating AI capabilities. Organizations using Superset with AI frameworks can readily develop machine learning models for predictions, automated insights, and enhanced interactive dashboards. Superset's flexibility allows integration with custom ML models, enabling more complex predictive analytics within sophisticated data visualizations.

- **Tableau's AI Integrations:** Tableau has introduced AI-powered features such as "`Ask Data`" and "`Explain Data`." "`Ask Data`" allows users to interact with data naturally through queries. "Explain Data" automatically provides explanations for data points, revealing potential causes for anomalies or trends. These features empower even non-technical users to interact with data intuitively and uncover valuable insights.
- **Google Data Studio with BigQuery ML:** The combination of BigQuery ML and Google Data Studio's data visualization capabilities offers significant AI potential. Users can integrate data directly into BigQuery ML to apply machine learning models and generate visualizations with quick predictions, trend forecasting, and anomaly detection. This allows businesses to leverage AI without requiring advanced programming expertise.

Real-World Use Cases

AI-based data visualization has been applied in industries, highly valuable in the following:

- **Retail:** Advanced visualization abilities by AI can help retailers predict consumer purchasing behavior, what is in hot demand, and how much to stock for replenishment. Artificial intelligence can help retailers optimize the shelf, price scheme, and marketing strategy through sales pattern analysis.
- **Finance:** Banks are employing AI-based visualization techniques that flag fraudulent transactions and can help predict markets or perform the risk analysis. It can easily display patterns that exist in huge financial data, indicate fraud or an investment opportunity.
- **Healthcare:** In healthcare, AI-driven visualizations help identify disease patterns, predict patient outcomes, and analyze treatment effectiveness. For instance, predictive analytics can be used to forecast patient admissions, enabling hospitals to allocate resources efficiently.
- **Manufacturing:** AI-based visualization can help manufacturers analyze equipment performance, predict upcoming needs in maintenance, and ensure optimum supply chain processes. An AI platform predicts downtime and reduces costs by detecting anomalies in production data.

Weaknesses and Controversies

AI-driven data visualization, although carrying many benefits also poses the following challenges:

- **Data Quality:** Artificial Intelligence models are only as good as the data they are trained on. Poor-quality or biased data gives wrong insights, so there is a need to focus on high-quality data and data governance.
- **Complexity and Skills Requirements:** Even though AI has made tremendous strides forward, the understanding and process of implementation is complex for machine learning models. Organizations will, therefore, have to invest in training or hire data science prowess to tap into the full potential of AI-based visualization.
- **Ethical Issues:** AI algorithms can introduce bias in the interpretation of data and related decisions. Ethical controls need to ensure data-driven analytics by AI systems is fair, transparent, and accountable.

The future of AI-driven data visualization, while still in its early stages, holds immense potential. As AI technology advances, we can expect to see:

- **More Intuitive Interaction:** Future tools will likely allow for more intuitive data interaction through voice commands, gesture recognition, or even augmented reality interfaces.
- **Hyper-personalization:** AI and visualization tools will evolve to provide more personalized insights. Visualizations may be automatically tailored to individual preferences, roles, and decision-making styles.
- **Richer Predictive and Prescriptive Analytics:** Improved machine learning models will move beyond simply forecasting trends to prescribing optimal actions. This prescriptive analytics capability will directly influence strategies.

Augmented Analytics and Natural Language Processing (NLP)

The phenomenal increase in data generation has spurred an overwhelming demand for analytics tools to facilitate efficient data analysis and interpretation. Traditional tools for data analysis and visualization are often intimidating and complex, requiring advanced technical skills or even data science expertise, making them inaccessible to many non-technical users. Augmented analytics and Natural Language Processing are revolutionizing this landscape, making Business Intelligence more accessible and transforming how people interact with data.

Definition of Augmented Analytics

The new trend in BI is the use of augmented analytics, which applies AI, ML, and NLP to enhance data preparation, insight generation, and data visualization. Advanced technologies in augmented analytics make any task of data analysis easier so that users gain insights without requiring deep technical knowledge. The goal is to extract actionable insights faster and more accurately, while also democratizing access to data analytics across the organization.

The Role of NLP in Augmented Analytics

Natural Language Processing (NLP), a branch of AI, enables machines to read, comprehend, and then produce human speech. Augmented analytics within BI tools incorporate NLP, allowing users to interact with their data in real time using conversational queries: text or voice command. This opens a window for users to query their data in plain, everyday language, much like asking a question on a search engine, simplifying data analysis considerably.

For instance, one no longer needs to trudge through the vast menu and filters of the system but just type or ask questions like, "*What were our total sales in the last quarter?*" or "*Show me the top-performing products in* 2023." The tool then automatically creates the needed insights and visualizations. This empowers users to explore data without needing technical expertise. Therefore, entry points are much more open, and there could also be a culture of data-based decision-making.

Augmented Analytics and NLP Reforming Business Intelligence

There are several transformational benefits as augmented analytics and NLP are tightly integrated into the BI platform.

One of the most important benefits of augmented analytics is that data analysis becomes accessible to any person, regardless of their technical skills. Now, users across all departments can explore data, generate reports, and make sense of insights, without relying on data analysts or IT teams.

- **Faster Insights:** Traditional data analysis is time consuming, involving multiple stages of data preparation, query building, and visualization. Augmented analytics automates all these processes, enabling real-time insights. The speed is important for decision-making in fast-moving industries where just-in-time insights make all the difference.
- **Automated Data Preparation:** The most time-consuming effort of any analytical data cycle is prep work. Augmented analytics employs machine learning algorithms to automatically clean, transform, and enhance the data, providing analysts with high-quality, accurate data for analysis.

Augmented analytics brings the ability to recognize hidden patterns, correlation, and trends that normally escape human analysis. Using AI and ML, tools can generate advanced insights, highlighting key drivers of trends, identifying anomalies, and suggesting opportunities.

NLP-driven BI tools create an interactive and conversational experience. Users can drill down into specific data points and refine their queries in real time, making data exploration more intuitive and user-friendly.

Key Examples of Augmented Analytics and NLP Tools

Several BI platforms have successfully integrated augmented analytics and NLP capabilities, making data analysis more intuitive and accessible. Here are some of the leading tools:

- **ThoughtSpot**: ThoughtSpot is a pioneer in augmented analytics, offering an intuitive, search-driven BI platform powered by AI and NLP. Users can interact with data using simple, conversational queries and instantly generate visualizations, reports, and insights. ThoughtSpot's AI engine, "*SpotIQ*," goes a step further by automatically generating insights, identifying trends, anomalies, and correlations that users might not have even considered.
- **Qlik Sense**: Qlik Sense incorporates augmented analytics through its "*Insight Advisor*" feature, which uses machine learning and NLP to guide users in exploring their data. The Insight Advisor can generate visualizations based on natural language queries, suggest the most relevant data insights, and even recommend actions based on the data findings. Qlik Sense's augmented intelligence capabilities empower users to explore data with ease, making it accessible to individuals across various skill levels.
- **Microsoft Power BI**: Microsoft Power BI integrates NLP through its "Q&A" feature, which allows users to interact with their data using natural language queries. Users can simply type or speak questions, such as "What are my sales by region?" or "Show me a trend analysis of monthly revenue," and Power BI will generate the appropriate visualizations instantly. Additionally, Power BI uses AI to provide automated insights, making it easier for users to identify patterns and trends in their data.

Augmented Analytics and NLP in Real-World Applications

Augmented analytics and NLP applications are disruptive for value streams across industries.

- **Retail**: Augmented analytics give a clearer understanding of what the customer prefers, in addition to trending sales. At the BI level, it will utilize NLP to question: "*What sells the most in New York?*" or "*Which age group spends most* *during holidays*." This leads to more intelligent decisions related to marketing campaigns, stock strategies, and custom er engagement.

- **Finance**: Augmented analytics helps financial analysts analyze transactional data, detect fraud patterns, and track investment performance. They can ask "*What were the top 10 transactions last month*?" or "*Which investment portfolios performed best in* Q2?" Such augmentation of analytics aids banks and financial institutions to better manage risk, optimize portfolios, and enhance customer service.
- **Health Care**: Augmented analytics can help in the analysis of any patient's data, either directly by doctors or by inferring patterns in disease outbreaks and monitoring treatment outcomes. For instance, in health care, doctors may query which treatments have the highest success rate for diabctic patients or what has been the rate of recovery that has changed over the past year for COVID-19 patients.

Augmented analytics also has applications in human resource, where it can be applied to track employee performance, trend hiring, and determinants of retention. For example, through such interrogation like "*which department has the highest turnover*?" or "*what contributes to employee satisfaction*?", HR personnel can identify strategies for improving workforce management.

Problems and Challenges

Despite the numerous benefits of augmented analytics and NLP, several challenges must be addressed:

- **Data Quality**: The quality of output from Augmented Analytics depends on the quality of the underlying data. Data governance practices must therefore be appropriately designed to prevent poor-quality or biased data from generating misleading insights.
- **Training and Adoption**: While augmented analytics simplifies data analysis, users still need training to feel comfortable with NLP-driven BI tools. Organizations need to introduce training programs to aid easy adoption.
- **Ethical Considerations**: All AI-driven technologies raise ethical considerations about privacy, data security, and propensity for algorithm bias. Responsible standards for augmented analytics are therefore essential.

Future of Augmented Analytics and NLP in BI

Augmented analytics and NLP in BI are very promising and offer multiple exciting developments on the horizon:

- **Voice-Activated BI:** The more sophisticated voice recognition, the faster voice-activated BI tools will advance. Users will interact with data solely by voice, so going through data will be much smoother and more intuitive.

- **Multi-Language Capabilities:** With new tools in BI, organizations can now work multi-linguistically. This will allow users from different geographies and origins to interact with data in their chosen language while democratizing access to it.
- **Context-Aware Analytics:** Advanced NLP models will become even more context-sensitive. BI tools understand the intent in questions and provide more relevant and precise answers. Consider the question, "*How did we perform last month?*" The system will understand "*here, in this case, by 'perform', you actually refer to monetary performance and 'last month' refers to the previous calendar month.*"
- **Deep AI:** Augmented analytics develops a profound capability using AI capabilities to include sentiment analysis, emotion detection, and more complex predictive modeling. It will, therefore, offer more insight and a holistic understanding of the data.

Real-Time Data Visualization and Streaming Analytics

Real-time data visualization and streaming analytics are revolutionizing the business world, mainly in today's fast-paced digital environment, by enabling the monitoring, analysis, and prompt reaction to data in real time. This capacity enables organizations to tap into immediate insights from constantly changing data, enabling them to respond to changing conditions, identify trends, and make data-driven decisions in real time. This shift has transformed revolution BI from static, traditional reports into dynamic, real-time dashboards that enable stakeholders with strategic insights based on current events.

Understanding Real-Time Data Visualization

Real-time data visualization is the presentation of data as it is generated, allowing users to monitor key metrics and patterns in real time. In contrast to this, static reports provide a historical view of information, while the real-time visualization extracts up-to-the-minute insights from a live data stream. This new approach empowers businesses to make real-time decisions without delays inherent in traditional data processing.

Streaming Analytics in the Visualization of Real-Time Information

Streaming analytics allows for the real-time examination of data, continuously processing the data from single or multiple sources to produce insights, identify trends and patterns, and initiate automatic actions. Applications, such as financial trading, monitoring of IoT devices, and management of supply chains, are the most critical ones, where time-sensitive decisions are crucial and missed opportunities or heightened risks can lead to significant repercussions.

It integrates data visualization tools with live streaming analytics to help businesses transform raw, unstructured data into meaningful visualizations, allowing trends and anomalies to be identified immediately as they happen.

Key Enabling Technologies of Real-Time Data Visualization

- **Apache Kafka:** This is a widely used streaming platform and forms the backbone of many real-time data pipelines. In fact, it is a kind of messaging system that ingests, stores, and distributes streams of data across various applications and systems. Kafka has fantastic ability to handle extremely high throughput with little latency; therefore, it is excellent for real-time analytics.
- **Apache Superset:** Superset is an open-source BI tool that integrates seamlessly with Apache Kafka to produce dynamic, real-time dashboards. Superset provides a flexible, interactive visualization layer which can handle data across sources, thus making it easier to build, customize and share real-time analytics dashboards. Its integration with Kafka allows users to better visualize their real-time data without much coding, broadening access to the benefits of real-time insights.

Superset and Kafka Working Together

Adding Apache Kafka to Superset will enable organizations to build real-time analytics dashboards with direct-live-visibility data. This is an extremely summarized explanation of exactly how they work together:

- Kafka accepts data from any source, including IoT sensors, monetary transactions, feeds from social networks, and streams it into designated topics.
- This stream of data is then processed in real time using Kafka Streams, Apache Flink, or some other processing engine to clean, transform, and enrich the data accordingly.

Data Visualization: Superset is directly connected to the data streams right from Kafka or from a database ingesting Kafka data and visualizes the processed data on interactive dashboards. These running dashboards update themselves with each new inflow, providing a live view of metrics, trends, and KPIs.

Key Advantage of Real-Time Data Visualization

- **Instant Decision:** Organizations respond to the change in conditions immediately through live data visualization without delay, which in turn makes decisions instantaneously. Such incidents are found among stock trading where a difference of a few seconds can be highly acute.

  Real-time monitoring and data detection can give companies the idea of whether something is wrong-whether it is system failure, anomalies, or security breaches in real time so that they may intervene as soon as possible.

- **Improved Experience to Customers:** Insights from customer behavior and preferences enable organizations to offer personalization, responsiveness, and thus an improved customer experience.

Uses of Real-Time Data Visualization Key

- **Monitoring IoT Devices**: IoT has revolutionized data visualization. Maintaining real-time awareness of the status of connected devices is important. Consider a smart factory, for example. Sensors attached to machines continuously stream data. Real-time visualization provides operators with insights into equipment health, including anomalies or maintenance, minimizing downtime and operational costs.
- **Financial Market**: Real-time monitoring stock prices, trends, and trading volume is in the financial market. For traders, real-time dashboards provide immediate visibility into price fluctuations, revealing potential trading opportunities and prompting timely transactions. Delayed analysis may then result in missing an opportunity or loss.
- **Supply Chain Management**: Real-time visualization plays a crucial role in supply chain management by providing insights into inventory levels, shipment tracking, and potential supply chain disruption. A logistics firm, for instance, could use real-time dashboards to monitor delivery trucks, traffic conditions, and optimize routes to keep deliveries up to schedule and save on fuel.

For real-time visualization, social media analytics is invaluable for tracking brand sentiment, trending topics, and customer engagement on any social media platform. Marketing teams could track live campaigns and respond to customer feedback in real time by initiating readjustments to improve brand visibility and customer interaction.

Challenges in Implementing Real-Time Visualization

While real-time data visualization offers significant benefits, it also presents challenges, including:

- **Volume and Velocity of Data:** Streams from real-time data streams generate enormous volumes of data at extraordinary speeds; hence, a strong infrastructure is needed in the ingestion, processing, and visualization of data. Scalable systems such as Kafka are therefore crucial in handling such data.
- **Data Quality:** Real-time data is usually noisier, inconsistent, and incomplete. Therefore, quality and accuracy of data will be critical in making reliable decisions based on real-time insights.
- **Technical Complexity:** Real-time data pipelines are somewhat technical in nature. It becomes challenging when attempting to integrate several tools such as Kafka, Superset, and other processing engines. Organizations need qualified people to manage the said complexities.

Future of Real-Time Data Visualization

With real-time visualization of data growing continuously, we will understand a few interesting trends, including:

- **Integration of AI and ML:** With integrated AI and ML, the real-time visualization tool will assist in producing predictive analytics, anomaly detection, as well as automated insights in real-time data.
- **Cloud-Based Real-Time Analytics:** More and more cloud platforms support data analytics in real-time, allowing for the hassle-free implementation and scaling of real-time visualization solutions without the investment needed for establishing on-premises infrastructure. This has, in turn, made edge computing create further proximity of processing to the source, further reducing latency for those applications of IoT that would have high requirements on real-time visualization.

Predictive and Prescriptive Analytics in Visualization

Business Intelligence refers to that area of activity, from which the simplest historical analysis of data has developed into more complex types: predictive and prescriptive analytics. The latter have transformed the way organizations understand and interact with their data better. Advanced analytics capabilities built into data visualization applications take businesses away from reacting decisions that place attention to what happened back then to strategies that are proactive, driven by foreseeing trends for the future and recommending an optimum action course.

Knowing Predictive and Prescriptive Analytics

- **Predictive analytics**: It involves statistics, machine learning (ML), and data mining from previous data to predict future events. Questions applied include "*What is likely to happen?*" and "*What may occur based on the current trend?*" It uses algorithms and models to forecast behaviors and anticipate future events, enabling companies to prepare proactively.
- **Prescriptive Analytics**: It is one step ahead of the previous state where it not only predicts the future outcomes but prescribes the best set of actions to be taken. To that effect, questions such as "*What must we do next?*" and "*Which strategy will promise the best possible outcome?*" are answered. Prescriptive analytics use sophisticated algorithms, optimization techniques, and simulation models providing specific actions that actually lead toward desired outcomes, guiding the decision-maker to find the best strategies.

Embedding Predictive and Prescriptive Analytics in BI Tools

By including predictive and prescriptive analytics in the BI tool, users will analyze historical data along with trends to predict the future and proposed actions to ensure a better understanding of the data and informed decisions for the future, using both historical data and forecasts. Here is how this analytics is part of BI tools:

- **Integration with Machine Learning Models:** The new BI environment can also be integrated with models created from machine learning using various programming languages. They are supposed to perform predictive and prescriptive analyses, run from within the BI environment. For example, an organization can construct an extraction of predictive sales trend forecasts and then display the output on interactive dashboards.
- **Automated Analytics:** Most BI tools adopt automated analytics engines that analyze data and give predictions or prescriptions through nonspecific technical acumen. These engines rely on embedded algorithms to identify trends, detect anomalies, and prescribe appropriate actions, thereby making nonspecific end-users use advanced analytics.
- **Interactive Dashboards:** Dynamic dashboards are commonly used to show predictive and prescriptive insight. Users can interact and adjust parameters to see how any other action may affect future outcomes. In this manner, users are enabled to make more informed and flexible decisions.

Key Examples of BI Tools with Predictive and Prescriptive Analytics

Many modern BI tools now include predictive and prescriptive analytics features, enabling users to forecast trends and receive data-driven recommendations. Tools such as Tableau, Power BI, and IBM Cognos integrate these advanced analytics capabilities, allowing businesses to make proactive and informed decisions.

- **Superset with Python/R Integration:** One is the Apache Superset, which actually is an open-source BI tool. It can leverage machine learning models written in Python or R. Users can now add predictive insights directly on the dashboard. For example, a data scientist might use scikit-learn in Python or caret in R to build a forecasting model. They might then connect the output of such a model to Superset and create real-time predictive visualizations. This integrates predictive insights to non-technical users without requiring them to code.
- **Tableau with Predictive Analytics Additions:** Tableau includes built-in predictive analytics features such as "*Trend Lines*" and "*Forecasting*". Users can derive predictions based on historical data straight from the tool. Moreover, it supports integration with R and Python scripts, enabling the use of more advanced predictive and prescriptive models.

Another BI leader is now adding seamless integration with Azure Machine Learning, allowing customers to add predictive models to their reports and dashboards in their applications. Companies can then use these machine learning models to their data, yield forecasts, and visualize predictions with the historical trends.

Applications of Predictive and Prescriptive Analytics in Real Life Through Visualization

Predictive and prescriptive analytics should significantly help the industries by alerting them to proactive strategies and smarter decision-making. Some examples include:

- **Retail and E-commerce:** Retailers use predictive analytics to forecast customer demand, require optimal level of inventory, and the sales trend. For instance, a predictive model may scan historical data of sales, seasonal demands, and the customer buying patterns to predict demand for certain items. Prescriptive analytics then offers optimal levels of inventory, price propositions, and promotional events to sell as much as possible and avoid stockouts.
- **Financial Services:** The finance sector applies predictive analytics for the advance prediction of credit risks, stock price, and frauds. In this area, the predictive models can be useful to the banks to identify probable defaulters on loans. Once that calculation is done, prescriptive analytics will recommend

strategies to be undertaken on risk, such as increasing the rate or payment plans tailored toward purpose.

Predictive analytics can predict the patient's outcome, outbreaks, and the effectiveness of the treatments in healthcare. For instance, using historical data, the hospitals can anticipate the admission of patients seasonally and hence use the same to optimize the staff and resource availability. Prescriptive analytics can outline the treatment plan based on the patient's medical history, symptoms, and genetic makeup to ensure better care and outcome by the patient.

Predictive analytics is utilized in supply chain management for demand forecast, potential disruption identification, and optimal management of inventory. For instance, the predictive model could predict raw material demand in terms of production schedules, weather patterns, and market trends. A recommendation can then be generated through prescriptive analytics regarding altering procurement strategies so that the correct amount of stock is available at the right time.

Predictive and Prescriptive Analytics Powering Organizations

It brings an army of changes into the organization by adding predictive and prescriptive analytics in a BI tool.

- **Anticipatory Decision-Making:** Organizations use predictive analytics to predict trends and challenges beforehand and make proactive decisions, rather than reactive decisions after something has happened. It ensures the market lead and opportunity-taking as soon as it occurs.

  This prescriptive analytics informs what the best course of action is, based on optimizing the outcomes from data-driven insights that are well-informed. Thus, organizations operate their optimized strategies while minimizing risk with maximum efficiency.

- **Data-Driven Culture:** It becomes quite easy even for application users with lesser technical skills to access, understand, and act upon the predictive and prescriptive insights. This fosters a data-driven culture within the organization, where information becomes the binding force of decision instead of intuition-based.

Implication of Using Predictive and Prescriptive Analytics

While the benefits are substantial, there are also some challenges to consider:

- **Data Quality and Availability:** Predictive and prescriptive models need high-quality, accurate data. Incomplete, inconsistent, or biased data can lead to incorrect predictions and recommendations, highlighting the importance of data governance for successful implementation.

- **Technical Expertise:** Building and integrating predictive and prescriptive models using BI tools generally require advanced data science skills. Organizations would need to invest in training or hire data scientists to fully utilize these capabilities.

Thus, the interpretation of results often becomes complex, making predictive and prescriptive insights difficult for non-technical users to understand. Improved visualizations and interfaces are needed to make these insights more accessible and actionable.

The Future of Predictive and Prescriptive Analytics in BI

As AI and machine learning technologies advance, predictive and prescriptive analytics will become even more deeply integrated into BI tools. Future capabilities are likely to include:

- **Real-Time Predictions:** This will enable businesses to become highly responsive to changing conditions, dynamically generating real-time predictions and prescriptions based on streaming data.
- **Automated Prescriptive Actions:** BI tools will not only suggest optimal actions but also automatically implement them, streamlining operations and decision-making processes.
- **Improved User Experience:** The integration of NLP will simplify user interaction with predictive and prescriptive analytics, allowing users to ask questions in natural language and receive actionable insights in real time.

Enhanced Data Storytelling and Narrative Visualization

From static reports to dynamic and engaging storytelling, it is transforming the way businesses and individuals engage with data. Data storytelling refers to the act of using data to tell a story is aimed at interpreting data that is not only informative but impactful, offering users quick clarity into complex information and enabling decisions made with confidence.

The Concept of Data Storytelling

At its core, data storytelling is the combination of data visualization, narrative techniques, and contextual insights as methods of expression. It transforms raw data and static charts into compelling narratives accessible to both technical and non-technical audiences, answering not only "what" but helping presenters answer "why" and "how," making it such a powerful vehicle for conveying meaning or action.

Data storytelling is defined by three components, including:

- **Data**: The primary facts and figures that constitute the raw material.
- **Narrative**: This is a story that contextualizes data, explaining its relevance and meaning.
- **Visuals**: Graphs, charts, and other illustrations that bring the story alive, enabling the reader to understand data in an easier and more digestible manner.

Benefits of Switching from Static Reports to Dynamic Storytelling

Switching from static reports to dynamic storytelling offers numerous benefits, including:

- **Engagement:** With static reports, a user easily gets confused with numbers and the meaning gets obscured. Data storytelling, on the other hand, engages a user so they can elicit a narrative from datasets, making it easier to track and digest.
- **Clarity and Understanding:** In a data-centric world, clear comprehension is paramount. Data storytelling unravels the complex datasets in a tale that brings clarity on trends, patterns, and relationships through it. For example, instead of just showing yearly sales figures, a good storytelling explains how those figures were influenced by seasonal changes and marketing strategies.

  Such actionable insights are the prime motive for data storytelling, that is, a quest to drive action. It is almost natural to explain the insights and highlight the takeaways or guide the audience toward actionable steps through a narrative presentation. Stories help stakeholders understand why these data points matter in their decision-making processes.
- **Emotional Connection:** People connect with stories on an emotional level. Presenting data within a narrative framework makes it easier for business professionals to engage. Whether it is a marketing team developing a customer journey or a financial analyst explaining market movements, stories will help connect the audience at deeper levels.

Many business intelligence tools are based on data storytelling that enables its users to build narratives using their data. Such tools, together with storytelling techniques, can offer dynamic interaction together with rich visualization, and present the data.

Following are some common BI tools used across organizations:

- **Tableau:** Tableau is basically leading the curve in data storytelling features. Its Story Points functionality allows users to create structured sequences of visualizations, similar to slides in a presentation, but focused on visual insights. Rather than presenting isolated graphs, Tableau enables users to weave them together into a coherent narrative that drives conclusions and actions. For example, a sales report in Tableau could start with a high-level overview of regional performance, drill down into specific areas needing improvement, and then propose actionable steps—all within a single storytelling sequence.
- **Power BI:** Microsoft Power BI combines storytelling capabilities with interactive reports and dashboards. It allows users to embed annotations, explanations, and drill-downs directly into visuals to create compelling narratives. Bookmarks enable step-by-step storytelling of key insights across different views. The Q&A feature further enhances storytelling by allowing users to ask questions in natural language and receive immediate visual answers, creating a more conversational experience. For example, a marketing team could use Power BI to narrate the success of a recent campaign, discussing real-time performance metrics, analyzing customer demographics, and even projecting future marketing strategies using data predictions.
- **Flourish:** Flourish is a specialized data storytelling tool that enables animated and interactive narratives. It offers various storytelling templates, from flow diagrams to scrollytelling. Flourish excels at creating immersive data exploration experiences. For example, a government agency could use Flourish to create an interactive story showing how policy changes impact public health, integrating data on healthcare utilization, economic well-being, and demographics.
- **Google Data Studio:** Google Data Studio focuses on making data storytelling accessible while maintaining customizable, shareable, interactive reports. It supports narrative visualizations through the creation of multi-page reports with embedded insights and commentary that guide the reader through a coherent data story. For example, a user could create an interactive report in Google Data Studio on quarterly performance, showing the source of increases by department, and embedding key takeaways and next quarter's forecasts.

Methods of Making Powerful Data Stories

An effective data storytelling goes beyond just some embellishment of visualizations to data; it develops a great narrative that resonates well with the audience. Some of the key techniques include:

- **Begin with a Clear Purpose:** A story always has an aim. Whether it is to project the business problem or trend, or recommend an action, working on the aim helps shape up the story in advance.

- **Structure**: A data narrative should consist of the classic beginning, middle, and end like every good story. It has context or the "why"; analysis or insight, the "what"; and then a conclusion or recommendation, the "how.".
- **Simplify the Images**: This means clarity. Images should unscramble confusion but not over shroud the audience. The charts should be very simple with more attention to the data that would give most relevance to your story.
- **Add Context with Annotations:** Add names, captions and annotations to help the reader understand the storyboard. That way, although the data could be complex, the story remains quite clear. There will be some engaging features that include click-through or drill-down, which engages the audience to explore it for themselves and makes them deep into understanding.
- **The Future of Data Storytelling:** As the BI tool keeps evolving, data storytelling will become ever more at the heart of how organizations communicate insights. Indeed, with progressing technologies in NLP and AI-driven insights, it would become easy for users to have narratives with such tools.

For example, AI generates storylines automatically from data, while NLP simply lets the user ask questions and gain responses in narrative form. However, AR and VR open up new frontiers in telling stories. The future will consist of actual storytelling of data in the real-time 3D environment, wherein users can explore data stories by walking through virtual models of their data.

Immersive Visualizations: Virtual Reality (VR) and Augmented Reality (AR)

Complex datasets, especially those with more than two dimensions, cannot be visualized properly with two dimensional methods. This limitation points to the future of data interaction: Virtual Reality (VR) and Augmented Reality (AR). This new phenomenon takes the experience of data visualization to a different plane altogether, from mere seeing to experiencing.

Rate of Evolution for Data Visualization Using VR and AR

Traditionally, data visualization was available only on flat, static screens - a laptop, a monitor, or even a mobile device. The tools are good enough for most use cases but never capture the intricate patterns, relationships, or insights that often lie hidden in large and complex datasets.

VR and AR enable users to:

- Interact with data in a 3D environment where they walk through, touch, and manipulate the actual points.

- Explore complex relationships in many ways; to bring out facets not present in the typical 2D view.
- Interact with the data in real time to drill down, zoom in on what is interesting by focusing on highlighting specific elements.

Knowing VR and AR in Data Visualization

Virtual reality creates a completely simulated environment that can be accessed via headsets such as Oculus Rift, HTC Vive, or Meta Quest. A data visualization via virtual reality allows one to navigate through points and graphs as if walking through a real space in a 3D world.

AR overlays virtual information onto the real-world data using a smartphone, tablet, or "*mixed reality*" headsets such as Microsoft HoloLens. It then maps this information over a 3D space within the consumer's environment, allowing them to view projections of data layered over their environment. Now imagine looking at your conference table. You might then simply see a 3D data model pop up right in front of you where you can interact through gestures or touch.

Benefits of VR and AR in Data Visualization

Virtual reality and augmented reality in data visualization provide an immersive, interactive experience with the data, giving the users the ability to explore difficult data in a more intuitive way. This is because it provides greater insights by depicting data in three-dimensional spaces, which makes patterns and relationships more understandable.

- **Improved Understanding and Information**
  - **Spatial Analysis:** The same data can be described spatially, meaning users can navigate multi-dimensional datasets in ways impossible on flat screens. This is particularly useful when looking for patterns, trends, or correlations in large data-sets.
  - **Better Understanding**: AR and VR allow the abstraction of data to become real, hence making complex relationships understandable quite rapidly. For instance, instead of trying to understand a big 2D network graph, the users would be immersed in a 3D version, making it significantly easier to comprehend the connections between nodes.
- **Interactive Discovery:** In a big way, user interaction can be made much more dynamic and interesting through hand gestures, voice commands, or controllers for data exploration. For example, within a VR environment, being able to "pick up" a data point, expand it, and examine its details closely would be significantly more informative.

- **Story Immersion:** With VR and AR, data storytelling can be a journey through the experience. Instead of using static slides, a data analyst can guide stakeholders through layers of 3D visualization, creating a memorable and more impactful experience for conveying insights.
- **Collaborative Data Analysis:** VR and AR enable real-time collaborative environments. It is possible to get people of all locations to enter a shared virtual space, interface with data, and brainstorm together, almost as if present physically in the same room, fostering better collective understanding and decision-making.

Practical Uses and Applications of VR and AR in Data Visualization

VR and AR are utilized in data visualization for simulation-based training environments, interactive dashboards, or to explore complex datasets. Such technologies are most crucial where comprehension of any intricate data set is required, such as in healthcare, engineering, and finance.

- **Healthcare and Medical Research:** For example, doctors and medical researchers can use it to visualize complex biological data such as patient anatomy in 3D. They could trace how various organs work together, understand how diseases develop, or even simulate surgery for help in diagnostics, training, or treatment planning.
- **Financial Services:** Financial analysts may make use of VR to virtually explore data on the market, investment portfolios, and stocks trends. Immersion in a 3D representation of financial metrics might allow better identification of trend, correlation, and anomaly than any other approach, furthering better-informed investment decisions.
- **Urban Planning and Smart Cities:** City planners can use augmented reality for the visualization of infrastructure projects in real-world settings, putting traffic patterns, energy usage, population density, and more over an actual city map. Such an immersive approach helps stakeholders understand what effects the projects will bring to an urban environment before their implementation.
- **Manufacturing and Supply Chain Management:** A manufacturer can use VR to view the lines of production, envision material flow, and note bottlenecks. All of this helps develop maximum efficiency for the processes to minimize downtime.
- **Education and Training:** VR can be applied by schools in teaching difficult subjects such as molecular biology and astrophysics; students can surround themselves with 3D models of molecules or of the solar system- a fun way of learning.

Tools and Platforms

The following tools offer powerful features and functionalities for building interactive, immersive experiences tailored to specific data visualization needs.

- **Microsoft HoloLens**: A leading AR headset, the HoloLens allows users to integrate data into their real-world surroundings. Businesses use it to visualize data dashboards in 3D data dashboards, overlay charts on machinery, or display sales data on a meeting room wall for a more immersive data experience.
- **Virtualitics**: Virtualitics is a data visualization platform specifically designed for VR data. Users will be able to explore VR data in a totally immersive 3D environment and support machine learning algorithms that automatically identify various patterns and trends, which can be visualized in VR, creating a multidimensional analysis experience.
- **Flow Immersive:** This web-based AR/VR platform lets people tell stories into data and engage and collaborate. Users can import datasets and then turn them into immersive visualizations accessible through a VR headset or mobile devices.
- **Tableau AR/VR Extensions:** These extensions bridge the gap between the popular BI tool and AR/VR technologies. They allow users to interact with Tableau dashboards in a VR environment, transforming traditional dashboards into VR-friendly experiences and generating deeper insights.

Technical Constraints and Concerns of Using VR and AR for Data Visualization

Using VR and AR for data visualization presents technical challenges, such as high processing requirements and limited accessibility on some devices. Also, security of data and the management of comfort for users in immersive environments are some of the crucial concerns that need to be addressed.

- **Technical Complexity:** VR and AR visualization definitely demands more technical skills in 3D modeling, coding, and user experience design, making them more complex to develop than 2D dashboards.

  For example, VR headsets and AR glasses can be expensive, limiting accessibility and widespread reach.
- **Data Overload:** The immersive nature of VR and AR can lead to data overload if not effectively realized. Poor 3D spaces confuse the user, degrading the effectiveness of visualization.
- **User Adaptability:** A user might not be open to embracing immersive

technologies, and sometimes the users are not accustomed to the environments in VR or AR, leading to an adaptation barrier.

Future of Immersive Data Visualization

The potential of VR and AR for enhancing data visualization is immense. We can anticipate further advancements, including:

- **Seamless Integration with AI:** AI-enabled analytics would provide real-time insight within VR/AR environments so that the users could interact with intelligent data models that adapt to their needs.
- **Increasing Adoption:** With further reduction in the price and usability of VR and AR hardware, increased industry-wide adoption is expected.
- **Augmented Collaboration:** More teams will use VR and AR to collaborate when analyzing data; they will share views on various discussions, consultations, interacting with 3D models, and making decisions in real-time virtual data rooms.

Integration of BI with Collaborative Platforms

In today's data-driven world, real-time collaboration and insights are essential for effective decision-making. Many organizations struggle to properly integrate data analysis with decision-making, often due to communication breakdowns.

Business Intelligence is transforming team work by seamlessly integrating with platforms such as Slack and Microsoft Teams. Embedding BI into the collaborative environments would enable the organizations to communicate much better by streamlining the decision-making process while making sure that insights are passed across teams easily and in real time.

The Value of Integrating BI with Collaborative Platforms

Integrating BI with collaborative platforms empower data-driven decision-making. When data is brought into these platforms using BI tools, it becomes part of the everyday conversation, indicating faster decisions based on data-based rationale, as users can discuss and act within a familiar environment.

- **Real-Time Data:** Teams receive alerts, updates, or visualizations in real time. This means everyone is working with the freshest data, really valuable for rapidly progressing industries where timely access to data can be crucial.

- **Improved Collaboration:** BI integrations allow many team members to view, comment on, and engage with data visualizations at once. Thus, it is a collaborative working environment where insights can be discussed and explored, with action taken in a group manner.
- **Data Democratization:** When these BI tools are pushed into the platforms teams use daily, data becomes accessible to everyone, not just data analysts or specialists. This promotes a data-driven culture throughout the organization.

Key Examples of BI Integration with Collaboration Platforms

Many BI tools, such as Microsoft Power BI, Tableau, and Superset, integrate with collaboration platforms like Microsoft Teams and Slack, enabling seamless data sharing and teamwork. These integrations allow users to discuss insights in real time and make collaborative, data-driven decisions.

Superset Integration with Slack

Apache Superset, an open-source BI tool, integrates with Slack, allowing teams to create an interactive data discussion platform within Slack channels. This integration offers benefits such as in-channel notifications, report sharing, and more.

- **Use Case:** A sales manager wants to track daily sales performance. Superset automatically shares daily sales reports or alerts about sales targets directly in a Slack channel. The team can then discuss the report, ask questions, and share insights in real time within the Slack workspace.
- **Benefits:**
    - Stakeholders receive real-time updates on key metrics.
    - Users can query Superset and receive answers directly in Slack, saving time and improving accessibility.
    - Teams can share data insights in Slack, tagging relevant stakeholders and decision-makers for prompt action.

Microsoft Power BI Integration with Microsoft Teams

Power BI offers deep integration with Microsoft Teams, allowing users to embed interactive reports into Teams channels for real-time discussions about data insights.

- **Use Case:** A marketing team uses a Power BI dashboard to track campaign performance, integrated directly into a dedicated Teams channel. Team members can view live data on clicks, conversions, and ROI within

Teams without switching applications. They can discuss trends, make adjustments, and plan next steps while staying engaged with current data.

- **Benefits:**
  - Power BI reports and dashboards are accessible within Teams, facilitating continuous collaboration.
  - Critical metrics, such as sudden drops in sales or website traffic, are readily visible, enabling prompt issue resolution.
  - Integration with the Microsoft ecosystem allows for leveraging other tools such as SharePoint, Excel, and Azure for more comprehensive data analysis.

Tableau's Collaborative Features

Tableau offers numerous collaborative features for sharing insights and conducting joint data analysis. These capabilities are further enhanced through integrations with platforms such as Slack and Microsoft Teams.

- **Use Case:** A finance team analyzing monthly financial reports creates a Tableau dashboard and shares it in their Slack channel. Team members can discuss the financial data, ask questions, annotate trends, and highlight key insights within Slack.
- **Benefits:**
  - Tableau's "`Ask Data`" feature allows users to ask questions about data in natural language and share findings directly in Slack or Microsoft Teams.
  - Users receive alerts in Slack or Teams when data thresholds are met or exceeded, ensuring timely attention to significant changes.
  - Interactive dashboards shared within collaborative platforms allow team members to filter, sort, and drill down into data directly from their conversations.

Practical Benefits of BI and Collaborative Platform Integration

- **Streamlined Workflows:** Integration eliminates the need to switch between multiple applications, streamlining workflows and consolidating information access.
- **Centralized Communication:** Data-related discussions, reports, and alerts are centralized, reducing miscommunication and missed insights.
- **Data Sharing:** Data visualizations are shared with stakeholders who may not have access to the BI tool, improving communication and understanding.
- **Real-time Notifications:** Integration enables automated notifications and alerts about critical data changes, prompting timely action.

Challenges of BI Integration with Collaborative Platforms

While BI integration with collaborative platforms offers numerous advantages, there are also challenges to consider:

- **Data Security and Privacy:** Sharing data-derived insights on collaborative platforms may expose sensitive information. Organizations need robust data governance and security policies to protect sensitive data.
- **Information Overload:** Excessive notifications and data alerts can overwhelm users, leading to alert fatigue. Careful configuration of alerts is essential to ensure relevance and actionability.
- **User Adoption and Training:** Effective use of integrated BI tools requires proper training and support to ensure users understand how to leverage the technology and communicate effectively with data visualizations.

Future of BI and Integration with Collaboration Platforms

As remote and hybrid work models become more prevalent, BI integration with collaborative platforms will become even more critical. Future trends include:

- **AI-driven Insights:** Collaboration platforms will increasingly use AI to analyze data shared from BI tools, automatically highlighting insights, trends, and anomalies for users, even those without technical expertise.
- **Voice-Activated BI:** Voice-activated technology will enable users to query data using voice commands directly within collaborative systems like Teams and Slack.
- **Workflow Automation:** BI will integrate with workflow automation tools like Microsoft Power Automate or Slack workflows, triggering data-driven actions automatically, such as alerts on KPI achievement, subsequent tasks, and even data-driven decision-making workflows.

Data Visualization in Edge Computing and IoT

The rapid development of technology will connect billions of devices, providing huge amounts of data through IoT and edge computing. These data streams offer businesses unprecedented opportunities to gain insights into their operations, assets, and environments. However, traditional data visualization methods are inadequate for handling the volume, velocity, and variety of this data. Data visualization in the context of edge computing and IoT is therefore emerging as a critical field, enabling organizations to cope with this flood of decentralized data and make better decisions by changing raw data into actionable insight.

Edge Computing and IoT Data

IoT describes an interconnection of physical and digital components, such as sensors, cameras, or inductive smart appliances, which can collect data based on the surrounding environment and communicate this data over the internet. This usually involves real-time creation of data, such as temperature readings from an industrial unit or heart rate data generated by a fitness tracking device.

The term edge computing refers to processing data at or near its source, often referred to as the "*edge*" of a network, rather than sending it off to a central cloud or data center. The decrease in latency, and therefore the response time, along with bandwidth conservation, makes it well-suited for use cases requiring real-time data analysis or visualization.

Role of Data Visualization in Edge Computing and IoT

Data visualization is crucial, especially for making sense of the large and complex datasets generated by the IoT devices and processed through edge computing. Good visualization helps organizations in following ways:

- **Real-time Monitoring:** Because data from IoT devices is real-time, visualizations enable live monitoring of assets, operations, and environments, allowing companies to respond immediately to events as they occur.
- **Data Exploration:** Visualization facilitates the exploration of data for patterns and anomalies, improving problem detection, enhancing performance, and enabling faster responses to opportunities.
- **Unified View of Geographically Distributed Data:** Organizations with operations or assets spread across multiple locations benefit significantly from data visualization. It provides stakeholders with a unified view of how various influencing variables are interconnected across different regions.

Major Examples of Data Visualization in Edge Computing and IoT

Visualization of data in edge computing and IoT helps monitor and analyze the inflow of real-time data coming in from connected devices. Examples include smart city traffic management dashboards or industrial IoT systems visualizing sensor data for optimizing operations and predicting maintenance needs.

Edge Computing Platforms for Real-Time Analytics: With edge computing platforms, the data can be processed and visualized in real-time, providing instant insights. A manufacturing company will most probably use edge computing while monitoring the output from its machines' sensors. These sensor outputs include temperature and pressure, even vibration. Real-time visualization allows operators to view anomalies and predict and avoid expensive downtime.

Example Platforms:

- **AWS IoT Greengrass:** This is an edge computing platform for processing the data from IoT. AWS IoT Greengrass is put together with visualization tools such as Grafana to help businesses build dashboards capable of monitoring data streams in real time.
- **Azure IoT Edge:** It is an edge-computing solution that processes data at the edge and integrates well with the visualization tool Microsoft Power BI, allowing an interactive dashboard to analyze trends, patterns, and anomalies of real-time data from IoT devices.

Apache Superset - Controlling IoT Data Streams: Apache Superset is an open-source Business Intelligence and data visualization tool that is increasingly being used to handle and visualize data emerging from the Internet of Things. The capability of Superset to connect with real-time data sources is quite beneficial for visualizing decentralized data coming out of edge computing environments.

Deployment example: A dozen sensors across a wind farm measure wind speed, power output, and mechanical health of the wind turbines. These sensors produce a constant data flow, which is processed near the edge to reduce latency in processing. For visualizing real-time performance metrics for each turbine and identifying those requiring maintenance, the company will integrate Apache Superset with its pipeline.

Challenges with Visualizing Data in Edge Computing and IoT

With edge computing and IoT unfolding the door to real-time insights, the visualization from such decentralized systems poses challenges in itself:

- **High-Volume, High-Velocity Data:** IoT devices generate massive amounts of data at high speeds, making real-time display difficult. Powerful visualization toolchains are needed to handle these data streams without compromising speed or latency.
- **Data Diversity:** Internet of Things devices produce various data types, from structured to unstructured and semi-structured. Visualizing this diverse data requires flexible tools capable of processing and presenting the data in the appropriate format.

- **Latency and Bandwidth Constraints:** In edge computing environments, visualizing data with minimal latency is critical, especially for applications such as autonomous vehicles, smart cities, or industrial automation. Any delay in visualizing data can hinder real-time decision-making.
- **Scalability**: As the organizations scale up their IoT deployments, the data generated can increase exponentially. The visualization tool should also scale up with the deployment to handle bigger volumes of data without impacting its performance.
- **Security and Privacy:** Typically, data coming from IoT devices is designed as sensitive or confidential representations. The visualization process must be capable of guaranteeing and maintaining data security and confidentiality, including healthcare, finance and manufacturing applications.

Data Visualization for Edge Computing and the Internet of Things

Despite the challenges presented by edge computing and IoT, there is significant potential for data visualization to unlock valuable opportunities:

- **Improved Real-Time Decisions** Businesses can react in real-time to changes or anomalies and thus can help minimize downtimes and improve the efficiency of operations. For instance, in the logistics industry, real-time monitoring of delivery vehicles using IoT sensors allows for maximization of routes and reduced fuel consumption.
- **Predictive Maintenance:** IoT data would make it possible for organizations to visualize predictive maintenance. By analyzing patterns in historical and real-time data, businesses can anticipate equipment failures and perform proactive maintenance, reducing downtime and costs.
- **Improved Operational Efficiency:** Organizations can track and improve processes with the help of edge computing or data visualization. For example, a farmer can make use of IoT sensors to monitor soil moisture, temperature, and crop health. This data can inform decisions regarding water supply, fertilization, and harvesting.
- **Intelligent Cities and Infrastructure Management:** IoT and edge computing facilitate real-time visualization of data from sensors monitoring city infrastructure, such as traffic lights, air quality monitors, or waste management systems. This enables optimization in resource allocation, reduction in traffic, and improvement in the quality of life for its residents.

Best Practices on Data Visualization of Edge Computing and IoT

Consider the following best practices on data visualization of edge computing:

- **Real-Time Dashboards**: Choose your visualization tools to ingest streams of real-time data, enabling stakeholders to keep track of what's coming in. Real-time dashboards can help resolve issues and take advantage of opportunities as they arise.
- **Simplifying Complexity:** IoT and edge data can be highly complex. Employ visualizations such as heat maps, scatter plots, and 3D models for making trends and patterns highly observable.
- **Prioritize Data Security:** Take proper measures to encrypt data associated with any form of IoT device. Implement access controls and also secure communication protocols, especially when integrating visualization tools.
- **Leverage Edge Analytics:** Preprocess data at the edge to minimize noise, bandwidth usage and latency, and prioritize the most insightful data points.
- **Future of Data Visualization in Edge Computing and IoT**: As the field of IoT and edge computing grows, data visualization tools must inherently support an increasingly large and complex dataset.

Emerging Trends

- **Augmented Reality (AR) and Virtual Reality (VR) Visualization**: AR and VR will enable rich visualization of interactive visualizations of IoT data in 3D space, where such complex insights will become accessible and intelligible. A significant focus will be on the implementation of artificial intelligence in the development of patterns and trends in IoT data, generating insights and recommendations that can be visualized to support faster decision-making.
- **Interoperability View**: Visualization tools will be able to integrate better, depending on the various edge computing platforms and IoT ecosystems, enabling smooth access to decentralized data across multiple sources.

Conclusion

This chapter has explored advanced technological mechanisms that enrich data visualization and business intelligence, enabling organizations to uncover deeper insights and foster more dynamic decision-making through AI-driven data visualization. Such an approach could unravel hidden trends and patterns in large amounts of data empowered by artificial intelligence. Similarly, augmented analytics and NLP have brought analysis within reach, bringing data closer to the decision-makers through intuitive, conversational interaction.

The growing relevance of real-time data visualization allows organizations to react instantly to changing conditions, while predictive and prescriptive analytics provide proactive insights and actionable recommendations. These advancements find real-world applications across industries, underscoring their potential not only to forecast outcomes but also to drive meaningful improvements.

With the rise of data storytelling, narrative visualization improves the messaging of insights by crafting compelling, relatable stories around data. On the other end, the immersive nature of VR and AR technologies is pushing the boundaries of traditional data visualization, providing users with more interesting means of exploring and interpreting data in 3D environments.

The integration of BI tools into collaboration platforms further enriches the data experience through teamwork and the promotion of real-time data discussions. The role of data visualization in edge computing and IoT demonstrates how critical insights can be derived and acted upon directly at the data source, promoting lean, responsive, and efficient operation.

These combined topics illustrate a rapidly growing domain, where technologies such as AI, VR, AR, and IoT are transforming business intelligence and shaping its future. As these technologies become more advanced and integrated into daily workflows, they will redefine the way we understand, share, and act on insights derived from data. This chapter provides a foundation for navigating these advancements, equipping you with the knowledge to leverage the latest trends and tools in data visualization and BI.

Index

B

C

D

E

F

G

H

S

T

U

V